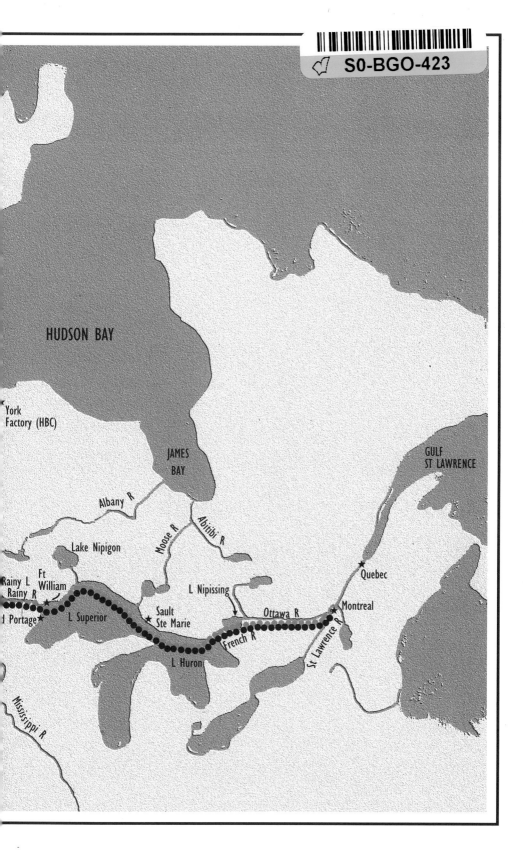

HUDSON BAY

York
Factory (HBC)

JAMES
BAY

GULF
ST LAWRENCE

Albany R

Moose R

Abitibi R

Lake Nipigon

Quebec

Rainy L
Ft
William
Rainy R

L Nipissing

Montreal

Portage

L Superior

Sault
Ste Marie

Ottawa R

French R

St Lawrence R

L Huron

Mississippi R

To Karen Yip

Best wishes

Ralph Brine

Canada's
Forgotten Highway

by Ralph Hunter Brine

Canada's Forgotten Highway

by Ralph Hunter Brine

For more information or to obtain a copy of *Canada's* Forgotten Highway, contact:

Whaler Bay Press
1201 Sturdies Bay Rd.
S 6, C 9
Galiano, BC   V0N 1P0.

(604) 539-2645 phone
(604) 539-9991 fax

Whaler Bay Press
c/o Copp's Shoes
P.O. Box 330
New Westminster BC
V3L 4Y6

(604) 521-6929 phone
(604) 521-6221 fax

ISBN #1–55056–362–9

PRINTED IN CANADA
by DW Friesen, Altona, Manitoba

♾ Printed on acid-free, recyclable paper

Dedication

C ystic Fibrosis (C.F.) is the most common life-threatening inherited disease affecting Canadian children. At present it is an incurable disease. One in every twenty-five persons in Canada carries the gene for C.F.

The greatest hope for prevention and cure lies in the hands of the people dedicated to the science of genetic research. Please, help us help them restore the *breath of life* to the innocent.

A royalty of $2.00 from each book sold will go to the Canadian Cystic Fibrosis Foundation. Thank you.

Whaler Bay Press

Ralph H. Brine
and
Marion E. Brine

Canada's Forgotten Highway is for those
who have been touched by the manitou of a river.

A Discourse Of Rivers

All rivers run to the sea,
Yet the sea overfloweth not.

A river glides at its own sweet will.
If left alone it will flow on still.

Find a river to follow,
From sea to shining sea.

May there always be a river to cross;
The river within is ever on the move.

A majestic river floats on and on,
Out of the mist and over the land.

Time moves up and down,
Like a river of events.

How I would love to have
A river at the end of my garden.

Rivers of crystal light
Flow across our land.

Though I know little about gods,
I believe every river has one.

In memory of Harvey Leslie Smith, canoeing companion.
His spirit was part of the Eastward Ho Canoe Expedition.

Ave Atque Vale, Harvey!

Acknowledgement

Many people have left their imprint on this book. The family has been most supportive, particularly my wife Marney. She typed the first draft several years ago, and has kept her critical eye on it all the way.

Several friends, and a few people in the writing profession, encouraged me to continue. Dr. W. Kaye Lamb, George Griffiths, Ron and Bee Thompson, Margaret Robson, Basil Benger, Mary-Jean Elliott, Naomi Miller, Marlyn Horsdal, Gray Campbell, Louan K. Carter, Dr. Bill Wickett, read and criticized the text. My thanks to local artist Bill Shead who did the line drawings for the maps. I am grateful to all.

The people on staff at New Westminster's Public Library were most helpful in tracking down reference material.

My thanks must go to George Macdonald and Harley McKibbin, the two stalwarts at my place of business. They made my involvement in Eastward Ho possible.

Permission to use the image of David Thompson is much appreciated. It was created by the 1961-64 art class of the David Thompson Secondary School in Vancouver, BC, under the direction of Mr. Leon Manuel.

Publications by the Champlain Society and the Hakluyt Society provided a deep well of knowledge which I drew upon to provide information about the canoe explorers contained between these covers.

No acknowledgement would be complete without mentioning the people and firms who gave financial and material support to Eastward Ho. Their names have been duly noted in the text, or listed in the appendix.

List of Maps

	Chapter	page
Canada		Inside cover
Mouth Columbia River	2	11
Canoe explorers of North America	2	16
Fraser River delta, Middle Arm	4	28
Fort Nisqually and Cowlitz portage	5	35
Harrison Lake – Fraser River connection	5	37
Fraser River – Hope to Ashcroft	5	38
Brigade trail Ft. Alexandria – Ft. Okanagan	5	44
Sicamous to Golden	8	78
Disposition of First Nations – circa 1800	11	116
North Saskatchewan River Edmonton to The Pas	12	126
Trading posts of the La Vérendrye Family	13	149
Map drawn by Auchagah	13	151
Map compiled by the La Vérendrye party	13	151
Winnipeg River	14	163
Rainy River	15	172
French and Mattawa Rivers	18	207
Ottawa River	18	214
Montreal	18	225
North America, Montreal to Pacific		back cover

List of Photos

	Chapter	page
Portaging the Talon Chute on Mattawa River		front cover
Aerial photo, mouth of Middle Arm of Fraser River	4	30
Swearing in the postman, Dave C, steps City Hall	5	32
Breasting the Skuzzy rapids in lower Fraser canyon	5	47
Lining canoe on Thompson River near Spences Bridge	6	56
D. Thompson's cairn in the Athabasca Pass	7	75
Log jam on the Columbia River, calls for a portage	8	79
Mud slide beside Columbia River takes out the road	8	88
Passing Mummery Glacier heading into Howse Pass	9	94
The Defile hides the Blaeberry River	9	95
Our feline guide leads to the B.C. – Alta. border	9	99
Canoe sledding on the North Saskatchewan River	10	106
Hard work on the North Saskatchewan River	10	114
Voyageurs or Border-Chain route – border post	15	173
Replica of canoe lock built for *canots de maître*	16	193
French River rapids below Récollet Falls	18	208
Eastward Ho and Parliament Buildings	18	222
One of the 2,000 canoe-mail envelopes carried	19	230

Contents

		page
Introduction		x
Chapter 1	The Search Begins	1
Chapter 2	The Last Link	10
Chapter 3	Eastward Ho	17
Chapter 4	Simon Fraser, *fifth man*	23
Chapter 5	Fraser's River	31
Chapter 6	The Thompson Connector	51
Chapter 7	David Thompson, *fifth man*	66
Chapter 8	The Road to Canada	76
Chapter 9	Across the Shining Mountains	92
Chapter 10	Ice	105
Chapter 11	People of the Prairie	115
Chapter 12	Edmonton to The Pas	123
Chapter 13	Pierre de la Vérendrye, *fifth man*	146
Chapter 14	Lacs des Prairies	152
Chapter 15	Up the Rainy River	167
Chapter 16	Two Great Lakes	186
Chapter 17	Samuel de Champlain, *fifth man*	196
Chapter 18	The First Road West	206
Chapter 19	Journey's End	226
Chapter 20	Summing Up	232
Appendix		237

Introduction

S amuel de Champlain initiated the search for a way to the Western Sea in the early part of the 17th century. He encouraged a generation of young Frenchmen to venture beyond the bounds of civilization by adopting the techniques of First Nations people, who were well versed in the art of wilderness survival.

Two centuries after Champlain's clarion call of Westward Ho!, David Thompson of the North West Company forged Canada's final link in transcontinental communication. He unlocked the secret of the twisting Columbia River by following it from the Rocky Mountains to the Pacific Ocean.

Canada's Forgotten Highway is about the development of the wilderness waterway that connected Montreal to the mouth of the Columbia River on the Pacific. This rambling 4300-mile track, suitable for canoes, in large measure determined the shape of Canada.

This book also contains the story of four modern-day canoeists who followed much of that ancient artery by canoeing from New Westminster, British Columbia, to Montreal, Quebec.

They called their adventure the Eastward Ho Canoe Expedition. In today's light, a canoe trip across Canada may seem unusual, but in the first half of the 19th century it was a common occurance.

Although *Canada's* Forgotten Highway is definitely *family fare,* it may be difficult to categorize. It is part history, part travel, part adventure; written by an amateur in all departments.

Ralph Brine

The Eastward Ho Canoe Expedition

*These islands mark the beginning
of the land and province of Canada.*
Jacques Cartier

Chapter One

The Search Begins

irst Nations people passed along their wilderness lore to new Canadians. They also supplied, according to Cartier, the name *canada*. Domagaya and Taignoagny, two First Nations lads, had wintered across the sea as guests of the French King and his Court. They returned to the St. Lawrence Valley aboard Cartier's ship La Grande Hermine in the summer of 1535. The Hermine, pushed by an east wind and in-coming tide, approached the narrows, (the quebec), of what Cartier had called La Grande Rivière.

The two boys, with their elbows on the starboard railing, watched the passing countryside intently. As soon as the ship entered the constricted river they began to nudge one other and point shoreward. Around one of the bends, they viewed the green fields and dwellings of their own people, and immediately broke into a foot-stomping dance of excitement, crying out: "Kanata!" "Kanata!".

The lessons received in France were remembered, and they added: "Le chemin de Canada", ("The way to home"). That day, Cartier entered in his journal: *"Canada means Homeland"*.

Cartier would be amazed today at the growth of those patches of green at the foot of the beetling rock of Quebec. Through the years they have formed a continuity from ocean to ocean. They have spread to become the second largest country in the world. Canada's land mass of 3.8 million square miles is exceeded only by that of Greater Russia.

Like her counterpart across the Pole, Canada is a *northern* country, with all that the name implies. Her climate is classified as 'Cool Temperate Zone', meaning, short summers and long winters. Much of Canada is an open air deep-freeze for half the year.

As a political unit, Canada defies geography. Her structures of mass follow lines of longitude, not latitude. The rugged Coast Range, the soaring Rockies, and the moderate Appalachian Mountains of the Atlantic, continue south to the Gulf of Mexico. We share the eroded Canadian Shield with southern neighbours in Minnesota and Michigan. The bald prairie sweeps south, to be drained by the broad Missouri and the mighty Mississippi.

Canada might have become divided into political bands of a north-south orientation, except for one key factor: *her rivers.*

Canada's mountains and plains may run north-south, but by and large, with the exception of the Mackenzie River, her internal waterways trend in an *east-west* line. The Columbia and Fraser Rivers emanate from the Rocky Mountains and ultimately flow *west* to the Pacific. Further north the Peace River belies its name by clawing *eastward* through the Rocky Mountains before joining the arctic-bearing Mackenzie system.

The Churchill River begins near Lake Athabasca and proceeds to wriggle and skip *eastward* to Hudson Bay. The Saskatchewan, through its north and south branches, takes most of the run-off from the prairie and carries it *east* to Lake Winnipeg.

Lake Winnipeg also collects from the south-western side of the Canadian Shield, and pours all of it down *east* into Hudson Bay via the Nelson River. The Great Lakes, the largest freshwater basin in the world, discharge *eastward* via the St. Lawrence River to the Atlantic Ocean. These *east* and *west* flowing rivers, used for centuries by First Nations, were the earliest avenues of transport and communication. *They* were the reason Canada eventually moved westward toward unity and independence.

In the summer of 1611, Samuel de Champlain waited on the island of Mount Royal for the return of his young aide Etienne Brûlé. Champlain had sent him westward up the Ottawa River the previous year to winter in the land of the Hurons.

With Champlain was a native youth by the name of 'Savignon', son of a Huron Chief. He had accepted the role of exchange student by travelling back to France with Champlain the previous year. If all went well, he and Brûlé would soon be with their own people.

This island had been occupied when Jacques Cartier first visited, but the meadow now lay deserted. Champlain's party had cleared some land in preparation for building, and he made this comment:

Patches of grasses hereabout would feed as many cattle as one could wish. All the varieties of wood which we have in our forests in France, along with vines, butternuts, plums, cherries, and strawberries, flourish here. Fish and game are abundant. We lack nothing while waiting at the foot of these rapids for Brûlé. This is the uppermost position on the River of Canada that can be reached by our pinnaces and shallops. Only by canoe and armed with the knowledge of the Native people can one continue westward.

Brûlé, dressed in animal skins, arrived with 200 Huron warriors. He spoke of the good treatment he had received, and said he had learned much of their language. He proceeded to demonstrate by translating some of the halting verbal communications between Champlain and several Huron Chiefs. The latter drew pictures in the sand and on birch-bark to describe rivers, falls, lakes, and the people who inhabited the land.

They assured Champlain they had seen a sea far from their country, but difficult to get to because of the continuous skirmishing between warring tribes. They described the country as being very wild in some parts. Champlain continued:

In short, they spoke in great detail, and I did not become tired of listening to them. I look forward to the day I can explore for myself the River of the West [Ottawa River], and journey further into the unknown in search of the Western Sea.

Worthy of the title "Father of Canada", Champlain laid his cornerstone at Quebec, the first continuously inhabited domain of the interior of New France. He forged the first section of the Long Road West by making treaties with the principal canoe societies, the Algonquin, Montagnais, Naskapi and Huron Nations. They had united to confront a common enemy, the fierce 'League of the Iroquois Confederacy'. With his Algonquian allies, Champlain ultimately explored the Ottawa-French River route to Georgian Bay on Lake Huron.

Champlain dedicated his life to Canada. When he died in Quebec City in 1635, New France was a fact that would endure. The farms and villages strung along the St. Lawrence valley would suffer years of hardship at the hand of the Iroquois, allies of the English, but Champlain's vision prevailed. By urging young men of his fledgling colony to become versed in wilderness survival, he formed the nucleus of a work-force that became thousands.

After Champlain, the fur trade industry continued to function as the main source of export and revenue for the struggling young country. It became the driving force that directed men out into the wilderness on a long march to the Western Sea. Generations of Frenchmen devoted their youth, and many their lives, to the mission of Westward Ho! In French-Canada their names are legion.

Brothers-in-law, Radisson and Groseilliers roamed the Great Lakes and ferreted out the Albany and Moose River connections to Hudson Bay. These original *coureurs de bois*, literally, *runners of the wood*, were individual entrepreneurs. They made their living by going out into the wilderness to purchase furs directly from native people.

After them, others came. Joliet and Father Marquette pointed the way to the Gulf of Mexico for La Salle to follow. The latter supplied the name "Lachine" to the rapids just above Montreal, hoping he was on his way to the Orient. Instead La Salle ended up claiming the entire Mississippi watershed for Louis XIV of France. He named it Louisiana.

Sieur Dulhut formed alliances with the Chippewa and established a presence in their lands from Lake Michigan to the western shore of Lake Superior. In 1688, Jacques de Noyon probed further when native guides led him through the intricate waterways of the Canadian Shield. They went up the Kaministikwia River, over the height-of-land to the westward-leading Rainy River, and on down it to Lake of the Woods.

Pierre La Vérendrye and his four sons followed on the heels of de Noyon. They heeded the advice of Auchagah, a far-ranging guide of the Cree Nation. He showed La Vérendrye the Pigeon River, a shorter route to the Rainy River. La Vérendrye anchored his westward penetration by constructing Fort St. Charles on the west shore of Lake of the Woods.

Jean-Baptiste, La Vérendrye's eldest son, accompanied by his cousin La Jemeraye, canoed down the exciting Winnipeg River. They entered the Canadian prairie, with its thousands of square miles of rolling meadow land. Guided by Cree and Assiniboine people through this veritable sea of grass, the La Vérendryes quickly laid to rest Pierre La Vérendrye's vain hope that Lake Winnipeg itself was the *Mer de l'Ouest*, (the Sea of the West).

Three more generations of canoe explorers, and another 2,000 miles of canoe routes would be required before such a dream could be realized. The La Vérendrye family did, however, locate the Saskatchewan River, the water link that would ultimately lead other canoe men to the formidable Shining Mountains, the final barrier to the true *Mer de l'Ouest*. The La Vérendryes also placed trading posts around Lake Winnipeg and on the banks of the Red, the Assiniboine and the Saskatchewan Rivers.

Nothing stays the same in human endeavours, and so it was with canoemen. The freedom-loving *coureurs de bois* of Radisson's day had gradually given way to a large and efficient industry that employed *voyageurs* as professional paddlers. They were hired for a set period at a fixed sum. From those ranks came the specialists; the *bouttes* who took their place in the bow and stern and named respectively *avant* and *gouvernail*; the *milieux* who sat between to paddle and portage; the *guides* who would be in charge of a brigade, or flotilla of canoes; and the *interprètes*, men well versed in native tongues. They all came under the control of the *bourgeois*. He was manager and sometimes financier of the enterprise, who in turn, would be assisted by one or more *commis* or clerks.

In communities such as Quebec City, Three Rivers and Montreal, large mercantile houses maintained profitability by controlling competition at the source, and by finding European markets for furs of all kinds. They cleaned, sorted and stored animal skins to minimize transatlantic shipping costs, and imported metal tools and trinkets from an industrialized Europe. The demand by native customers for the good things in life never slackened. Like mankind everywhere, native North Americans wished to ease the hardships doled out by Mother Nature. Large commercial firms supplied credit to the far-off fur hunters, often waiting three to four years before realizing a return on their investment.

By the 18th century, canoe men of New France had constructed and occupied over fifty outposts on the rivers flowing south from the eastern slope of the Appalachian Mountains. They were on the Ohio, the Illinois, the Wisconsin, Minnesota, Missouri, Wabash, Arkansas, and the Alabama Rivers. There were over twenty on

'Ole Miss' herself. Added to La Vérendrye's dozen, along with those on both sides of the Canadian Shield from Lake Winnipeg to Labrador, they could be listed in the hundreds.

Not all the posts were in operation at once. The majority were seasonal, or closed when the particular area they had been erected to serve became denuded of fur-bearing animals.

In 1760, with the turnover of political power in Canada from the Court of Versailles to the Court of St. James, the situation changed very little for the average citizen. Most were engaged in fishing, agriculture or fur-gathering. The English pound sterling gradually replaced the French livre, and overseas marketing moved from Paris to London, but the mechanics of the fur trade in Canada stayed the same.

French speaking merchants formed liaisons with English speaking counterparts who had moved up the Hudson River from the former Province of New York. Below that level, the personnel in the field, and consequently the *lingua franca*, remained basically French. Skills in action, not of words, was the important ingredient. Men who could handle canoes on wind-swept lakes, or on rivers steaming with white-water rapids; those who knew how to live through winters in a wilderness that could kill the uninitiated; they remained on the payroll.

In early Canada, First Nations, French, and English peoples accommodated each other. By doing so, they were able to put together North America's transcontinental waterway.

In Canada, the fur trade always depended on native people. They knew the terrain and how to survive in it. Their men made the canoes, trapped and hunted the wild animals, and protected the family unit. The women did the cooking, made the clothes, looked after the youngsters and broke camp. Without their input, men-folk would not have travelled so freely throughout wilderness North America.

The first contact with Europeans saw coastal First Nations trading their excess fur and leather garments to the white-skinned strangers in exchange for useful tools and adornments. As the volume of trade grew, the demand for animal pelts reached far into the hinterland, and many native groups became involved. The carrot that continually pulled French and English westward was the incentive to by-pass the middleman and reach the source. They sought top quality at the lowest price available.

Generally speaking, in Canada, native people served as the actual harvesters of furs, an arrangement upheld by the monarchies of both France and Great Britain. This social policy was not without cost.

In fact it was adherence to such dictums that twice brought about tremendous political upheavals in the power structure of the New World.

The first significant event took place in New France. Radisson and Groseilliers had been punished by local authorities for entering 'Indian Country' without a permit. Vexed by this treatment, in 1663 they set sail for France to find redress. They petitioned the Courts at Versailles, but got nowhere with their plea.

Thoroughly frustrated, Radisson sought financial support in London, England. The result was a Royal Charter from Charles II blessing the formation of the 'Governor and Company of Adventurers Trading Into Hudson's Bay'. The occupation of Hudson Bay by the English was ultimately the death knell of France in North America.

Another example of regal policies provoking social upheaval was the *Quebec Act* of 1774. This well-intended piece of legislation, voted in by the British Parliament, was implemented partly to protect the indigenous population. Instead, it became one of the sparks that ignited the American Revolution.

Shortly after political control of New France passed into English hands, Pontiac, Chief of the Ottawa Nation and friendly to the French, made an alliance with the Senecas, Ojibwas and Hurons, to wrest control of the Great Lakes from the English. With the exception of Fort Detroit, all the garrisoned outposts fell to his forces. It took several months of intense counterattacking by General Amherst to get the situation under control. Amherst's main fear was that this insurrection might lead to a general uprising throughout the new Province of Quebec.

At the peace treaty, British authorities assured Pontiac that boundaries would be established beyond which settlement would not be allowed. As well as protecting the interests of First Nations, the Quebec Act granted certain rights to the people of Quebec. It also put direct control of the entire Mississippi watershed into the hands of government officials in Quebec City. Governors James Murray and Guy Carlton, who followed General Amherst, disliked the rough-and-ready fur traders moving in from New York. They sympathized with the French-Canadian gentry.

To the English colonists, who had been fighting the French for over a hundred years, the Quebec Act was a damnable sellout. When the Quebec Act was piled on top of the Sugar Act, the Stamp Act and the Tea Act, they become known collectively as The Intolerable Acts.

The Intolerable Acts provided the rallying cry for people fed up with what they saw as heavy-handed government.

In Canada, after the passing of political power from France to Great Britain, the fur trade entered a period of flux similar to the free-for-all days of the coureur de bois. The system soon stabilized again with the formation of the North West Company (NWC) in 1783.

The NWC quickly grew into an aggressive partnership organization that carried on the French tradition of taking the trade out into the wilderness. This consortium of wintering partners and mercantile houses in Montreal provided the final impetus for our wilderness highway.

The most noteworthy exploration work in this period was done by Peter Pond, Alexander Mackenzie, Simon Fraser and David Thompson. We will speak of them later.

By the end of the 18th century there were three large firms exporting tremendous amounts of fur from North America; the newly formed North West Co. (NWC), the Hudson's Bay Co. (HBC), and the Astor Fur Co. (AFC).

The HBC had been around a long time, with outposts on Hudson Bay since 1670. Headquartered in London, England, they were the nearest and most direct competitor of the NWC. Their principal port was Fort York at the mouth of the Nelson River, on the west side of Hudson Bay. The HBC people liked to belittle the upstart Montreal-based fur traders as: "those peddlers from Quebec."

South of the new Canada-U.S. border, the one-man show of John Jacob Astor had grown to prominence. Astor, who had arrived penniless from Germany at the age of 20, ended up one of America's richest men. He controlled most of the United States' fur trade from New York, through his Astor Fur Co.

During the rapid twenty-year growth period of the NWC, when glossy beaver pelts from northern Canada were fetching sky-high prices in London, the intrepid Alexander Mackenzie became the first person to cross North America from the Atlantic to the Pacific. His expedition set out from the junction of the Smoky and Peace Rivers in May of 1793.

They had quite a struggle portaging their canoe past the wild Peace River canyon, and again over the height-of-land from Arctic Lake, the source of the Parsnip River.

Mackenzie finally came to a broad, fast-flowing stream which carried them west, then south. Mackenzie called it the Tacoutche Tesse.

Further south, near what would become Fort Alexandria, he heeded the advice of local inhabitants and retraced his steps to the West Road River where his guide picked up a well-used overland trading route to the Pacific Coast. They hiked over what was called a *grease* trail. People of the interior used it to trade animal skins for oolichon oil from natives on the coast.

When Mackenzie had attained his objective he wrote on a rock in a small bay off Dean Channel, west of Bella Coola: *From Canada by land, 22nd of July, 1793.*

Mackenzie drove himself and crew unmercifully, but he accomplished a superhuman feat of exploration. Their course was 1200 miles, 960 by water, 240 by land. The west-bound trip took 75 days, the return 34. It is doubtful if that return journey could be matched even by today's top competitive paddlers. We have become unaccustomed to twenty hour workdays.

After his return to civilization, and from a study of Capt. Vancouver's 1792-3 coastal explorations, Mackenzie conjectured that the Tacoutche Tesse might have been the Columbia River and a possible trade route to the Pacific.

Simon Fraser followed Mackenzie's track a few years later. He established trading posts from MacLeod Lake, through Stuart Lake, to Fraser Lake. Then by sticking to the river Mackenzie had veered from, Fraser found a way down that tumultuous stream until it emptied into the Pacific Ocean at the 49th parallel.

Both Fraser and Mackenzie were disappointed that their discoveries had seemed to have been in vain. This was not the hoped-for Columbia River which Capt. Gray had discovered from seaward in his ship the Columbia. Worse still, the Fraser River was not a navigable stream for canoe traffic.

Two years after Fraser's expedition, John Jacob Astor, with key personnel enticed away from the North West Co., formed the Pacific Fur Co., (PFC). This new corporation set sail for a round-the-horn voyage to the Pacific Ocean, arriving at the mouth of the Columbia River at the end of March, 1811. They erected Fort Astoria there, and inadvertently set the stage for the arrival of the canoeman who soon would complete Canada's transcontinental waterway.

We camped a short distance above Point Vancouver,
from which place to the Sea,
the River has been surveyed by Lieut. Broughton.
David Thompson

Chapter Two
The Last Link

On a midsummer's day in 1811, near the mouth of Oregon's Columbia River, eight men in a lap-strake cedar canoe could be seen heading toward the open Pacific. A flag of Montreal's North West Company streamed astern. They had passed Pacific Fur Co.'s Fort Astoria on Tongue Point to their left. Up ahead, low-lying Point Adams appeared on the port bow. Further away, Cape Disappointment loomed to starboard. As they neared the rows of surf tumbling in between Point Adams and the Cape, a neatly dressed man of weather-beaten visage gave the command to cease paddling. The canoe coasted to a stop on the heaving river.

Spellbound, the crew saw each approaching wave rising higher and higher against the sky, only to plunge into oblivion. A twist of foam would remain to highlight the ocean beyond.

The new arrivals were from Canada, and they had just made history by completing a water route across the widest part of North America. With this transcontinental waterway in place, the fur trade emporiums of eastern Canada would be able to export their valuable beaver and sea otter pelts directly to the lucrative markets of the Orient. Canada had its window on the Pacific.

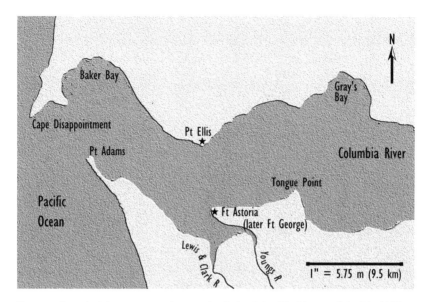

Thompson's arrival by canoe at the mouth of the Columbia River — July 14, 1811

A practical north-west passage across the continent had been a Holy Grail for Canadian canoe explorers for some 200 years, and now the centuries-old quest had been fulfilled. Measured in the convoluted ways of canoe travel, the distance from Montreal to the mouth of the Columbia River was 4300 miles. In a straight line it would be half that.

This newly proven route was the first transcontinental expressway between the Atlantic and Pacific Oceans, and it remained in use for half a century. The canoeway would be instrumental in delineating the boundary between two westward expanding nations. Ninety-five percent of it was a wilderness waterway, suitable for canoes or double-ended boats. The remaining five percent was overland.

The seven *voyageurs* in the canoe were Michel Bordeaux, Pierre Pariel, Joseph Côté, François Grégoire, Michel Boulard, and two excellent Iroquois paddlers, Charles and Ignace. They were all in the employ of the North West Company.

Their leader was David Thompson, fur trader, surveyor, map maker and wilderness traveller sans pareil. He was in charge of the Columbia District, an area which lay between the Rockies and the Cascades, and from the 46th to the 52nd parallel of latitude.

As his canoe rocked on the turbulence where river and sea met, Thompson might have reflected on the significance of the occasion. Through persistent effort he had located a safe and usable pass through the Rockies, and he had canoed the entire course of a river that led from the Rocky Mountains to the sea. He would be the last canoe explorer to be involved in the search for a practical passage to the Pacific.

Canada's Forgotten Highway will talk about many canoe explorers, but it will focus on four who put their own special imprint on the wilderness highway. They are, Samuel de Champlain, Pierre La Vérendrye, Simon Fraser, and David Thompson. Canada's Forgotten Highway also highlights the important contribution made by First Nations people, the incremental discoverers of the continent-wide waterway.

The endeavour by Canadian canoemen to produce a continent-wide highway was a combined effort of First Nation and European people. Fitting together the many pieces of this winding corridor was done by ferreting out information already possessed by local native groups. With their made-in-Canada birchbark canoes, they had been travelling and trading via the waterways of this vast northern country for centuries. But it took some time to assemble all the bits and pieces needed to solve the gigantic jig-saw puzzle of a million square miles.

On his day of victory, David Thompson repeated his oft-used prayer: *Thanks to All Merciful Providence for granting us safe passage.*

Such piety was unusual when contrasted with the average rough-and-ready fur trader, but Thompson was unique in many ways. He was well educated for a person of his time, having attended school in London, England until the age of fourteen. Possessing a scientific turn of mind, he became a keen observer of his environment, as evidenced by a book he wrote when he was in his late seventies. Entitled simply, "Narrative," it was his record of twenty-eight years spent travelling throughout western British North America.

Thompson's "Narrative" lay buried in obscurity for many years until unearthed by J.B. Tyrrell, noted Canadian geographer and historian. Through his examination of Thompson's field notes and unfinished document, Tyrrell discovered a heretofore unknown fur trader who had crossed and recrossed Canada many times, from Hudson Bay to Lake Athabasca, from the St. Lawrence River to the Pacific Ocean. Tyrrell estimated Thompson had rambled some 50,000 miles; on foot, in canoe or on horseback, performing a multifaceted role of fur trader, explorer, and surveyor, throughout a vast and lonely land.

By breaching the Rocky Mountain barrier, and unlocking the secret of the twisting Columbia River, Thompson completed Canada's centuries-old dream of a way to the Western Sea.

The Pacific Fur Co.'s venture at the mouth of the Columbia River, initiated by Astor, collapsed two years after it began. As a result of the 1812-14 War, the PFC was forced to sell out to the North West Co. and the name of the outpost was changed from Astoria to Fort George.

Ten years later the two main Canadian combatants, the NWC and the HBC, practically ruined themselves in their determination to eliminate the other. Something had to give. Economics dictated that it should be the once proud and fiercely independent North West Co. They were forced to amalgamate with the Hudson's Bay Co. under the latter's banner.

In 1821 George Simpson of the new HBC took over management of all the waterways used by both former companies. He soon made several major adjustments in the name of efficiency. The most noteworthy was elimination of the 2,000-mile haul between Lake Winnipeg and Montreal for the transport of heavy, bulky items. From then on trade goods and fur bales to and from the *pays d'en haut* would enter and leave Canada at York Factory on the bleak western shore of Hudson Bay. With York boats being used almost exclusively on larger rivers, express canoes would be limited to carrying passengers and correspondence between distant posts.

In order to better control the fur trade of the Pacific Rim, Simpson enlarged and strengthened Fort Vancouver, 100 miles inland from the coast, on the Columbia River. Montreal retained its position as the financial and administrative centre so that the Montreal to Fort William to Lake Winnipeg connection remained in use for express purposes.

Simpson, with two whirlwind tours across Canada in 1824-25 and 1828, established a record for travel time. He also made it quite clear that others should try to keep up the high standard he had set. For instance, every spring, a HBC clerk with correspondence and account books, would leave the Pacific terminus of Fort Vancouver. Two months later *voyageurs* would deposit him at the Company's offices at York Factory on Hudson Bay. At the end of summer the same person would return to Fort Vancouver with the annual fall brigade, his books all marked and cleared for another years operation in the Columbia District. This portion of the trans-Canada highway was referred to as "The Communication."

For the next quarter of a century the HBC held sway over the largest dominion ever controlled by a single entrepreneurial body. Other forces were at work. Land-hungry settlers began flooding into the Willamette Valley of Oregon. This tide could not be stemmed by the HBC without military support from Great Britain, which was not forthcoming.

During the boundary negotiations of 1845-46, the Americans managed to gobble up all the future State of Washington. The HBC was supposed to have access in perpetuity to the entire Columbia River, including the lower portion from the 49th parallel to the Pacific Ocean, but the Americans would not honour the agreement signed by both parties.

Eventually the HBC was forced to pull up stakes and move its 'window on the Pacific' to Fort Victoria on Vancouver Island. The Columbia River ceased to be the western leg of Canada's transcontinental highway. This was a significant loss to the HBC, and to a future Canada.

To help firm up an overall picture of the ocean to ocean canoe highway, it can be broken into four segments.

Described from east to west, the first segment was from Montreal to the north-western shore of Lake Superior. Roughly 1,000 canoe-miles in length, the route included the Ottawa River, Mattawa River, Lake Nipissing, the French River, Lake Huron and Lake Superior. It was only on this section that the huge thirty-five foot, *canots de maître*, the mother of all canoes, were used. After exchanging trade goods for furs at either Grand Portage or Fort William, the same crew of *voyageurs* would turn around and head back to Montreal.

The next section covered the greatest distance. Close to 1400 miles, it included the Rainy River, Lake of the Woods, the Winnipeg River, Lake Winnipeg, and the Saskatchewan River to Fort Edmonton.

The third section was less than 400-miles in total, but it included two lengthy overland portions. From Fort Edmonton, horses generally carried supplies and personnel to Fort Assiniboine on the Athabaska River. Canoes then took over for a 200-mile run up into the heart of the Rocky Mountains. The last leg of this segment was a 70-mile trek through Athabasca Pass to the Columbia River.

At Boat Encampment, on the northernmost loop of the Columbia River, the fourth segment began. Here canoes or double-ended river boats called *bateaux*, waited to transport goods and people all the way to Fort Vancouver.

One rather surprising fact of the long journey was that it made little difference in time whether one travelled east or west. Either way, under the care of an experienced crew of *voyageurs*, and barring accidents or extremes of weather, the 4300-mile highway could generally be completed within five to six months.

Tyrrell's edition of David Thompson's 'Narrative', published by the Champlain Society, introduced a new concept of Canada's development. It came as a minor revelation to learn that canoemen had once criss-crossed so much of British North America. And further, as the journals of traders after Thompson would show, they had put together a waterway that functioned as the main communication line between east and west for half a century. Workers and executives of the fur trade travelled over it, as did soldiers, scientists, priests, women and children; all propelled by the muscular arms of Canadian *voyageurs*. The Pacific terminus was in Oregon Territory, an area Great Britain once considered part of her domain. The whole enterprise was a Canadian affair, and the existence of this canoe road ensured that Canada would be one nation from sea to sea.

Canadian *voyageurs* established North America's first transcontinental communication forty years before covered wagons squealed down the Oregon Trail into Fort Vancouver; fifty years previous to Wells Fargo or the Pony Express; sixty years before the Union & Central Railroad reached the Pacific; and seventy five years ahead of the Canadian Pacific Railroad.

Awareness of the artery that helped set the boundary line between Canada and the United States has dimmed over time, but the waterways are still there. With the exception of dams on the Columbia, Saskatchewan, Winnipeg and Ottawa Rivers, the route remains virtually the same as the day Thompson completed it on July 14th, 1811.

When the 'iron-horse' arrived in North America in the latter part of the 19th century, the general public soon forgot the continent-wide highway developed by Canadian canoemen, and the spirit of our rivers faded rapidly away.

Perhaps we should listen more closely to our First Nations people. They tell us that the *manitou* of our rivers are part of a *Great Manitou* that can help unite us all, if we but recognize the stories of our past, our History.

Canadians often display a reluctance to blow their own horn. It is time to remove the mute and speak with pride about our national accomplishments. Our wilderness waterways deserve recognition for the major role they played in Canada's development. "Canada's Forgotten Highway" means to dislodge some of time's accumulated debris in order to uncover more Canadian traditions. Links with the past provide strengths for our future.

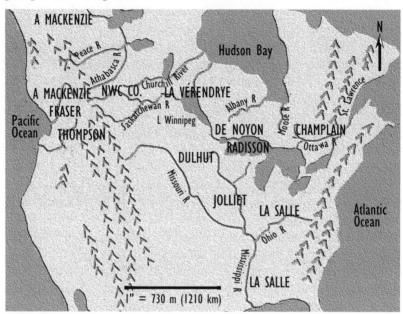

Canoe explorations in North America

1609-15   Champlain: L. Huron & L. Ontario via Ottawa River
1650-60   Radisson: L. Michigan & L. Superior, Moose & Albany R.
1669-71   La Salle: L. Ontario, L. Erie, & Ohio River
1673   Jolliet: Wisconsin & Mississippi River
1678   Dulhut: L. Nipigon & Siouan Nation near the Mississipi
1682   La Salle: Mississippi to Gulf of Mexico
1688   De Noyon
1731-43   The La Vérendryes: 9 forts (Rainy L – Saskatchewan R)
1760-90   Free traders form NWC. Men like Frobisher, Henry, Pond, explore the Athabasca River to the Rockies
1789   Mackenzie: To the Arctic Ocean on Mackenzie River
1793   Mackenzie: To the Pacific at Bella Coola
1805-08   Fraser: To the Pacific at mouth of Fraser River
1807-11   Thompson completes the Forgotten Highway

*They could be swung
on the pendulum of an idea.*
T. E. Lawrence

Chapter Three
Eastward Ho

David Thompson's 'Narrative' prompted four men to retrace much of the waterway that had spanned 200 years of Canadian history. In order to prove the existence of a water connection between New Westminster B.C. and Montreal, Quebec, they paddled, motored and portaged a 20-foot canoe across Canada. Their 1967 venture was entitled the 'Eastward Ho Canoe Expedition'. They vowed to follow by *shoe and canoe*, a 4,000-mile wilderness trail from Pacific to Atlantic tidewater.

As well as focusing on Eastward Ho, "Canada's Forgotten Highway" looks at interesting highlights by travellers who preceded them on the wilderness trail; explorers, adventurers, employees of the fur trade, and regular passengers.

If the waterway Eastward Ho followed becomes more widely known, others may wish to share the experience. It is a challenge to be sure, but those who embark on such a venture will have a deeper appreciation of the moving spirit, or river *manitou* that helped forge this country we call Canada.

As Eastward Ho progressed eastward across the face of the land, they journeyed backward in time and deeper into history. A strange sensation began to envelope them. It was as if they had become infected by the spirit of the rivers, and were being pulled along by a stream moving on a predetermined course. As one of the four commented along the way: "Events seemed to take control of us, and not we of them."

This curious feeling strengthened with time and distance, and its increase helped minimize the dangers and difficulties that lay in the way.

The Eastward Ho route followed a path laid out by four principal canoe explorers: Fraser, Thompson, La Vérendrye and Champlain. Some of the hazards were shared; the cold, the wet, the dangers of wild rivers, and the muscle-straining agonies of portaging. Later in the venture, a feeling of camaraderie with those who had gone before began to assert itself upon the members of Eastward Ho. At times the presence of former canoe explorers seemed almost palpable, creating, as it were, a *fifth man* in the canoe.

When the Eastward Ho adventure was over, everyone resumed their various occupations. Stimulated by our trans-Canada journey, I began to delve more deeply into the journals of fur trade men who had travelled on Canada's forgotten highway. Reading about those perilous times was an exhilarating experience. Early Canadian history became *alive*, which was something that had never happened during my years of formal education. I found the North America that once was nature's paradise; harsh, beautiful and challenging,

After retirement, I wanted my children and grandchildren to experience the thrills I had received from delving into our country's past. This book is the result. It is an attempt to tell a simple but exciting story; the development of the long road west that shaped Canada.

"Canada's Forgotten Highway" has been structured by combining the log of Eastward Ho with the journals of earlier canoe men. I also use a *fifth man* theme to detail remarks made by Champlain, La Vérendrye, Fraser and Thompson. Text printed in *script* indicates extracts from their journals. Some poetic license was taken, which I trust will not upset historians unduly. Comments made of the route by other early canoemen, who are labelled *observers*, are also included. Their comments, french terms and emphasized words are printed in *italics*.

Before proceeding up Fraser's river in company with the first fifth man, let's take a look at the seven Eastward Ho members; starting with the four canoeists:

At forty-three, I was the oldest of the canoe foursome, and engaged in the retail shoe business in New Westminster. My interest in David Thompson was the spark which ignited the enthusiasm of the others. My great good fortune was in having a wife willing to bear the responsibility of five teen-agers, and a father-in-law able to take charge of the store, while I dashed off across the country in pursuit of a rather unusual quest.

Dave Chisholm was a young physician of twenty-eight who hailed from Saskatoon, Saskatchewan. He managed to squeeze a four-month absence between his locum in New Westminster and a three-year post-graduate course in Aero-space Medicine at the University of Ohio. It was Dave's interest and commitment that turned the 'idea' from talk to reality.

Next to come aboard was Don MacNaughton. A family man, living and working in the New Westminster area, Don also had an understanding wife. He was thirty-nine, stockily built, with the long-armed strength of a wrestler. A native-born Montrealer, he learned to cope with the out-of-doors as a lineman in his early days with B.C. Tel.

The three of us connected at New Westminster's YM-YWCA through a mutual interest in physical fitness.

The fourth crewman was twenty-two year old Jim Reid. Although the youngest, he was the most experienced in the proposed type of canoe travel, having made a 1200-mile motorized canoe trip down the Mackenzie River to the Arctic ocean the previous summer. Jim signed on late in February, a month before the scheduled departure date of April 1st.

The three members of the land party who were to carry supplies and liaison with the canoe at prescribed intervals, were Bill Gifford and Edo and Lorna Hemmes.

Bill Gifford, a native son of New Westminster, had recently retired, but he was still physically active. His duties were to drive a station wagon and communicate between the canoe and trailer with supplies of food and gasoline. He would also scout ahead for various unforeseen problems, and make contact with civic groups who might be interested in the venture.

Edo had emigrated from Holland with his English wife Lorna after the war. They made a great husband and wife team. As well as driving a camper-truck with attached trailer, Edo planned to record the trip on 16mm movie film.

A shortage of time was the greatest hurdle to overcome. The longest the participants could devote to this project was four months. The problem therefore was to devise a method whereby the passage to Montreal, traditionally taking five months, could be covered in the allotted time.

One way to achieve this objective would be to shorten the distance. Eastward Ho decided to forgo the portion of the Columbia River that was in the U.S.A., and instead head eastward on the Fraser River. This would save 300 miles. This new route would follow the Fraser to Lytton, the Thompson River to Shuswap Lake, then the Eagle River through Eagle Pass to join the Columbia River at Revelstoke.

This switch from the established all-Columbia River route had two advantages. No one had ever attempted to go upstream through the Fraser canyon since Fraser's hair-raising journey of 1808, so it would make an interesting canoe challenge. Secondly, there was a certain satisfaction, particularly in Canada's Centennial Year, of keeping to an all-Canadian route wherever possible. Oregon Territory is not the Canadian preserve it once was.

Another proposed change would be to cross over the Rocky Mountains at the Howse Pass rather than the Athabasca Pass. The former was Thompson's first breakthrough of the Rockies. Its eastern end puts the traveller close to the North Saskatchewan River, thus negating the 100-mile-long overland portion from the Athabasca River to Edmonton.

If travel time estimates were correct, approximately half a month could be saved by these two changes to the traditional transcontinental route.

A sure way of shrinking the time element would be to go faster. That could best be accomplished by using an outboard motor on a V-stern canoe, the mode of transport for present-day fur traders throughout northern Canada. Some purists may scorn this wrench from tradition, but the constriction of 'time' was crucial. To break the expedition into halves and do it in two years was complicated and too difficult to hold together.

Rivers the *voyageurs* couldn't possibly ascend, except by portaging, could be climbed by the use of motor power. Larger bodies of water could be crossed in half the time.

The first trans-Canada waterway, when in use, was organized from beginning to end. Food, horses, and transport vessels of various sizes were provided for the *voyageurs* at specific locations. Most importantly, the men who propelled canoes of the fur trade were full-time paddlers.

The Eastward Ho crew was in fair shape, but not in the same class as those who paddled for a living. Amateurs could not equal the strenuous labour of professionals. From dawn to dusk *voyageurs* paddled, poled, and lined canoes loaded with goods and passengers. They portaged 300-lb. *north canoes*, or if east of Fort William, 600-lb. *canots de maître*. *Voyageurs* strained over rugged terrain under two or more ninety-pound packs. They often had to put up with short rations.

When approaching or leaving land, bark covered vessels couldn't be allowed to touch bottom. Hence, lower extremities were soaking wet most of the day. *Voyageurs* were a hardy breed.

As a balm to authenticity, it should be borne in mind that the canoe explorers, such as Champlain, La Vérendrye, Fraser or Thompson, never paddled, except in dire emergency; nor did officers and clerks of the established fur trade. Explorers and officers directed, *voyageurs* paddled. A 20 h.p. Johnson would serve as *voyageur* and Eastward Ho would save some time.

Although an outboard motor may save time, it does not necessarily make travelling easier. The extra weight of portaging a ninety-lb. machine, and fuel at ten lbs. per gallon, is an obvious drawback; as is sitting all day exposed to an inescapable motor-induced wind. Paddling may be monotonous and relatively slow, but it does keep you warm.

Another difficulty was the lack of first-hand information available, from a canoeist's point of view, of the dangerous canyon sections of the Fraser and Thompson Rivers. To our knowledge, no one had ever canoed *up* them. The only written account was Fraser's party, and they hiked most of the way. The ability to move upstream at more than double the speed of a paddled canoe will increase the tendency to tackle more difficult waters, thus raising the risk considerably.

Eastward Ho will copy the *voyageurs* in one respect. When going *downstream* through white-water rapids, we will be paddling.

An overall concern was the sheer power of the three B.C. rivers we planned to follow. To be ahead of spring freshet on all three meant departing no later than the beginning of April.

A great deal of equipment was needed. When an appeal for assistance went out into the business community, many came forward to help. Eastward Ho did not ask Government for financial aid, but rather, we sought assistance from people willing to dip into their own pockets.

Dinty Moore, western agent for Chestnut Canoe Co., helped choose a twenty-foot V-stern freight canoe. A cruiser model, it had a keel and reinforced transom. He then inveigled Chestnut into loaning it for as long as it took Eastward Ho to reach Montreal. The canoe required a long-shafted 20 h.p. outboard which a local Johnson dealer was able to borrow from Outboard Marine.

In spite of help from many businesses, there was still a shortfall in Eastward Ho's financial situation. Not wishing to incur debt, the members put their heads together for a money raising scheme, finally settling on the idea of serving as canoe-mail couriers. To this end they had printed 2,000 attractive envelopes and presold them at $5.00 apiece; along with the promise to: "carry them all the way to Montreal, *en canoe*."

Eastward Ho's journey is about to begin, but before embarking, a closer look at Simon Fraser is in order. He is the first *fifth man* whose footsteps and paddle strokes Eastward Ho plans to follow come April Fool's Day morning.

I named my canoe 'Perseverance'
Simon Fraser, 1776 – 1862

Chapter Four
fifth man Simon Fraser

Simon Fraser was the ninth child of Simon and Isobel Fraser. He first saw the light of day on his parent's farm near Bennington in the present State of Vermont. He was ushered into the world in the year that saw the birth of a nation, the brand new United States of America.

The Frasers, recent immigrants from Scotland, had become enmeshed in local politics which saw family pitted against family, neighbour against neighbour. Simon Sr. took up arms to defend the King's authority. He was an early victim of the revolutionary war, dying in prison from neglect on the part of his goalers.

Widow Fraser had her hands full. Her eldest son had followed his father into the British Army, leaving the next lad in line barely able to take over a man's work. There was little help from other farmers as the majority in their area sympathized with the rebel cause. Over the years, much of their livestock and farming equipment was stolen or broken by local bully boys who tormented the Frasers unmercifully. Mrs. Fraser didn't resort to arms, but demonstrated her fighting spirit by seeing to the survival of the eight children who remained under her care.

Even after the cessation of hostilities, persecutions continued. To escape harassment the Frasers joined the line of United Empire Loyalists streaming northward to obtain grants of farmland in the Cornwall area of Upper Canada. Young Simon's life was typical of a stump-ranching farm boy. There was neither time nor money for schooling. The whole family spent long, hard hours from sunup to sundown, clearing, breaking ground, cultivating the soil, seeding and cropping it. Farm animals had to be attended to as well.

Then Simon had a lucky break. He was brought to Montreal by an uncle who paid for a year's education, enough for him to become articled as clerk with the North West Company. At age 16 he was off into the wilds of Canada. A brawny lad of stocky build, blue eyes, a turned up nose, and a head of tousled red-tinged hair. His father had told the children their name was French in origin, and once spelt 'Fraise', a reference to the preponderance of redheads in the clan.

Ambitious and hardworking, Simon was soon assigned to the high country of Lake Athabasca. Nine years after his entry into the NWC he was made a wintering partner, entitled to a share in profits.

In 1804 Fraser was asked to lead an expedition in the footsteps of his illustrious predecessor, Sir Alexander Mackenzie. Fraser was ordered to establish trading posts on the western side of the Rockies, then make an assault on the large south-flowing river which Mackenzie had only explored part way.

The fall of 1805 saw Fraser's party ascending the Peace River, then the Parsnip River. Instead of continuing to the headwaters of the latter, as Mackenzie had done, they turned west up a small tributary, later called the Pack River, a stream Mackenzie seems not to have noticed. Fraser threw a small jab at his senior partner by suggesting: *Sir A.M.K. used to indulge himself sometimes with a little sleep.*

The Pack River drained a small lake where a trading post was erected. It came to be called Fort McLeod and holds the record of the longest standing white man's habitation in present day British Columbia. Fraser left a small party to conduct the winter's trade with the Sekani people, then went back down the Parsnip and Peace Rivers to the eastern side of the Rockies.

Fraser returned to MacLeod Lake as soon as the rivers had flushed out the ice of winter. He explored more country, then constructed posts on Stuart and Fraser Lakes, and at the junction of the Nechako and Fraser Rivers. To honour his mother's often repeated memories of her native Scotland, Fraser named the country New Caledonia.

Fraser's right hand man was John Stuart, a most capable fellow, and only a couple of years younger than Fraser. Hailing from the Highlands of Strathspey, Scotland, he had joined the NWC eight years previously. Stuart could build canoes, he wrote well, and thanks to a year with the Royal Engineers in Great Britain, he knew the rudiments of surveying. He would eventually rise to be a Chief Factor for the entire north-west area. Fraser needed Stuart to do the field notes, so essential for mapping, and wanted him to keep the official log. Fraser himself felt insecure about his own writing skills.

Fraser and Stuart were each in charge of posts on Fraser and McLeod Lakes, putting up with another winter's diplomacy in dealing with the Carriers and Sekanis. The latter often preferred a little inter-tribal fighting to working on traplines.

Business matters occupied most of the letter writing, but social news crept in. Fraser appraised Stuart of his winter marriage to a local belle, when he wrote: *My friend, I have once more entered upon the matrimonial state.*

In the early days of the NWC, it was common practice for traders to enter into marriages of convenience, an arrangement welcomed by native maidens and their parents. But in a cost cutting move, the NWC began to frown upon the practice. Feeding an ever expanding band of camp followers was causing a heavy drain on profits. Some of these liaisons were short-lived, but many were broken only at the grave.

Fraser's men, with a multitude of health problems, were a long way from professional medical aid. Strenuous work brought on torn and bruised muscles, judging by the number of sore back and hernia complaints. Stomach problems abounded, due perhaps to the almost exclusive winter diet of dried salmon. A medicine chest of sorts was part of the baggage of expeditions such as this. Fraser himself had need of a remedy when he wrote to John Stuart during the long winter of 1806-07:

I would thank you for some of that Medicine you made use of Last winter with Directions how to take it, as I have a small Touch of come riddle come Raddle.

Venereal diseases were probably the most debilitating of all the sicknesses visited upon the *voyageurs*, and they were generally treated with compounds of mercury. The phrase *come riddle come raddle* is probably a Scottish shepherd's euphemism for such an illness. *Raddle* was the red ochre painted on a ram's brisket to mark a ewe's rump, letting the farmer know when she had been serviced.

By May 28, 1808, Fraser was ready to investigate the great unknown. He chose Fort George, at the forks of the Nechako and Fraser Rivers, as the departure point for his southward journey:

Having made every necessary preparation for a long voyage, we embarked at 5 o'clock A.M. in four canoes.

The crew consisted of twenty-four: three officers, Fraser, Stuart and Jules Quesnel; two interpreters, and nineteen *voyageurs*. The canoes were loaded with such necessities as pemmican, stuffed into bags of sewn buffalo hides called *taureaux*; gifts to please the people whose lands they would be entering; stacks of dried salmon; and equipment for repairs and for building shelters. There was little room for personal effects, but Mr. Stuart took his wooden writing desk and navigational equipment.

For the first two days they made excellent time, covering 100 miles to stop at the mouth of a tributary coming in from the east which Fraser named Quesnel River. But progress slowed to a snail's pace upon entering the first canyon. They eventually gave up their bark canoes due to the violence of the river. A few miles north of Lillooet they made a log platform to cache the canoes: *We placed them under a shade of branches to screen the gum from the sun. Such articles as we could not carry, we buried in the ground.*

Under eighty-lb. packs, an ammunition belt slung over a shoulder, and a rifle clutched in one hand, the men had to scramble up and down the seemingly endless jagged cliffs for untold miles. Occasionally, where river conditions warranted, friendly natives would give them a lift in dugout canoes.

At Camchin (Lytton), they paused at a turquoise coloured river entering on their left. Mr. Fraser reported:

Twelve hundred people live here and they call the forks 'Camchin'. I had to shake hands with every one. They gave us salmon, berries, oil and roots. Our men ate six dogs. They possessed European articles - a copper Tea Kettle, brass camp kettle, strip of common blanket, and clothing such as Cree women wear. The Indians said they were brought from our settlements beyond the Mountains. From an idea that our friends of Fort des Prairies department (Columbia Department under David Thompson) *are established upon the sources of it, among the mountains, we gave it the name of Thompson's River. Some of the people of Camchin appear very old. Cleanly inclined they enjoy pure mountain air, and make use of wholesome food.*

Further downriver the terrain became much worse. They had to use native-made vine ladders and bridges to scale the vertical walls of Hell's Gate. Next, the precipitous cliffs of Saddle Rock Mountain formed another obstacle.

When they reached a widening Fraser Valley they were carried along the river by a taxi-like canoe service which took them from one settlement to the next. At each stop they had to bargain with strangers to obtain food and further transportation, a laborious process which slowed them down considerably.

Three days out of the final canyon, canoes of the Whonnock tribe deposited Fraser in front of a large village at the mouth of the Coquitlam River. Fraser eyed a 40 foot long dugout canoe drawn up on the beach. After much wheedling and shouting between the owner and himself, Fraser obtained the craft, which was large enough to carry his whole party.

At midday Fraser's men were opposite a steep hill of the future New Westminster. He wrote: ...

We came to a place where the river divides into several channels. Seeing a canoe following us we waited ... One Indian of that canoe embarked with us and conducted us into the right channel.

By the afternoon of July 2nd, Fraser's westward journey was practically at an end: *At last we came in sight of a gulph or bay of the sea; this the Indians call 'Pas-hil- roe'. It runs in a S.W. & N.E. direction. In this bay are several high and rocky islands whose summits are covered with snow. On the right shore we noticed a village called by the Natives 'Misquiame'.*

The Fraser River terminates in a broad estuary of several channels, none of which were investigated by Capt. Vancouver in his 1792 circumnavigation of Vancouver Island.

An examination of David Thompson's 1814 map, and Capt. Richards' 1859 surveys aboard the HMS Plumper, indicate that Fraser entered the Straits of Georgia from a channel south of Sea Island, today's Middle Arm.

He probably continued west over Sturgeon Bank until Howe Sound came into view around the high sand cliffs of Point Grey. His *Pas-hil-roe* that ran in a N.E. direction would be Howe Sound with its islands in the foreground and the snowcapped mountains of Sky Pilot, Garibaldi and Sedgewick beyond.

Fraser then turned north and followed the west shore of Sea Island until sighting the long-houses of the Musqueam community behind Iona Island. After a brief inspection tour of their settlement, Fraser's party returned to their canoe and continued north-west for approximately two miles until opposite a smaller native habitation.

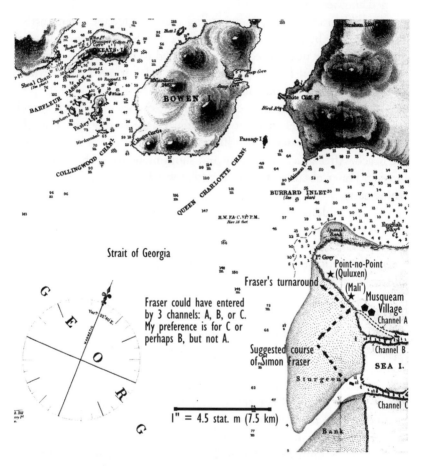

Survey by Capt. Richards and Lt. Mayne – 1860

Dr. Michael Kew of the Department of Anthropology and Sociology at UBC has given me an accurate description of the area where Simon Fraser ceased his westward voyage. Dr. Kew stated: "It is clear from Fraser's journal that he entered a shallow creek on a falling tide and landed at that portion of Musqueam village called Stselexw. After examining the site, his crew ... then made a brief run downstream, refraining from landing at a second village. This may have been the settlement area at Musqueam known as Mali' or it may have been further west at another site at Point-no-Point, known as Quluxen. This was a palisaded house-site which served in times of trouble as a look-out station. They then turned back, heading up-stream, and by the time they came abreast of Musqueam, the tide had turned in their favour."

Simon Fraser stated in his log: *After two miles we came opposite a second village. Here our curiosity incited us to go ashore; but ... it was thought neither prudent nor necessary to run further risk. We therefore turned our course.*

From Fraser's journal and from Dr. Kew, it would appear that Point-no-Point marked his most westerly penetration.

On their return upriver, after darkness had forced them to shore, Fraser's men lay on the sand exhausted by a long, stressful day. To rub salt in the wound, in the middle of the night a rising tide roused them from their rest. They arrived back at the Coquitlam Village at five a.m. to find the inhabitants bathing in the river. The reception was not cordial. Obviously something had turned the natives against them which led Fraser to feel that nothing but problems lay ahead if they forced their luck by staying longer. Eventually someone would go too far and even their firearms might not prevent a massacre.

Fraser wrote: *We saw nothing but dangers and difficulties in our way. We therefore relinquished our design and directed our thoughts towards home. ... The latitude is 49° nearly, while that of the Columbia is 46°20'. This River, therefore, is not the Columbia. If I had been convinced of this fact where I left my canoes, I would have returned from thence.*

As far as Fraser was concerned, this was the River of Disappointment. For purposes of the fur trade, it was not a navigable route to the ocean. His dreams of glory and the hope of achieving a title like that of his fur trading partner, Sir Alexander Mackenzie, crumbled overnight.

History would exonerate him, as in a sense, Fraser did achieve more than 'Sir Knight'. By constructing a permanent chain of forts in the interior, and exploring from there to the 49th parallel, he established the boundaries of a future British Columbia, which ensured a Canada from sea to sea. Canadians are indebted to Simon Fraser. Without his claim on the land, British Columbia might well have become part of another country.

Fraser remained in the Athabasca department for ten more years, then retired to take up land near the village of St. Andrews in the township of Cornwall, Ontario. Two years later he married Catherine Macdonell in the Roman Catholic Church at St. Andrews. Simon was forty-four, his bride twenty-nine. They had five sons and three daughters.

One of the last of the famous Nor'Westers, Simon Fraser died at the age of 86. Catherine passed away the following day.

At one point in time I gave a copy of the text to Dr. W. Kaye Lamb, former Dominion Archivist and a leading authority on Canada's early western development. He took the trouble to make several written comments. One such referred to the theory of Fraser's turnaround position: "My chief doubt is whether it is conceivable that Fraser would comment upon as relatively small a waterway as Howe Sound, when he was faced with the infinitely larger Strait of Georgia. I grant you Howe Sound would appear to run to the north-east, but my own feeling is that for once Fraser made a mistake and really intended to write south-east to north-west for the lay of the land."

"But if I still differ about this, I am quite sure you are right about two highly important matters: (1) the location of the "look-out" at which Fraser turned back, and (2) the fact that he followed the Middle Arm, not the North Arm, when he came to Sea Island."

Midnight of March 31 saw everything in place for Eastward Ho. The next morning, with a gap of over a century and a half, we were ready to embark in the footsteps of Simon Fraser and his *voyageurs*. We expect to follow their tracks as far as Lytton, then choose a different course to Montreal.

Aerial photo — mouth of Middle Arm of Fraser River

After returning to the forks of the river,
we made the decision to relinquish our design
and direct our thoughts homeward.
This River of Disappointment is not the Columbia.
Perhaps my friend Thompson will be more fortunate.
Simon Fraser

Chapter Five
Fraser's River

One hundred and fifty nine years after Simon Fraser, his 'River of Disappointment' would become Eastward Ho's 'River of Challenge'. There were several dissimilarities between the two expeditions, but they had one thing in common. Within 100 miles, both would have to combat the most powerful and dangerous stretch of waterway west of the Rocky Mountains.

Some of the differences should be enumerated, not the least of which was timing. Eastward Ho had purposely chosen to make their assault before the melting snows of summer had increased the river's volume, speed, and turbulence to gigantic proportions. Fraser's calendar brought him close to the maximum freshet periods of June and July. His river would have been galloping along at quite a clip, making it about the worst time of year to investigate the awesome Fraser Canyon.

A further difficulty relative to Fraser's timing was that he arrived during the munificent summer salmon runs which took place every year on this river of bounty. As a result, during July and August, the lower Fraser valley from the Straits of Georgia up to Yale, was inundated with large groups of Coast Salish fishermen from Vancouver Island and Puget Sound.

The visitors, away from home ground, tended to be less accommodating than the regular residents who dwelt along the river. The latter referred to themselves as *Stalo*. According to anthropologist Wilson Duff, *stálu* was *river* in *Halkomelem,* the Coast Salish language.

Another difference was in the vessels the two expeditions used. Fraser's *voyageurs* had to leave their bark canoes at Leon Creek north of Lillooet. They were completely dependent on the goodwill of the people whose territory they had entered. The borrowed canoe which Fraser's party obtained in the Fraser Valley was the largest model of dugout on the river. It was heavy, it leaked, and the owner kept badgering Fraser for its return.

The food supply was tenuous for Fraser's men. While Eastward Ho had the latest in packaged basics and delicacies, Fraser had to negotiate for every meal; not an easy matter when you're on the run. Bargaining for transportation and food in unintelligible tongues called for patience and understanding from both parties. The pale-faced strangers satisfied their most pressing needs with sign language, and on occasion, a loud voice.

A delightful spring morning augured well for Eastward Ho. It lightened the air and the spirits of the participants. On the steps of City Hall, Mr. S. Murphy of Canada's postal service designated Dave Chisholm a pro-tem mail carrier, without pay of course, then presented him with four locked canvas bags of canoe-mail for delivery to Montreal Post Office.

Mayor Stuart Gifford bestowed his official blessing, and asked the members of Eastward Ho to carry greetings to Canadians across the land.

A large crowd had assembled on the waterfront to say goodbye. Dozens of bobbing canoes carried young people dressed in native costumes, simulating the water-borne presence of the original inhabitants of the river, the Stalo people. Sights were set for Ruby Creek, 70 miles upstream.

It was not long before Eastward Ho encountered problems Fraser's *voyageurs* did not have. The outboard running at full speed exposed us to a chilling head wind that brought on a rapid loss of body heat. A hasty change was made into wool fisherman pants, shirts, sweaters and ski-toques. In the confined space of an open canoe there was no escaping the self-created stream of cold air.

Another problem encountered was that a double ended canoe has virtually no planing surface. Under acceleration the bow rises higher and higher out of the water, while the stern digs an equally deep hole. To maintain speed the canoe had to be leveled, which meant three of the crew sat as close to the bow as possible. At slow speed the heavily weighted bow would nose down into the water, prohibiting the helmsman from steering properly. With each major change in throttle setting, therefore, the three up front had to shift back and forth as moveable ballast in order for the canoe to attain equilibrium.

When underway, the three at the bow could carry on a conversation, but it was a lonely existence for the helmsman. Huddled at the stern in front of his roaring motor, he could only communicate by sign language. The helm turned out to be an unenviable position for another reason. At cruising speed, a high spume of spray curved into the air close beside the gunwales. The slightest cross wind turned it into a perpetual shower, spewing cascades of water into the stern of the canoe and onto the lap of the hapless helmsman.

Eventually the helmsman learned to steer with one hand on the throttle while the other pushed a hand-pump to minimize the ever present pool of water. Slowing the canoe lowered the bow, but if the water hadn't been removed, those up front would soon feel moisture creeping around their derrières. Then the helmsman heard from his forward friends, mostly in the form of extremely loud curses.

Their *fifth man,* meanwhile, had his own troubles.

Mr. Fraser: *It took us four days to reach friendly Indians near where the river narrows, a distance of 80 miles. In a heavy cedar dugout canoe that leaked badly, and for which the owner demanded an exorbitant price, we had to force our way through several flotillas of threatening natives. We were fortunate they were not a united political unit, but rather a series of large family groupings interspersed every ten miles or so along both sides of the river. The largest cohesive assembly numbered about 400 souls.*

According to Wilson Duff, Fraser would have passed dozens of Stalo settlements between Yale and Point Grey. Each had minor differences with neighbours that increased with the distance between them. Today the Stalo have close to fifty separate Land Reserves set aside along both banks of the Fraser River.

Fraser also witnessed three distinct kinds of dug-out canoes manufactured from tall cedars of the lower Fraser Valley. The largest, like the one bartered from the Chief of the Coquitlams, would be over 40 feet in length, and shaped out of three quarters of the circumference of a large tree. Generally paddled by twelve men, it obviously had room for more as it carried all Fraser's party.

The most common canoe, and the type Fraser's tormentors would have given chase in, were adzed out of half a cedar log. Between 15 to 30 feet, they carried up to a dozen people.

The third one was very specialized and designed for fishing over shallow, wind-protected water. It had a shovel-nosed look with wide platforms jutting from both bow and stern which allowed the fisherman to night-fish by torchlight.

Eastward Ho's morning run was easy enough. On their right, hidden behind MacMillan Island, they passed historic Fort Langley, established by James MacMillan of the HBC in 1827.

Fort Langley was the first coastal trading station north of Columbia River's Fort Vancouver. Archibald McDonald, who we'll be hearing more about further upriver, took over the management of Fort Langley from MacMillan. A few years later McDonald supervised the building of Fort Nisqually at the foot of Puget Sound.

Before losing control of the Oregon Territory in 1846, the HBC had maintained a north-south transportation corridor between Fort Langley and Fort Vancouver. A canoe route lead north from the Columbia via the Cowlitz River to Fort Nisqually, then to the Fraser River through Canoe Passage.

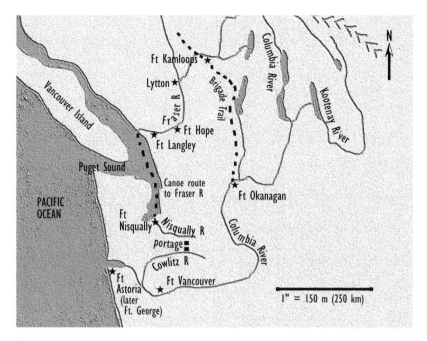

The Nisqually – Cowlitz portage

Eastward Ho passed Whonnock, then Matsqui Island, First Nations settlements both then and now. On the south side of the river Mt. Sumas appeared. Fraser had described the knob-shaped hill on his down-river passage :

Mr. Fraser: *The river ran fast for nine miles then slowed into a lake. Here we saw seals and a large river coming in on our left. On the same side a round mountain is visible which the natives have a name for and which sounds like 'shemotch'.*

The large tributary Fraser saw was the delta of the combined Sumas and Vedder rivers which enter between Sumas and Chilliwack Mountains. The area has been diked and drained since, but the Fraser River still slows appreciably along this section.

Travelling down his 'Great River', Fraser had invaded the country of the Salish who dwelt in southern British Columbia and the western part of Washington State. According to anthropologist Wilson Duff, salish language was an Algonquian tongue, indicating the first Salish may have migrated west through the mountains. Anthropologists divided them into Interior and Coast Salish.

At the upper end of its lake-like portion near the base of Chilliwack Mountain, the Fraser spreads out into numerous gravel-strewn channels. Its opaque waters make it difficult to judge depth. By an island studded bend near the mouth of Harrison River, where Fraser had trouble keeping clear of harassing natives, our propeller struck an unseen rock.

Repairs were made on a gravel bar near Agassiz, directly south of Harrison Lake. *Observer* Archibald McDonald wrote of that large body of water, saying:

Francis Ermatinger, my subordinate when I was in charge at Fort Kamloops prior to my assignment at Fort Langley, made a circular trip through there in 1827 to investigate the 'Lillewaite Tribe'. With the help of an experienced Indian guide, Ermatinger witnessed the Seton, Anderson, and 'Lillewhit' [now Harrison] *Lakes' connection with the Fraser River.*

A.C. Anderson explored the same route 30 years later when it became an alternate way to the gold fields of Barkerville. It would appear from McDonald's journal that from a point of 'first discovery', Anderson Lake should have been called Lake Ermatinger.

As we neared the end of our first day and our goal of Ruby Creek, temperatures dropped with the sun. Wool liners were slipped under rubber mitts and ski toques pulled down to cover stinging ears. To our right, on the south side of the river, Mt. Cheam and the snow clad Skagit Range lay burnished in gold, the peaks catching and flinging back the cold, sinking rays of the sun.

Evening sky turned to indigo. A few stars peeped out. A bonfire lit by friends at the mouth of Ruby Creek on the north side, flickered across the now ink-dark Fraser river. We headed toward our rendezvous.

Gem prospectors had once gathered garnets from the gravel of that mountain stream. The surrounding area is Reserve land for the Tait people. Their Chief, Alex Peters, greeted the frozen canoeists with a warm handshake. His ancestors had shaken hands with Simon Fraser and had supplied his hungry *voyageurs* with freshly caught salmon.

It was very near this location that Fraser and his officers had their first taste of open rebellion. Some of the men, stressed out by lack of sleep, insufficient food, and an endless series of confrontations since arriving at the delta of the river, refused to continue up the Fraser River. On the face of it, such behaviour might seem foolhardy, but there may have been some sense behind the rebel's action.

Voyageurs, raised to a life of wilderness travel, understood the art of sign language. Perhaps they had found out from friendly Tait people of an escape route via Harrison Lake. At the head of that lake, an easy rise along Douglas Creek leads to the headwaters of the Nahatlatch River. The Nahatlatch is a tributary of the Fraser River which it enters just north of Boston Bar.

Our *fifth man* Simon Fraser said: *Mr. Stuart informed me that several of the men were bent upon going by land across the mountains to the place where we had slept on the 24th of June.*

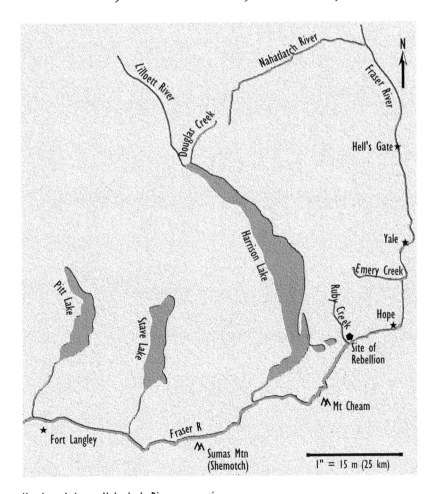

Harrison Lake – Nahatlach River connection

Although Fraser and his officers eventually persuaded the men to stick together, the incident does point out the extensive geographical knowledge possessed by local inhabitants. It also demonstrated the generosity of the people who shared this information with strangers.

Eastward Ho had arrived at Ruby Creek in one day, but as we made ready for day two, we knew that such progress wouldn't last. Already the river could be felt pulsating with new-found power. Threading the Fraser's lower canyon section will put everything to the ultimate test. If we had embarked on a fool's errand, we certainly would know by the end of this day.

Expecting some portaging, we travelled light; an extra five gallon gasoline container, plenty of rope, spare paddles, the canoe mail, and sandwiches. No one needed urging to put on life jackets.

Open aspects of the Fraser Valley are left behind as you approach the mountains enclosing the town of Hope.

Originally Fort Hope, its title implies a wish, which it did when its location satisfied the quest of A.C. Anderson of the HBC. Thanks to Blackeye, a Chief of the Interior Salish, Anderson was able to establish the Coquihalla route to the interior.

When Americans threatened to cut off Canadian use of the lower Columbia River in 1846, officials of the HBC hoped that a satisfactory route could be found from B.C.'s interior to the Fraser River. The Coquihalla trail satisfied that wish.

Furs from New Caledonia, originally consigned to Fort Vancouver on the Columbia River, were transported instead by pack-horse to Hope. They were carried from Hope to Fort Langley by canoe, then

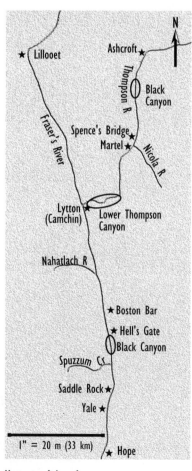

Hope to Ashcroft

on to Fort Victoria in sea-going vessels for trans-pacific shipment. Provincial highway # 5 followed Blackeye's rugged horse trail.

For Eastward Ho, the first rapid of any consequence after Hope is at the mouth of Emory Creek. This rapid fluctuates markedly with different heights of water. We were told that two young men had lost their lives here recently, when their canoe foundered in the large standing waves brought on by the annual spring freshet.

Fraser's men made a *décharge*, lining their heavy canoe up past it. For Eastward Ho, however, in April there was only one moderate wave which we rode over quite easily.

A *décharge* is when the canoe's lading is removed for paddling or lining the canoe past an obstruction. A *portage* is a full carry of everything, including canoe. To *line* a canoe is to propel it forward from shore by means of attached ropes.

After a few bends of the river the town of Yale came into view. Nestled into the crook of a dog-leg, it used to be a great salmon-drying area. During summer and fall, long tiers of drying fish lined rocky shelves on both sides of the river. A smoldering fire produced wisps of smoke that wafted about the dehydrating mass, ostensibly to repel hosts of hungry flies.

On his return trip Simon Fraser had spent a night near present day Yale, immensely relieved to be amongst a more amiable group of people. Here he had given up his large dug-out, and was hitchhiking back up through the canyon. He and his men took an occasional ride in small dugout canoes when the situation warranted, but mostly they struggled on foot along the rim of the precipitous canyon.

Mr. Fraser: *The Indians received us kindly. They called us over to the other side of the river, gave us salmon and berries and showed us how they fished with nets. The mesh was constructed from nettle fibres and hung between ends of two long poles. They resembled purse seines and were dragged between two canoes.*

During the gold rush of 1858, Yale was the head of river navigation for the stern-wheelers huffing and puffing in from New Westminster. At the height of the gold fever it was a jump-up place. Scores of saloons and dance halls soaked up the pokes of thousands of miners fresh in from the gold fields.

The town was named after James Yale, another HBC officer. He had joined Gov. George Simpson's 1828 trans-Canada tour at Fort St. James on Stuart Lake, in New Caledonia.

Eastward Ho could see that the river was beginning to rise after its winter doldrums. Our timing was right. In a few days much of it would be impassable. It was now or never. With trepidation we entered the canyon.

Above Yale the river shoots viciously through a narrow channel between the highway and a jagged barren island called Lady Franklin Rock. Men of the fur trade called the chute formed by this restriction 'The Falls'.

This condition happens when a portion of the river is raised by an underwater obstruction, such as a large immovable boulder. The water immediately above the obstacle increases in velocity as it falls the extra distance, thus creating a hole in the river. The size of hole depends on the volume and speed of the waterfall. The water pouring out of the hole creates a series of standing waves which line up in parallel rows across the river.

When working upstream, the first trick is to get through the parallel waves. Then you have to skirt the outer rim of the water-hole to climb the slope above it. You gradually change the angle of the canoe so that your stern misses the void. Once clear of it you swing the canoe straight into the stream of falling water, open full throttle, and hope there is enough power to climb the slope. When the canoe is hovering above the hole, the die is cast. The only choice is forward; with any backward slippage the canoe will drop into the hole.

This rapid was not the worst to be encountered, but as the first major one it was a challenge. I felt that the success of the expedition hinged upon it. At the helm, my knees shook, my hand on the throttle wouldn't stop twitching. Preparation highlights of the past six months flashed through my brain like rapid-fire video clips. I had begun this action that now threatened the lives of others. Was it all to blow up in my face? I was one worried guy. This was indeed the moment of truth.

The canoe hesitated at the top of the falls, bow in the air, stern hovering over the gaping hole below. Everyone unconsciously grabbed the gunwale, squeezed, and leaned forward, willing the canoe to escape the hold of the river.

Gaining momentum, we slowly drew away from the hole in the river, and reached the top of the chute. With a whoop of relief everyone relaxed.

"I clung to the woodwork so hard I expected a piece to come off in my hand." Don laughed.

Watching from the highway, Harvey Smith, friend and canoeing companion, who had arranged the departure ceremonies, sensed our thoughts, and said afterwards, "Your stomachs must have been in knots. What a relief to see you get through that first 'Big One'. When you did, I knew you'd handle the problems ahead."

Though less sanguine perhaps than Harvey, we were now confident the canoe could take it, and that we had picked the right combination of size and power. It was also gratifying to find out that 'fear' would not likely be a threat to our continuance. However, some joy was held in reserve. Over-confidence can swiftly provoke Nemesis and the river gods into retaliatory action. They demand constant respect.

In camp that night we talked about the challenge of Lady Franklin Rock and its association with the Arctic explorer, Sir John Franklin. Dave read an account from a tourist brochure.

"In 1847, after Franklin perished on his third attempt to find a seagoing North-West Passage, his wife spent a fortune stirring up world attention on his behalf. One of her more impractical schemes was an attempt to reach the Arctic via Simon Fraser's river. It may look feasible on a map but the logistics of a full-blown search party trying to cope with the 'impossible canyon', wasn't too sound. The HBC tried to dissuade her, but she was adamant and found someone either ignorant of the terrain or without scruple for spending her money. Predictably, her expedition met with disaster when attempting to breast the rapids opposite that rocky island. A fully-laden canoe, stuffed with precious equipment for the relief expedition, along with an unfortunate crew member, slid into a watery grave."

Fifth man Simon Fraser had something to say about the Rock: *Natives from the village where the rapids end told us that white men like us had come to this 'bad rock' from below.*

The reference was probably to some unheralded traders who had made their way up the Fraser River from the coast. They could have been Spanish, British, American or Russian. All these nations had sailing ships cruising the Pacific north-west coast before Simon Fraser's arrival.

After the Rock, Eastward Ho bounced through four miles of turbulent water, intent on safety rather than speed. Towering mountains began to pinch in the river, increasing the awareness of powerful forces that so disdainfully buffeted the canoe. Slithering around another bend we met a rocky island in the middle of the river.

White water cascaded down two equally tumultuous channels. Progress by river was impossible at this point.

The old 1860's road to the Cariboo was close to the west rim of the canyon so the rock wall was anxiously scanned for a break. Keen-eyed Don spotted a narrow cleft down at water level. He pointed it out to Jim who steered over, nudging our bow into the crack in the wall. The motor was removed and passed hand over hand to Don who had managed a foothold on the slippery rocks; then the fuel. The canoe with its stern out in the current, rocked from side to side, making things difficult. The last bit of cargo, the mail, was passed forward like buckets in a fire brigade.

As we sat wondering how to extricate the canoe in this confined area, a shout came from above. Friends had followed our progress from the highway and figured we might be having a few problems. A search brought them to the defile.

Ropes were made fast to the thwarts, and several pairs of willing hands hoisted the canoe up the ravine to a level patch of ground. Volunteer packers might carry equipment, but Dave the postman called out, "Nobody but canoe crew totes the mail bags!"

The motley group of portagers crossed a trail leading to Sawmill Creek where Eastward Ho re-entered Fraser River at the base of Saddle Rock Mountain. In Fraser's day this mountain marked the dividing line between the Interior-Salish Thompson River Indians and the Coast-Salish Stalo people of the Fraser River delta. Highway engineers have since rammed a tunnel through the innards of Saddle Mountain whose precipitous cliffs once provided a barrier between the Thompson and Stalo Nations.

Mr. Fraser: *We were now back in the area of the Hacamaugh, having left most of the Ackinroe people at the 'bad rock'. We saw many fishermen poised on rock ledges, working the back eddies for salmon with long-handled dipping nets made of hemp-fibre, supplied by the Hacamaugh. This was the source for much of the Stalo's netting material and it served many purposes. Some nets were made of thread the size of cod lines. They were eight fathoms long with meshes 16 inches wide. The Natives caught deer and other large animals with them.*

Saddle Rock Island is plainly visible from the trail above the river. Shaped exactly like a saddle, this moss covered mound of granite is about the length of a football field. Two rounded horns sit in line with the river. The concavity in between is perfectly shaped to seat a giant river man such as the mythical Paul Bunyan.

Observer Archibald McDonald, when running this part of the Fraser with the Simpson 1828 expedition, wrote:

Started at broad daylight, low water, in 25 minutes came to head of Simpson's Falls where the river is choked up by a most solid rock of about half an acre in extent. Examined it along the west shore, but conceived the run along that side extremely dangerous, and owing to the immense rocks all over, to carry was impossible. The east lead was then determined upon, crossed, and run without landing on that side, by the Guide. He rushed on with his bark canoe, and a safe arrival below was effected, but not without much risk in the whirlpools against the rocks that hung over us. The boat followed, but did not suffer by the eddies so much, as it did by being swallowed in the swell of the Fall, out of which the power of 12 paddles could not keep it.

Spuzzum Creek entered on the west side. It was once the settlement of sixty people who befriended Fraser's party. Spazum or Spuzzum, meant 'little flat'. When tombs of a curious construction caught Fraser's eye, he asked to inspect them.

Mr. Fraser: *This the Chief granted, conducting me himself. These are the best 1 have seen. They are constructed like chests of drawers 15 feet long, with well proportioned carvings of birds and animals upon boards and posts.*

In 1858, when the Cariboo Road arrived here from Yale, Spuzzum served as a depot for a western branch-line of the north-south fur brigade that moved between Fort Alexandria on the upper Fraser and Fort Kamloops on the Thompson River. A spur line led from Merritt to this point on the Fraser River, which supplanted Anderson's Coquihalla route. Here the HBC operated a ferry across the Fraser.

John Stuart, after his return from the 1808 Fraser River Expedition, had remembered what some First Nations people said about a well-used horse trail providing a by-pass for much of the tumultuous Fraser Canyon. In 1813 he followed their advice, and established a winding brigade trail from Fort Alexandria through Kamloops to Vernon, and down Okanagan waterways to Fort Okanagan on the Columbia River. Each spring, canoe brigades from Fort McLeod, Fort James and Fort George converged on Fort Alexandria with their winter's accumulation of animal skins. Waiting pack animals would receive two, ninety-lb. tightly packed bales of fur, balanced one to a side. A return trip would be made in the summer with the cargo done up in ninety-lb. *pieces.*

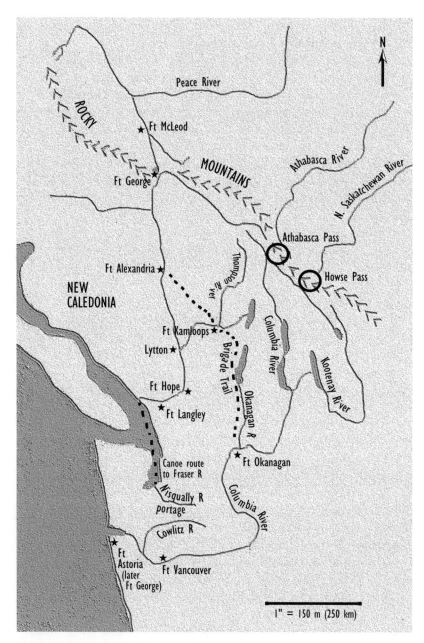

Brigade Trail: Fort Alexandria to Fort Okanagan

What a spectacle those semi-annual mile-long pack-trains between New Caledonia and the Columbia would have made. Swearing packers and hundreds of sweating horses raised a train of dust visible for miles. With a little imagination, a map, and a couple of reference books, one can follow that colourful caravan of old. Today it is Highway 97.

The next landmark for Eastward Ho was Alexandra Bridge, the third bridge of that name constructed for the Cariboo Road. A few more miles brought us to the ominously named Black Canyon whose upper end terminated in the narrow gorge of Hell's Gate. Fraser had to scale perpendicular walls to circumvent this three-mile stretch. It must have been a spine-tingling exercise for the *voyageurs*, loaded down with guns and packs.

Mr. Fraser: *The road was unbelievable; a rudimentary path over rocks, defiles and precipices, made passable by shaky primitive scaffolding and ladders. With heavy loads to carry and hands occupied the men had to summon up courage to attempt passage. The ascent of sheer cliffs was by means of ladders consisting of two parallel poles interlaced with cross-sticks tied with twigs for steps. These ladders were placed end to end for any height. Tied together loosely, they swayed in the smallest breeze. The worst was climbing a rock projecting out over the one you were leaving. But the Indians went up and down like sailors in the rigging.*

The people were generous, giving us two dogs which the men enjoyed eating. They passed on hand-carved wooden tools and woven baskets and a blanket of soft Dog's hair. We observed amongst them pieces of iron and brass and a bunch of brass keys they said came from the crew of a ship destroyed by Indians of the sea.

Eastward Ho had not been able to examine this deep canyon at first hand. With fingers crossed, we edged gingerly into its gloomy aperture, darkened by the rock-loving black lichens which adorn the walls.

In the confines of the canyon the river tilted and accelerated in a series of gigantic steps. Progress slowed considerably. At this particular water level a rocky shelf was exposed which enabled two men to scramble along its slippery surface, each with a tank of gas. Lightened by 400 pounds, the canoe was able to squeak through.

Then came the final rise at the top of Black Canyon. Here no shelving was present. Either we went through fully loaded or retreated several miles back to the bottom of the canyon. We decided to run it.

We had to evade a black hole in midstream. The helmsman twisted on full throttle to ascend the incline. Too late, he discovered there wasn't enough power to escape the pull of the river. The canoe barely held its position, the river streaking by at 14 m.p.h., the canoe's maximum speed. Even with the motor howling at its highest pitch, we just couldn't pull away from the maelstrom.

The helmsman started to sweat. He could hear nothing over the screaming motor, but could see a small conference going on at the bow. Presently Jim began shifting his weight from side to side, swaying the canoe into a gentle rocking motion. The other two followed suit, maintaining a slow, regular rhythm. Almost imperceptibly the canoe began inching forward, creeping up the incline, drawing away from danger. Jim had remembered a trick his party had picked up when ascending the Nahanni River the previous year. When we finally attained the top of the fall, victory yells released our pent up tension.

The flying buttresses of Hell's Gate presented themselves next. Here the torrent rips through towering ramparts at velocities up to twenty mph., which left no doubt about what had to be done. We drew into a tiny bay on the east side below the barrier. It was portage time.

When all the equipment had been hauled to the top of a steep bank of boulders, evening was coming on. It had been a long exhausting day, physically and mentally. Food and sleep were the top priorities. Then some one noticed that a life jacket and light meter were missing. None could recall leaving the articles.

"Perhaps Don and I left them by the river when we made that last carry on the west side," Dave remarked.

Dog-tired though they were, the two of them left immediately to cross Hell's Gate suspension bridge to follow the C.P.R. tracks downriver in search of the missing gear. They returned after dark with Don having a tale to tell.

"We were well into a tunnel when steel rails telegraphed the 'clickity-click, clickity-clack' of an approaching train. The tunnel curved so you couldn't tell which way it was coming. Since we were heading south, we ran that way, hoping we had picked the right direction.

"A pin-point of daylight at the end of the tunnel began to grow as our feet pounded down the ties. Then a rhythmic beat pulsated hollowly in the chamber behind, indicating the train had entered the tunnel. The gyrating headlight of the engine flung our leaping shadows down the long hall as we ran for our lives. We won the race with seconds to spare, leaping clear as the hissing locomotive thundered by. After catching our breath, we found the missing articles."

"Yes, but at almost too high a price," Lorna said quietly.

Next morning, a carry was made around Hells' Gate. The rapids took their name from the Steam boat 'Skuzzy', used in 1880 as a supply depot for the construction crews laying the C.P.R. tracks. Large black eye-bolts, employed to winch the vessel through the Gates can still be seen sticking out of the granite cliffs beside the river.

Breasting the Scuzzy rapids in lower Fraser canyon

There are several Hell's Gates on the rivers of North America, but this one that Eastward Ho and Simon Fraser had to scramble over must have been the original. Precipitous sides of the canyon are squeezed so closely together they almost form a coffer dam. The volume and the violence of the river surging through the narrows is something to behold. *Observer* Archibald McDonald called these narrows the *Gate Dalles*.

The river here is faster than it was in Fraser's day. Early in this century the Canadian National Railway blasted, without forethought, a tunnel along the river's east side. Thousands of tons of rock slid into the river, sunk to the bottom and formed an inaccessible plug. The increased slope boosted the velocity of the river dramatically at that point.

At certain critical water levels, the flow is such that even salmon, who are capable of leaping five foot high waterfalls, and whose hydraulically perfected bodies defy the laws of gravity, can't make headway. The present *fish-ways* were constructed during and after World War Two.

Eight miles above Boston Bar the Nahatlatch River comes in on the west side. Fraser had camped at its mouth when going downstream on June 24th. It was the upper reaches of this river that his *voyageurs* had wanted to head for, when they mutinied near the mouth of Ruby Creek on July 6th.

Further on the river began to twist and form rapids once more, forcing us to make several décharges and portages. The toughest section was an area called Kanaka Bar. It was named after the Hawaiians who arrived as sailors on HBC vessels, but jumped ship to pan gold.

A narrow canyon cast the river into deep shadow. Strong eddies and up-wellings hurled us from side to side, forcing the helmsman to constantly change speed and heading. We sat with paddles in-hand, ready to fend off a sudden crash against the overhanging cliffs. This short canyon was probably the one Archibald McDonald called 'McDonald's Dalles' in his 1828 Trans-Canada tour with Gov. Simpson.

After the canyon it was back to battling the flumes of whitewater that roared around each bend. Every turn brought a different kind of problem, depending on slope and tightness of the curve. It was in this area that D'Alaire, one of Fraser's men, almost drowned as the result of an upset. In spite of half a lifetime spent on water, no *voyageur* wore any type of flotation equipment. Few knew how to swim.

Light fades early at the bottom of these soaring canyon walls, making it increasingly difficult to pick a line through the rapids. Just when we thought the goal of Lytton would not be met, meaning a cold and hungry night without food or sleeping bags, Don spotted the overhead trestle of the Canadian Pacific Railway. A check of the map indicated we were only a couple of miles from Lytton. The east, or Lytton side of the Fraser was sheer cliff. The only choice was a steep ascent of loose gravel that lay on the west side. Canoe and equipment were dragged well above the river in case a cloudburst should provoke a sudden upsurge in water level. Taking only the canoe mail, we scrambled up the steep embankment to the C.P.R. tracks, then crossed over the Fraser on the railway bridge.

Darkness settled in as we stepped along the ties leading to the lights of Lytton. The town was named after Bulwar-Lytton, Secretary of State for the Colonies, and the man who appointed the legendary Judge Begbie, Chief Justice for British Columbia. Walking along Main Street, we wondered where the land party had made camp. Jim glimpsed Bill Gifford's car turning a corner, and stopped him with a whistle.

Bill backed up. "Well, if it ain't the canoodlers! I've been driving up and down that canyon all afternoon trying to locate you. Thought you'd drowned by now".

"No such luck", we replied, hopping into the station wagon. The land party had camped on the flats at the junction of the Fraser and Thompson Rivers. The canoe crew tented beside them.

Lytton is on the edge of the great interior plateau, bounded on the west by the Cascade Range which the Fraser River furrows through, and on the east by the Monashee Mountains. This plateau extends 250 miles south from Williams Lake to the U.S. border, and it is 100 miles across. Here one breathes the dry, exhilarating air of the high country, scented by pine tree and sage brush.

Fraser made reference to David Thompson's explorations of the Columbia River. It must have been a severe disappointment to have struggled so valiantly that summer of 1808, only to hear rumours that his partner had beaten him to it. Manfully he named the river after the apparent winner. But as Fraser learned on his return to Canada, although Thompson had broken through the Rockies at Howse Pass, he wouldn't decipher the peculiar configuration of the Columbia River for another three years. Nor would he ever witness the river Fraser had named after him.

In the morning Eastward Ho returned along the railway tracks to the cache on the Fraser. Everything was in order. The Fraser River portion was completed by canoe within the hour. Daily mileages had been 76, 36 and 38, a total of 150 in three days. It was a feather in Eastward Ho's cap to have wrapped up the first and most dangerous of three British Columbia rivers. Yet we had to stand in awe at the achievements of Fraser's men and officers. When you consider the differences in technology, local knowledge, and access, their coverage of the terrain in seven days was truly quite remarkable.

What can be said of their *fifth man,* Simon Fraser, as Eastward Ho prepares to leave their guide and book companion? A rough-hewn individual, he was steady as a rock under the press of adversity, as his journal amply demonstrates. For example, his entry of June 15, 1808, when he realized the impossibility of carrying on without adequate canoe transportation:

Mr. Fraser: *Here we are in a strange country, surrounded with dangers and difficulties among numberless people who never saw the face of a white man. Our situation is critical and highly unpleasant; however, we shall endeavour to make the best of it; what can not be cured must be endured.*

A noble homily, simply stated. Upon departure from Fort George, Fraser had christened his canoe 'Perseverance', the motto of the NWC; surely an apt description of the owner's personality.

*This part of the river is all rapids, the walls of the
canyon so precipitous there is no hope of portaging.
We ran them because we had to. White faces of the bravest,
even our partly amphibious Iroquois bowman,
reflected everyone's concern.*

Gov. George Simpson

Chapter Six
The Thompson Connector

overnor Simpson and Archibald McDonald have been credited
with the first descent of the entire Thompson River. The
peripatetic governor was on his way to the Columbia River
from Hudson Bay. He made an incredibly fast business trip
of 3,000 miles in just over 100 days.

HBC man, James Yale, waited for Simpson at the junction of
the Fraser and Thompson Rivers, the site of a First Nations settlement
called Camchin, today's Lytton. Simpson had put Yale in charge of two
canoes at Fort Alexandria on the Fraser River, 100 miles north of
Camchin.

He had also given Yale his number one bow-man, Jean
Baptiste Bernard. Yale and Bernard were to investigate the Fraser down
to these forks, while Simpson and McDonald went overland along the
interior horse-brigade trail to Fort Kamloops. The plan was for
Simpson and McDonald to run the Thompson River from Kamloops,
in a boat constructed expressly for the purpose, and meet Yale at the
forks.

The plan sounded fine, but there was a small catch. The canyons in question had never been navigated before. We know the problems Simon Fraser had, who saw all of his river firsthand. We have Archibald McDonald's report of his inspection of the Thompson River by horseback two years previously. He had been unable to assess the canyon immediately above Camchin because the near vertical terrain would not allow access to the river.

Here we have the manager of the most powerful company in Canada willing to risk his life for a bit of geographical information. Simpson demonstrated great courage by placing himself in jeopardy and relying solely upon the skills of his men. Yet the question might be asked, "Was he heroic or just plain foolhardy?"

Part of the answer is that the Governor of the HBC in Canada was desperate. On his 1824 trip to the Columbia he had seen the handwriting on the wall; access to the lower Columbia might well be lost to the Americans. This was why he had ordered the immediate construction of Fort Vancouver on the Columbia River, 100 miles from the sea. Fort Langley was erected shortly after on the Fraser River, as a possible fall-back. Now, if he could find an alternate route to the sea that remained north of the 49th parallel, New Caledonia's problems would be solved.

It was not to be. Simpson's decision, made as a result of his hair-raising runs down both the Thompson and the Fraser rivers, had an immediate affect on HBC policy in the Oregon Territory. Since the boundaries of Western Canada hinged in large measure on the conduct of the HBC, it is appropriate to review a report he made to his superiors, the all powerful 'London Committee'. He wrote from Fort Vancouver, March 1, 1829:

The lower half of the Thompson is full of frequent and formidable rapids. It consists of many rugged precipices with no possibility of portaging. We only lightened for two rapids but had narrow escapes. In one, the river poured over our gunwales. In this unmanageable state we immediately entered another which threw us out of control. A flick of the current drew us back from the brink and providentially we got out safely. The continual plunging from one rapid to another kept us as wet as if we had been dragged through the river. At the forks of the Fraser we were happy to meet Mr. Yale and his party.

Mr. Yale's report of the Fraser river from Alexandria to here is favourable, arising perhaps from the lowered state of the water, and because he had my bowman, the best judge of river navigation in Canada.

Following Mr. Yale's recounting I was optimistic. We remained at the Forks an hour then started down [the Fraser River]. Immediately the character and appearance of the river totally changed. Every new reach brought fresh and more alarming dangers. The banks erected into perpendicular mountains soaring from the river to their cloud enveloped peaks.

In many places there was no possibility of landing to examine dangers, consequently we were hurried into rapids before we could ascertain how to run them. Our craft would shoot like the flight of an arrow into deep whirlpools which seemed to sport in wheeling us about, leaving our water logged craft in a sinking state." *"I will no longer think of Fraser's River as a practical communication. It had never been canoed before in its entirety. We ran all the rapids successfully through the lower canyon, i.e. from Thompson River down. But we were travelling light and had three of the most skillful bowmen in the country. And we were lucky. I would consider the passage certain death in 9 out of 10 times.*

Simpson's hope that Simon Fraser had exaggerated his difficulties proved to be wishful thinking. Now, having learned at first hand how unsuitable the Fraser River was for commercial transport, he realized that the retention of Fort Vancouver and the use of the lower Columbia must be actively pursued as long as possible.

Under Simpson's iron fist many wasteful habits of the Columbia District were eliminated, forcing American competitors to temporarily withdraw from the field. The HBC retained control of Oregon for another decade. By the mid 1840's, however, the inexorable push of migrants into the lower Columbia was forcing the Company's hand. In 1845, much to their regret, they had to shift their base northward. They established Fort Victoria on Vancouver Island. That retreat also made it easier for the conciliatory Peel-Aberdeen government to give in to the Americans. It allowed the border to run from Lake of the Woods through to the Straits of Georgia on the 49th parallel, rather than backing the Canadian position of having the border dip south and follow the Columbia River to the Pacific.

At Lytton a new river and a fresh set of problems faced Eastward Ho. Eighty miles of fast water, interspersed with two canyons, lay between Lytton and Savona on Kamloops Lake. Seasonal low water, which had been a boon on the Fraser, would prove a handicap on the Thompson River. There was not enough water in the lower canyon to use the long-shafted motor. Nor could any shelving be seen that might afford an opportunity for lining or portaging the canoe. To wait for a foot rise in water level could mean a delay of days or weeks.

A reasonable alternative was 'shanks mare'. The decision was made to hike the highway until a favourable point of entry to the river could be found. No time was wasted. Breaking camp, we tied the canoe on top of the camper, placed the canoe mail into our back packs and started humping the road to Spences Bridge.

A view from the high bluff above Lytton affords an arresting sight. A panorama of mountain beyond mountain fills the northern horizon. Lower down, two ragged-edged canyons of the Thompson and Fraser Rivers converge in a Y-shaped embrace to mingle their disparate rivers. The turquoise water of the smaller Thompson resisted with a sharply defined line for several hundred yards, but eventually became absorbed by its clay-colored partner.

On Thompson River's west side, Painted Canyon greets the eye. A vertical, variegated cliff, it appears to have been a mountain torn apart by some cataclysmic force, with half of it thrown away heaven knows where. Jackpine and poplar trees dotted its lower valley where a herd of elk foraged.

Trudging along a highway eventually loses its appeal. One begins to dwell increasingly on monotony and sore feet. The others had accepted my "guesstimate" of ten miles to a launching site. Twenty miles later we staggered into Shaw Springs. It was dark, and it was raining. Eight hours marching on asphalt had produced blisters on top of throbbing feet.

The others were understandably annoyed. My only rebuttal to criticism was a lame, "I didn't mind the walk."

Three successive days of tense situations had the old adrenaline running. Boredom and sore feet proved a sudden anticlimax.

An interesting historical reference was missed on the hike. About midway we had passed the mouth of a small river called Nicoamen. *Observer* Archibald McDonald, who had scouted the Thompson River between Kamloops and Lytton on horseback, reported to John McLoughlin, his superior stationed at Fort Vancouver:

In conformance with your desire, I set out accompanied by eight men and Nicholas the upper Okanakan Chief Am happy to inform you that in seven days we were back after performing the desired object. This river (the Thompson) *to the mouth of the Coutamine is not bad, and indeed to the little Nicaumchin there are no very dangerous places: but from there for about five miles down it was nothing but a continuation of Cascades and strong Rapids.*

On his return from the forks of the Thompson and Fraser, McDonald was guided up the valley of the Nicola River which he said was: *... an Indian track that leads to the upper forks of the Okanagan river.*

Obviously McDonald's guide Nicholas knew this country like the back of his hand. His access trails predated highways 8, 5A and 97 by many years. Nicola River and Nicola Lake were likely named after him.

According to McDonald's memo of 1827 the First Nation population of the Thompson Valley District was estimated to be 3500 souls.

For *Coutamine,* read Nicola River, which enters the Thompson at Spences Bridge; for *little Nicaumchin,* read Nicoamen River. Note also the use of the syllable "chin", as in Camchin, Nicaumchin and Wallachin. Fraser referred to the "chin" people of Camchin as being members of the "Atnah" Nation.

The rain came down in torrents on Eastward Ho's campsite, a pale dawn eventually permeating the steady drizzle. Breakfast was a standup affair, huddled around the coleman. During dish washing, the mists hanging low on the hillside began to lift. It seemed odd the first rainfall should have been in the dry belt, but as we would discover, 'unusual' weather became the norm.

The previous night's rainfall had not raised the river appreciably, but clear water of the Thompson was an improvement over the muddy Fraser. You could at least see the bottom coming up to meet you. "Perhaps we won't nick so many propellers now", remarked Jim.

The canoe sat in a back-eddy while the mail and necessities of the day were tossed in. Shortly after launching, two divergent channels of white water confronted us, neither deep enough for the long-shafted motor. We decided to 'line' the canoe.

With ropes tied fore and aft the canoe drifted out into the current, trimmed at a 25 degree angle to the river. Taut ropes create a vector affect, forcing the canoe upstream. The method works well with lightweight canoes, but Big Red had a keel and it was relatively heavy with 300 lbs. of fuel and motor aboard. These factors inhibited the necessary side-slipping action.

Progress was by inches. When capping waves from rough water beat against the bow, or when the man on the bowline allowed the canoe to nose out just a little too far, the pull on the arms became unbearable.

An additional difficulty was the dark-green scum growing on the boulders lining the shore. It made secure footing impossible. The bow line got away from Jim once. Flat out on his stomach, head hanging over the river with Dave grasping his heels, he was unable to prevent the nylon rope from slipping through his clenched fists. The canoe, released from its sideways pull, shot into mid stream, heading across the river. The stunned crew watched helplessly as their vessel executed a 180 degree turn. Then like a wild steed under the hands of a skilled cowboy, it came tremulously back to shore, checked by Don pulling in the safety line, hand over hand.

Lining canoe on Thompson River near Spences Bridge

Passing under the highway at Spences Bridge, we went over to a group of youngsters who stood waving from the shore. Alerted to Eastward Ho's arrival, they had been let out of school to inspect these men who had embarked on a river journey across Canada. Their principal called out. "You've come at the right time. This class is studying the history of our canoe explorers." An enjoyable half hour was spent discussing stories from Canada's past.

The last set of rapids for the day were the noisy Martels, a mile of continuous white water. Following a lengthy inspection, we carried our gear to the top of the rapids, making two return trips. The thought of struggling with the canoe over that stretch of uneven boulders was too much for Jim and Dave. They decided to run the rapids. Jim draped himself over the bow to weigh it down and pick out a channel.

The swiftly moving waterway was interspersed with patches of foam bubbling up from large rocks strewn along the bed of the river. Soon all was confusion. The propeller, cavitating loudly in the froth, prevented Dave from catching a word of Jim's shouted commands. Jim would swing his arm in one direction, then another. Did he mean, "go that way?" or, "don't go that way?" It was like skiing out of control on a giant slalom course. The situation would have been laughable were it not for the worry of wrecking the equipment.

They came out at the top unscathed. Drifting into shore, with a touch of pride in his voice, Jim said, "That worked pretty darn well. We'll have to do the same next time".

"When I figure out what your signals mean," was Dave's reply. "Blind luck got us through that lot."

Eastward Ho grounded on a sandbar in a hook of quiet water. The area, called Martel on the map, used to be a watering site for the C.N.R. in the days of steam engines. Now diesels whistle by a lonely watchman's house flanked by acres of sterile dunes. We had only covered eight-miles from Shaw Springs to our campsite at Martel.

The river, peaceful here, gurgled past the doorway of our tent, but muffled sounds from the Martel Rapids rumbled through the night. They were serving notice that their 'big brothers' up ahead were ready to repeat the challenge. Stars shone through the sharp, dry air with a steady brilliance, forecasting a sunny day.

A rosy-fingered dawn saw everyone up knocking frost off the tent, the crisp morning air as clear as a cup of spring water. Between Martel and Ashcroft, a distance of twenty miles, the highway leaves the Thompson River.

The morning run was easier than expected. A dunking is less worrisome in the Thompson River than in the Fraser. It is generally a more accessible river, except for its lower canyon, and it contains a smaller volume of water.

At lunch time, easing of tension allowed a relaxed examination of the surroundings. The river, its waves fringed with white collars, swept by our feet as it dashed around serpentine gravel bars. An eagle soared lazily over the rim of the cliff across the way, telescopic eyes searching for a noonday snack of field mouse or marmot. Behind, a squirrel scuttled through the brush.

Drowsiness followed a satisfying snack of sardines, rye-crisp, cheese and a chocolate bar. With gumboots off, toes wriggling in the warm sand, Jim echoed Ralph's thoughts. "Too bad we're always in such a hurry".

Eager Dave's reply was "Yeah, but we still have three thousand, eight hundred miles to go, so let's keep at it." Reluctantly, the others heaved themselves up from their soft granular couch.

There were two rapids below Black Canyon. We stopped to examine the first one, then went through as planned, threading our way past some rocks. I was feeling a little cocky. Creeping up on the next one, I slowed to call, "Looks okay, lets go for it."

The rapid appeared innocent enough as it descended around a 45-degree bend. Our bow edged past the waves at the bottom of the schuss, then nosed into the incline as the throttle opened up. To everyone's astonishment the river came tumbling in over the bow. The men of ballast up front yelled in consternation as cold water poured over a prow that refused to lift.

No time to look for causes. With the canoe wallowing badly, we cut the motor and tilted it up to avoid cracking the transom during any backward drift. The two men sitting forward, wedged tightly together in the bow, didn't dare scramble to their feet. The slightest roll could cause the canoe to turn turtle. With cautious movements of our paddles we managed to gain some control. Water poured over the transom as the canoe backed down beside the gaping maw. Fortunately a back-eddy held us momentarily, allowing a precious couple of minutes to paddle shoreward in crab-like fashion.

A ton of water had to be sloshed out before our half-filled bathtub could be dragged high enough to tip out the remainder. Fortunately the mail had been sealed in plastic bags.

Launching again, after the fact, we took a closer look at the rapid for a second attempt. Two chutes merged at ninety degrees to form a deep trench filled with non-supportive froth. The canoe couldn't rise due to lack of buoyancy. Figuring the river had us on this one, we carried around the obstacle.

The spectacular L-shaped Black Canyon followed. The dark red, volcanic walls of this Black Canyon were not at all like the Black Canyon of the Fraser River. The walls of the latter were of grey granite, and came much closer together. Here the river had gouged deeply into the land, leaving red rubble cliffs spaced two or three hundred yards apart. The wash from the motor cut a cream colored furrow on the surface of a deep quiet pool where the river temporarily slows its downhill rush.

In the stem of the L, the river reverted to its surly, shallow ways, its bottom covered with rock ridges and chest-deep depressions. The crew had to jump out and align themselves along the gunwale and pull with all their might to work the canoe from one water filled pot-hole to another. Razor-sharp ridges caused repeated stumbling.

The tilted motor, with its shaft and propeller projecting two feet straight back from the transom, was a hindrance when trying to move quickly from one side of the canoe to the other. During the struggle, a hand slipped. On the opposite side, Don managed to retain his grip, preventing the stern from landing on a sharp rock, but he bore the full weight of the canoe. The result was a severely wrenched back. He said nothing at the time.

The uphill struggle continued until the channel narrowed and the river deepened, allowing use of the motor. Behind, the sun sank quickly beneath the rim of the canyon that had given us such a hard battle. Ahead, the Ashcroft bridge loomed against a darkening sky. The solitary figure standing vigil at one end was Bill Gifford, the kind of man who would remain at his cold perch all night if necessary.

The next day posed no difficulties. Lunch was in the Wallachin area where the hand of man had once triumphed temporarily over nature. Viewed from the river, deserted wood-framed houses stood with sagging doors and gaping windows. Weather-loosened tar-paper flapped in the moaning wind. Rusting farm equipment lay half buried in the parched earth, evidence that man had been an innovator in this now deserted village. On the north side of the Thompson Valley, intermittent remnants of a wooden irrigation flue ran downhill across several miles of sun-baked, metallic hills.

From a Kamloops brochure came the following: "Early in the 1900's an ambitious and dedicated group of young people from England settled in this sagebrush country to create abundant life. They built long flumes up into the hills to catch precious water; planted trees, ploughed fields, seeded crops and raised families. In 1914, hearing the bugle call of World War 1, the men returned to fight for Mother England. None came back to Wallachin."

Eastward Ho entered Kamloops Lake, passing Savona shortly after one o'clock. Then it was on to the lake's eastern end where the Thompson River enters. In late afternoon, our prow grounded with a sibilant hiss on the south shore of Thompson River, waterfront for the City of Kamloops.

Kamloops, at the junction of North and South Thompson Rivers, was once a gathering place for Shuswap people, part of the Interior Salish group. When fur traders first entered this area in 1811 they recorded the pronunciation as *Cum Kloops*. Old Fort Kamloops was at the forks, but on the north side of Thompson River.

The first recorded white person into this country was a trader by the name of David Stuart. He was a former Nor'wester but no relation of our John Stuart. David Stuart had signed up with Astor and his short lived Pacific Fur Co., and was part of the group that had sailed from New York aboard the ship Tonquin, bound for the Columbia River, arriving near the end of March, 1811. He was present at Fort Astoria when David Thompson arrived in his canoe. He accompanied Thompson's return up the Columbia as far as the Okanagan River. Stuart erected Fort Okanagan beside the falls, then proceeded along Okanagan River to the land of the *Sheewaps,* (the Shuswap Nation), where he wintered.

David Stuart was with a canoe brigade that left Astoria on April 4th, 1814, bound for Montreal. The North West Co. had bought out Astor's Pacific Fur Co., and the party contained members of the PFC who did not wish to sign on with the NWC. There were 76 people seated in ten vessels, with five to six paddlers per vessel. They reached Montreal on schedule five months later.

Kamloops has long served as a transportation centre. As well as a stopover for the Okanagan-Coquihalla horse brigades, the North Thompson River gave access to the Yellowhead route to Tête Jaune Cache and Jasper. The open, grass covered hills became the feeding and breeding grounds for horses needed in the brigades, and later for the *argonauts* of the Cariboo Gold Rush.

The next river for Eastward Ho was the South Thompson which emanates from Shuswap Lake. A pleasant, lazy stream, it winds through cattle country. Brown and white Herefords graze along the river bank, farm buildings alternate with summer cottages.

Marshlands bordering the river provided feeding grounds for hundreds of Tundra swans, which the approaching canoe kept pushing up into the air. They didn't circle back, but with great white wings flapping ponderously would rise only to glide down again to the water around the next bend. After a few miles the canoe entered a widening of the river, where thousands of the large snowy birds had massed together. Stirred into action, all the swans took flight en masse. Overhead the sky filled with their beating wings, the air with a cacophony of protesting squawks. Now with more maneuvering room they were finally able to wheel about. Flock after flock poured back downriver, relieved to escape the disturbing hornet buzzing underneath.

A large mission church lay at the entry into Little Shuswap Lake. Across the lake was Little River, a half-mile stream draining Shuswap Lake. Referred to as the richest river of its size in the world, its value is measured by the millions of dollars worth of sockeye salmon which travel through here on their way to the spawning grounds of Adams River.

Little River is also a popular fishing area for the trout angler, particularly on weekends. Fishermen stared sourly at the passing canoe which was disturbing the sanctity of their favourite pool. They seemed unaware their fishing holes were part of a Vancouver to Montreal waterway.

Friends had invited Eastward Ho to spend the night at their cottage on Shuswap Lake. That evening, "the Doc" busied himself making minor repairs to fellow crew members, handing out jokes as well as band-aids. Turning to his canoe mail, he became very serious. He discovered some envelopes had received water marks. After sorting and re-packing it all, the *Postman* announced sternly, "All right you guys, from now on there's no more using mail bags as cushions."

Mid-morning of the next day, Eastward Ho glided onto the beach near Sicamous. We had hoped to canoe up the Eagle River, but its twisting course was covered with windfall. 'River' rather over-dignified its description; 'small winding creek, cross-hatched with fallen trees', would be more accurate. To save time we decided to hike the forty-five miles to Revelstoke.

Lunch-time respite next day was spent beside the road with boots off to cool our burning feet. The others kidded me with, "It must be the shoeman and his poor fitting boots." Dave finally resorted to wearing runners a size too large. Sloppy in the morning, the running shoes were tight at the end of the day.

Malakwa was passed, a Shuswap word for 'mosquito'. Next was Craigallachie, where Lord Strathcona drove the last spike for the C.P.R., completing Canada's first transcontinental railway and bringing British Columbia into confederation.

Before receiving his title, Lord Strathcona was plain Donald Smith, nephew of John Stuart of Fraser River fame. On the recommendation of his uncle, Donald had secured a position on the bottom rung of the

Hudson's Bay Co.'s ladder. The young lad arrived fresh from the hills of Strathspey to work in icy Labrador. There were no thoughts of titles in his head, surely, but eventually he became Governor of the HBC and President of the Bank of Montreal. He later received a baronetcy for his sponsorship of the Strathcona Horse, a regiment that saw action in the Boer War.

Popular belief has it that the 'last spike' was made out of gold or platinum, spawning recurring speculation as to its whereabouts. The C.P.R. claims it was just an ordinary forged steel spike, like millions of others. Practical men like Smith might have suffered sleepless nights at the thought of such a valuable asset stuck in a railway tie. British Columbia reaped a harvest of real gold from the sustained period of growth following on the heels of the new transportation system that opened up the West.

Many passersby beeped horns and waved encouragement to the hikers. Late in the day an overtaking truck honked at us. Automatically the hiker's heads nodded acknowledgment. Around the next bend, a piece of cardboard lay beside the road. On it was scrawled, "Good luck boys, from Sno-Boy of Penticton, Des Reigh". Underneath were four large oranges. It was touching that a man would take the time to stop his truck, get down out of the cab and make this simple gesture.

Bob Tustin, President of Revelstoke's Chamber of Commerce drove out to pay a call. "The whole town is excited about your coming," he told us. "We're planning an evening reception on your arrival, and a royal sendoff at departure time. A scroll has been prepared for you to carry to Mayor Drapeau of Montreal. Our schools will have a morning closure so the kids can cheer you on your way. And don't worry about accommodation," Bob continued, "The Travelodge is putting you up gratis".

Most importantly, Bob brought along Eric Neilson, a river-boat man familiar with the Columbia River between Revelstoke and Boat Encampment. Eric spoke only of what he knew from personal experience. He proved a reliable informant.

Mile-to-the-inch maps were brought out. Revelstoke to Boat Encampment was 100 miles by water. At that time, before flooding from Mica and Revelstoke dams, Boat Encampment was a bus stop on the two hundred mile Big Bend Highway that paralleled the Columbia River. A summer-only road, it looped around the northern Selkirk mountain range. Further back in time, in the early 1800's, Boat Encampment had been an important staging post on the road from Canada which crossed the Rockies through Athabasca Pass, then continued down the Columbia River to Fort Vancouver.

Eric's descriptions of the various rapids were pencilled onto the map; which ones to run, which to portage, where and how. "The valley is narrow," he stated, "Hence the river changes constantly and significantly under varying weather conditions. What I'm telling you are generalities. Just bear in mind that water levels affect each bend and gravel shoal. A quiet back eddy can change into a violent whirlpool overnight."

"The river rose two feet last night. My advice is to head north from Revelstoke as quickly as possible. The annual spring run-off could begin any time. I wouldn't attempt an ascent of the Columbia during its flood," warned the experienced river man.

After digesting Eric's information, we felt reasonably sure of reaching Mica Creek, providing no monstrous upsurge of the river took place. Our land party could drive that far too, the road being open for construction vehicles.

We learned that on the Rocky Mountain Trench side, the road paralleling the Columbia River was still buried under several feet of snow. With air temperatures lower on the eastern half of the Big Bend, it was likely to remain so for another month at least. The big question mark remained. Should the eastern section be skied, snowshoed or canoed? The answer would have to wait.

Our trek continued past Clanwilliam Lake to the height of land at Eagle Pass, two thirds of the way through the Monashee Range. Mountain peaks began to soar. Walter Moberly had discovered and named this pass as surveyor for the C.P.R. when rail construction was taking place through the Rocky, Selkirk and Monashee Mountains.

The last few miles, winding downhill to the Columbia River seemed interminable. Steel girders of the bridge into Revelstoke finally materialized, but the sight of so much snow laying along the river bank was disconcerting.

Dinner was in a nearby restaurant where the strain of the past eleven days surfaced. A heated argument began over the method of paying for ordered meals such as this one.

Don raised his voice in anger. Ralph got testy. Sparks flew across the table. Dave, blue eyes blazing, snapped, "For heaven's sake, stop airing our dirty linen in public! If we have to argue, let's keep our bloody disagreements to ourselves."

We all returned to the motel to cool off. The blow-up had a therapeutic affect. Next morning, while making arrangements for the days that lay ahead, we were laughing at our antics in the restaurant.

A freezing rain had enveloped the higher reaches of Columbia Valley, wiping out several recently installed microwave towers. All phone communications were severed. It was rumoured that crews from Lenkurt Electric had been working 24 hours a day. They hoped to have some service lines operating by mid-afternoon. Flying conditions were practically zero.

Back at the motel Jim and Dave re-sorted the trailer. Fumes from a leaking pump attached to a 45-gallon drum had contaminated all of the unsealed stock of food. We munched gasoline flavoured Dad's Cookies for weeks afterwards; but fresh air creates ravenous appetites.

While we scouted around for information of the river above Boat Encampment, someone said, "B.C. Hydro has a bombardier based at Mica. Perhaps they could be persuaded to take your canoe part way up the Columbia while you ski the snow-covered road."

After a series of delays and relays, Don managed to reach Gordon Tanner. Between bouts of static and total silence Don outlined the problems besetting Eastward Ho. Repeating the rumour of a 'bombardier', Don asked, "Can we beg, borrow or steal it for a day to take our canoe to Kinbasket Lake?"

"Yes, the bombardier is here," Gordon Tanner's voice crackled, "but I don't know what kind of shape it's in. It hasn't been in service for some time, nor can I authorize its use. By the time you get here maybe we'll have something figured out."

With that slender hope, the decision was made to tackle the Columbia River the next morning. Of course the whole Columbia River loop of the Big Bend could have been by-passed with a 70 mile hike through Rogers Pass to Moberly, but that was a last resort. The intent was to follow David Thompson who had paddled through this very place in 1811.

At the civic banquet that evening Mayor Lundell and several aldermen were present. One of the latter was George LaForme, a native son who had trapped and guided in the Selkirk Mountains. George was familiar with the Columbia between Boat Encampment and Kinbasket Lake. He said, "Its a steep canyon all the way up to the lake. My advice for this time of year would be to ski the whole bit. Unfortunately I can't advise you on the Surprise Rapids further up-river. My trap-lines didn't extend that far south."

The next day Eastward Ho would attempt an ascent of the Columbia River, the third and final river to be encountered in British Columbia. Damming the Columbia at Revelstoke and Mica Creek, since Eastward Ho's passage through here, has removed much of the danger and excitement. Today two lovely emerald lakes graced by green-clad timbered slopes are there for canoeists. Two hundred miles of pleasant paddling surrounded by magnificent peaks of the Selkirk and Rocky Mountains is some compensation for the drowning of a river.

This is David Thompson country and Eastward Ho will presently be embarking on the river he explored in its entirety. A biography of the second *fifth man* is the subject of the next chapter. His writings inspired the Eastward Ho journey.

Everywhere his work was found to be of the highest order,
especially considering the means and facilities at his disposal.

J.B. Tyrrell describing David Thompson, 1770 – 1857

(image taken from the wall mural at the David Thompson
Secondary School, Vancouver, BC)

Chapter Seven

fifth man **David Thompson**

he first child of Welsh parents, David Thompson was born in the parish of St. John the Evangelist, Westminster, England. Two years later a brother John arrived. The father of the two boys died shortly afterwards and was buried in a paupers grave, paid for by the parish. The widow was left penniless.

It seems odd that a city lad, born and raised within walking distance of Westminster Abbey, with cobblestoned streets as a playground and the Abbey's monumental inscriptions to read for mental exercise, should find his niche in a distant Canadian wilderness. Such did fate decree for fourteen year old David Thompson, upon departure from a charity institution known as Grey Coat School. The school's building was a former monastery belonging to Westminster Abbey, and, as they do to this day, the Board of Governors of the ivy-covered school paid annual rent of 'one pepper corn' to the Dean of Westminster Abbey.

After a seven-year tutelage, Thompson's teachers thought he had absorbed enough knowledge. His name appeared in a minute book of 1784:

"On the 20th of May, David Thompson, a mathematical boy belonging to the Hospital, was bound to the Hudson's Bay Co. as an apprentice for seven years. The Treasurer paid the said Company five pounds for taking the boy in."

That year a wide-eyed David viewed a new world aboard the Hudson's Bay Co.'s sailing ship 'Prince Rupert'. He sailed from Gravesend on the Thames, bound for Stromness, Scotland. From there a course was set for the snowy northern wastes of Canada.

In September young Thompson sighted the bleak western shore of Hudson Bay and the granitic coastline of the Canadian Shield at the mouth of Churchill River. The scar on the skyline was the gutted skeleton of Prince of Wales Fort, the calling card left two years previously by the daring French naval commander La Perouse.

There was no time for contemplation. Winter was coming on. Capt. Tunstall had only allowed 10 days for stores to be taken off and his ship's holds filled with the bales of fur piled on shore. Everything had to be transported by rowboat to and from the Prince Rupert anchored in the Bay, a time-consuming process. When the ship sailed away, a small group of men and one boy were left in solitude for a year.

Thompson was made of tough fibre and soon adjusted to the new regime. He had received an unusual amount of formal schooling for one of his age and station. Seven years of the Three R's, and a dollop of religion, had left its mark. Because of this training he was asked to do secretarial work for the Fort commander, the intrepid Arctic explorer, Samuel Hearne.

Many years later he wrote of those early days:

All our movements, more or less, were for self-preservation. The wood that could be collected for fuel gave us only one fire in the morning and another in the evening. The rest of the day, if bad weather, we had to walk in the guard room with our heavy coats of dressed beaver, but when the weather was tolerable, we passed the day in shooting grouse. The interior of the walls of the house were covered with hoarfrost four inches thick, pieces of which often broke off and to prevent this we wetted the whole extent and made it a coat of ice after which it remained firm and added to the warmth of the house. The cold is so intense that everything, in a manner is shivered by it; the very rocks are split with a sound like the report of a gun.

He went on to describe the habits of aquatic birds, polar bears, seals and other animals, as well as the customs of Inuit and First Nations people. This introduction to the world of nature brought forth his acute powers of observation that were coupled to a scientific turn of mind. His 'Narrative' detailed living on the Bay so succinctly, that if you were preparing to spend a year there without modern conveniences, the information needed for survival could be found in the first thirty pages of his book.

A born story teller, he created graphic verbal pictures for his readers. Many years after Thompson's term in the far west, Dr. J.J. Bigsby, a geologist from England, and working with Thompson on the International Boundary Commission, drew him thus in his book 'Shoe and Canoe':

'His figure was short and compact, his black hair worn short all around and cut square just above the eyebrows, as if by one stroke of the shears. His complexion was of the gardener, ruddy brown'.

'He has a very powerful mind and a single faculty of picture-making. He can create a wilderness and people it with warring savages; or climb the Rocky Mountains with you in a snow storm, so clearly and palpably, that only shut your eyes and you hear the crack of a rifle and feel snowflakes on your cheeks'.

Thompson had a strong religious streak in his nature, an unusual trait for a fur trader. It gave him a moralistic, and at times, an intolerant view of human activity. He took an early aversion to the devastating affects of liquor on the behavior of native people. In 1785 during Thompson's first year at York Factory, over 2,000 gallons of English brandy were brought to that station alone. Ten years later the quantity had quadrupled. To lessen overhead, the Company opened a small distillery at York. With a disapproving tone he wrote:

No matter what service the Indian performs, strong grog is given to him, sometimes for two or three days. Men and Women are all drunk and become the most degraded of human beings.

Twenty years later when Thompson was in charge of trade on the western side of the Rocky Mountains, he took a stand and refused to allow spirits into the area under his jurisdiction. Although contrary to the methods of his partners, who railed against his stiff-necked puritanism, he had his way. Eventually Thompson's attitude was vindicated. When the HBC amalgamated with the NWC in 1821 to eliminate cutthroat competition, the incentive of promoting drunkeness as an inducement to trade finally ceased.

Thompson's apprenticeship provided many experiences that taught him to cope with a harsh and unforgiving land. He toured the west on horseback as far as 'The Shining Mountains', learning survival techniques. He observed at first hand the disposition of nomadic Plains Indians; how to trade fairly with Cree, Assiniboine, and people of the fierce Blackfoot Nation. The latter, made up of three groups named Piegan, Blood, and Blackfeet, led a warrior's life similar to the freedom-loving Bedouin of Lawrence of Arabia.

When Thompson was eighteen he suffered a nasty accident. While carrying a heavy load down a steep bank of the North Saskatchewan River, he fell awkwardly and broke his femur. Writing about the incident fifty years later, he said:

Which by the mercy of God turned out to be the best thing that ever happened to me.

Thompson was an invalid for almost a year. Spending the following winter at Cumberland House, he met and became an assistant to Mr. Philip Turnor, a practical astronomer and surveyor for the Hudson's Bay Co. Under Turnor he applied his mathematical skills to learn the art of surveying. During long winter evenings he applied himself with such zeal to solving reams of arithmetical problems that his right eye suffered a temporary blindness.

The events of that year firmed Thompson's personality by bringing on a maturity of purpose. Henceforth he would focus his ambition around the new-found knowledge of surveying. No more the carefree gallop on horseback, or idle chit-chat beside the camp fire. He began to keep day books wherein he consistently recorded his position, distances and direction, with astronomical observations for latitude and longitude. In the future, throughout the length and breadth of Canada, he would keep detailed weather reports, record ethnological details of native people, and make scientific observations of the environment .

Thompson served his seven years apprenticeship with HBC, then contracted for two additional three-year terms. There may have been a personality clash between Thompson and fellow workers toward the end of his tenure, or perhaps he did not fully appreciate the financial difficulties the HBC was experiencing due to Britain's involvement in European wars.

In any event he was dissatisfied with management's lack of enthusiasm toward surveying at that time. In the spring of 1797 he signed on with the opposition, the hated NWC, a rapidly expanding firm that promised Thompson plenty of survey work and an opportunity for partnership status. This was an act which the HBC, particularly the hypercritical Gov. George Simpson, never forgave.

His first mapping assignment was a threefold one spread over a thousand miles. First he had to locate the villages of the Mandan Indians of the upper Missouri River. Secondly, he had to find the source of the Mississippi River. Thirdly, he had to identify specified trading posts, particularly Grand Portage on the western shore of Lake Superior.

Prompted perhaps by the desire to make a good impression on his new employers, Thompson set out on an incredible feat of surveying. Travelling through a strange country, under difficult conditions of a prairie winter, he completed all three assignments in less than six months. When Alexander Mackenzie, a senior partner in the NWC, and a man who knew a thing or two about wilderness travel, received the full report at Grand Portage, he was astounded at what their new man had accomplished. He wrote: "I would have been happy to have had it done in two years!"

The next task was to the far north-west, mapping trade routes and positioning trading posts along the upper Churchill River and lower portions of the Athabasca River. He paddled to Lake Ile-à-la-Crosse, an important connector to Peter Pond Lake. Then to Lake La Loche and the historic Methy Portage that first put Montreal fur traders into the Arctic-seeking waters of the Clearwater River. From there he travelled to Lake Athabasca, home of the largest and sleekest beaver in North America.

Thompson also surveyed the fair sex at Ile-à-la-Crosse, for he paused there long enough to marry Charlotte Small, age fourteen. She was the comely daughter of a Cree mother and Patrick Small, a founding partner of the NWC. Like many other 'bourgeois', Small had made his fortune in 'Indian Country', then returned to civilization leaving his western-built family behind, 'in the manner of the country' – à la façon du pays.

The Thompson nuptial, celebrated in a NWC House, was perhaps as simple as the statement that Thompson recorded in his notes when he wrote:

The event took place on June 10, 1799 at Lat. 55.26.15N, Long. 107.46.40.W.

The year 1804 was an important one for the NWC as well as David Thompson. It was during that year the 'grand old man' of the fur trade, Simon McTavish, died. His place was taken by his hand-groomed nephew, William McGillvray, who brought fresh ideas and new vigor to the partnership. He healed the breach with Sir Alexander

Mackenzie, who in opposition to McTavish had formed the XY Company six years previously. Competition had become ruinous to both houses. That same year, several new partners were added to the firm, one of them being David Thompson. He was declared the official astronomer of the NWC.

With the change in management, the NWC embarked on its last great expansionary move, a two-pronged thrust to the western sea. One was led by Simon Fraser, the other by David Thompson. In the spring of 1807, based on information supplied from two of his scouts, La Gasse and Le Blanc, Thompson found a way through the impenetrable looking mountains with their lofty wind-swept peaks and glacier-filled valleys. The route he chose became known as Howse Pass.

When Thompson first reached the river flowing *north* between the west side of the Rockies and the Selkirk range of mountains, today's 'Rocky Mountain Trench', hope for it being the Columbia appeared nil. It was running the wrong way. The parallel mountain ranges which contained it streamed northward as far as the eye could see. Thompson knew that the Columbia River entered the Pacific 300 miles south of his present position. So he turned south and went upstream. He realized from the terrain that this river's headwaters were not far away. He sought a south flowing river.

Thompson built Kootenay House, a few miles downstream from Columbia Lake, the uppermost reservoir of the Columbia River. He would move Kootenay House later to a site overlooking the lake, but it was the first of half-a-dozen trading establishments he would construct west of the Rocky Mountains. He concentrated for the next three years in developing a viable trading area in the future states of western Montana, northern Idaho and eastern Washington. It was a program similar to what his partner Simon Fraser was conducting in New Caledonia.

He made several attempts to find a navigable canoe route to the elusive Columbia, but the rivers of entry were beset with impenetrable canyons. Thompson had got himself into a cul-de-sac. On a map, access to the main Columbia looks easy as the Kootenay, Pend d'Oreille and Spokane rivers all rush through to service the Columbia River. The problem was all those tributaries had long portions which prevented their use as canoe passages.

Lewis & Clark, after crossing the Rockies in their 1805 expedition to the Pacific Ocean, had struck the Snake River which led them to the Columbia at what is now Pasco, Wash. From there they carried on to the sea. Thompson's trading posts were near the Spokane area, roughly 100 miles north and east of Lewis and Clark's entry to the lower Columbia River.

It wasn't until the spring of 1810 that Thompson found the key to unlock the riddle of the Columbia River. In late April, after attempting a second but equally fruitless descent of Pend d'Oreille River, he climbed a high crag above the canyon. From its peak he could see the Pend d'Oreille running west to enter a large river flowing south towards his position. This new river lay between two parallel mountain ridges that continued north until out of sight.

With a native guide to hold his surveying instruments Thompson sighted the mountain range that lay east of the river. To his surprise he found it to be on the same longitude line as the snow-capped peaks he had sighted across the valley when he first crossed the Rockies. The mountain range, which he named Nelson Mountains in honour of the great British Admiral, we know today as the Selkirks.

Thompson hypothesized that the glacial-green stream he had come upon in 1807, the one which flowed in the wrong direction, was in fact the very same river he now saw flowing southward. He premised that the river must have doubled back on itself to loop around the Selkirk Mountains.

Thompson had no time for further investigation as he had to dash east for an important meeting at Rainy Lake. In September, on his return, he was turned back near the NWC's post of Rocky Mountain House. There a human barrier blocked his way to the Howse Pass. A large contingent of Piegan warriors had returned from patrolling the upper Missouri River where they had been stationed in the wake of the Lewis and Clark expedition that had killed some of their people. The Piegans were now determined to stop Thompson from carrying guns and ammunition to the Kootenay Nation, their traditional enemy. The Kootenays had occupied the high valleys of the Rocky Mountains before being driven westward by tribes of the Blackfeet Confederation.

Acting upon information picked up from free-traders, in January of 1811 Thompson succeeded in opening a second pass through the mountains. It was 100 miles north of Howse Pass, away from the reach of the Piegans, yet it still came out on the Columbia River. This breakthrough became known as the Athabasca Pass. It worked its way into history by becoming, for half a century, the recognized mountain crossing for the canoe road to the Pacific.

That summer Thompson made his celebrated trip down the lower portion of the Columbia River to the ocean. At Fort Astoria he spent a few days with Duncan MacDougall, an old friend and former Nor'Wester in charge of Astor's Pacific Fur Trade Co. The Astorians had arrived at the mouth of Columbia River four months previously, aboard the sailing ship Tonquin.

Thompson showed MacDougall a letter from the wintering partners, given to him at Rainy Lake. It outlined acceptance of an agreement to purchase a one third interest in the PFC by the NWC. Unbeknownst to Thompson, that agreement had become null and void after his departure from Rainy Lake.

The two men exchanged letters of mutual association stating that the NWC would have unlimited access of the Columbia River to its mouth, but would restrict its fur gathering to the country east of the river. Two years later during the 1812-14 war between Canada and the United States, the NWC bought out the entire Columbia River holdings of the PFC.

When Thompson left Fort Astoria that summer of 1811, he stayed on the Columbia River all the way north to Boat Encampment, thus completing exploration of the entire 1200 mile river. In the vicinity of present day Revelstoke, on Sept. 11, he records being soaked to the skin from heavy rainstorms, his men having lined and poled most of the way against a full river and heavy current.

Carrying on to Boat Encampment, Thompson continued to probe for other canoe-road connections. He explored northward up Canoe River to near present day Valemont. He obviously was aware of a third breakthrough of the Rockies, the one now called Yellowhead Pass.

In the spring of 1812, at the age of forty-two, Thompson made his last crossing of the Rocky Mountains. Picking up his family on route, he canoed to Fort William to learn that Canada and the United States were at war. With eyes skinned for American naval patrols on the Great Lakes, his *voyageurs* hightailed it to the safety of the mouth of the French River in Georgian Bay. The French-Ottawa River link carried Thompson and his family to Montreal.

Thompson's hard-headed partners appreciated his achievements. They awarded him a generous severance pay of 100 pounds sterling, a goodly sum for those days, plus three years share of profits. As an added bonus, after completing his maps for the Company, he was to be considered retired, but entitled to one share's worth of profit for a seven year period.

Thompson took up residence in Terrebonne, Quebec, where he completed his great map of Western Canada. It was a compilation from surveys he and others had made during the previous two decades. The Ontario Provincial Archives possess the original copy.

From 1816 to 1826, the British Government employed him to survey and define the Canada-U.S. boundary line from the St. Lawrence to Lake of the Woods. In his mid-fifties, Thompson settled back to a modest living as a farmer and business man in Williamstown, Ontario, with hopefully some spare time to devote to the detailed drafting of his many valuable maps.

Unfortunately, loans made to members of the community were not as easy to collect as those made to First Nations people. Neighbours, business acquaintances, and family, tarnished their honour at his expense. The NWC, coming upon hard times, did not live up to its commitment. Out of capital at sixty-five, Thompson returned to surveying.

He had no time to pursue publication of his map-making achievements. This failure not only cost him recognition as a cartographer, it also meant no royalty money would come his way. His straitened circumstances did not prevent the HBC, Arrowsmiths, or the Government of Canada, from plagiarizing his creations. Instead of a well-earned retirement, he had to survey Francis Lake, the St. Lawrence River, even city lots, in order to provide for himself and his wife.

Living in Montreal at age 75, Thompson was confined indoors. He then set about to write the memoirs which he called simply, 'Narrative'. Ill health and blindness prevented completion. At eighty years of age, Thompson put down his pen. He died in 1857. His life's companion, Charlotte, followed him to the grave three months later.

Thompson's great map of the North-West has been much improved through modern technology, but his 'Narrative' will live on as long as Canadians take pride in their fellow countrymen. His pages became a canvas on which he painted vivid scenes from his mind's eye.

As with many people of his time, recognition came posthumously. Thompson's incomplete and unsold 'Narrative', was edited by J.B. Tyrrell and published by the Champlain Society in 1916. A copy of that edition, long out of print, is now worth several hundred dollars.

Like the rest of us, Thompson had his personal foibles. Somewhat careless perhaps about money-matters, he died in penury. As head of the Columbia Department for several years, he obviously possessed managerial ability, but he could be intransigent at times.

To sum up: an eye for detail, a retentive memory, the patience to record monumental amounts of data, and above all, a relentless drive contained inside a resilient body, made Thompson the ultimate wilderness traveller and map-maker. He deserves a high position in Canada's Hall of Fame.

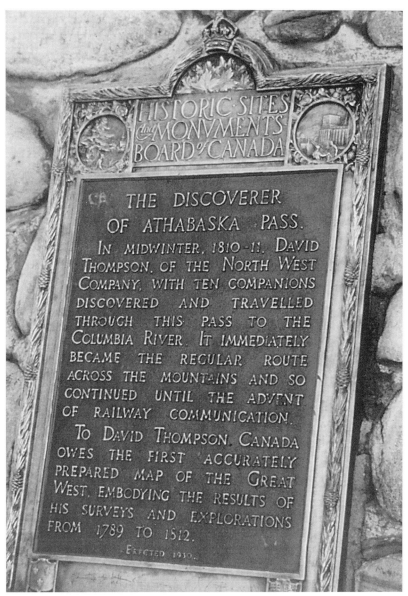

David Thompson's cairn in the Athabasca Pass

With the help of my guide I was able to survey
the Columbia River emanating from the north in a deep valley.
At last I begin to comprehend the strange course of
this sinuous river.

David Thompson

Chapter Eight
The Road to Canada

n April, 1810, Thompson had climbed the western slope of the Selkirk Mountains, which he had labeled the Nelson range. He was about to unravel the secret of the Columbia River, finally realizing that it made a 200-mile detour to reach the Pacific Ocean.

The Columbia and Kootenay Rivers form a geographical oddity. This pair of glacial-coloured streams are part of the Rocky Mountain Trench. Starting within five miles of one another, but separated by the Brisco range of hills, they flow in parallel, but opposite, directions.

The Kootenay, subverted by some glacier of the previous ice age, runs south-west, missing Columbia Lake, the source of the Columbia River, by a hop, skip and jump. The Columbia River courses northward. Both rivers carry on their separate ways for 200 miles; then both change their minds at the same time. The Columbia turns south at Boat Encampment, while the Kootenay bends northward into Canada, near Libby, Montana. The latter forms Kootenay Lake, then exits via its West Arm to roar down and join forces with the Columbia at Castlegar, something they could have done more easily 300 miles sooner. There is no accounting for rivers, but therein lies their attraction.

In its 200-mile detour between Golden and Revelstoke, through an area commonly referred to as The Big Bend, the Columbia River drops an average of 5.5 feet per mile, the same gradient as the lower canyon of the Fraser River.

At present-day Revelstoke on the Columbia River, in mid-April of 1812, *fifth man* David Thompson faced conditions similar to those of Eastward Ho. He stated: *We had six canoes, each with 1800 lbs. of fur, 300 lbs. of pemmican, and paddled by five voyageurs. The depth of snow was distressing. After working with the line all day, at night we had only the snow to lie on, feet and legs numb with cold from pulling the canoes up the rapids. There was no help for it we had to go on.*

Eastward Ho made an early start in a mist enshrouded dawn, shivering inside wool clothing and water-proofs. The day's goal was Downie Creek, 45 miles upstream. A helicopter pilot, slipping under the heavy cloud cover the previous day, had a look at the massive log clusters grouped at each river bend, and sent us a warning. "The river has been rising for three or four days now and the large bundles are beginning to shift out into the main channel. They're big enough to block your canoe. Time is of the essence. Your expedition could become cut off."

As Eastward Ho's canoe slid under the main highway bridge, a crowd of young people let out of school for the occasion lined the railing to shout encouragement: "Go Man! Get There! Yeah Montreal!"

The air was raw with the smell and feel of winter. More snow threatened from clouds smothering the mountain tops. This valley receives a heavy annual snowfall squeezed out from moist Pacific air being raised and cooled by the Selkirk Mountains. Ever increasing amounts of it covered the gravel bars, as we proceeded northward.

By late spring the river steams through Little Dalles Canyon. Whirlpools and combing waves beat frantically against unclimbable walls. Before freshet, however, the turbulence is minimal and the passage surprisingly easy. It was in marked contrast to Thompson's first ascent of this part of the Columbia.

Mr. Thompson: *Camped last night below the Dalles to where Finan McDonald had ascended a few weeks previous. We lined our canoe; the river full of currents and rapids.*

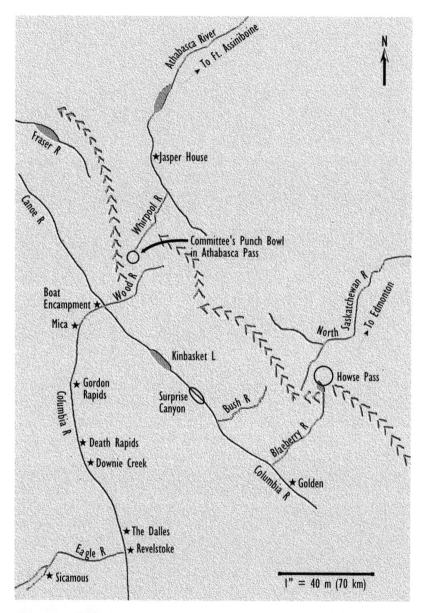

Sicamous to Golden

The first hurdle Eastward Ho encountered were the log bundles. They consisted of a dozen or more logs wrapped together with steel cable, scattered randomly along the valley floor. Towering several feet above our heads, the hulking brutes were intimidating obstacles to pass when maneuvering against a ten m.p.h. current.

Once past the end of a bundle projecting into the main channel, the helmsman would have to quickly swing the canoe ninety degrees and run parallel to the logs on their upstream side. This was the breath-catching part. If the motor should suddenly fail, the current sweeping beneath the logs would suck the canoe under in a twinkling. A leap for safety to the logs wasn't on because the latter were sheathed in snow and ice. There was no way to obtain a hold on them.

Log jam on the Columbia River calls for a portage

Flirting with this danger continued throughout the day. Lining or portaging began whenever the river became completely blocked. In these circumstances we were glad of the snowbanks which allowed us to drag the canoe past the obstructions.

The luxury of pulling a canoe over snow wasn't available to *voyageurs*. Tender birch-bark hulls couldn't stand the abrasion. After 1821 the HBC used York boats built on the Columbia River. Double-ended and planked hull, they were rowed rather than paddled. York boats were heavy, but seaworthy and durable. Most importantly, they carried a much larger payload than canoes. *Voyageurs* could load three tons of freight into them.

The log bundles often lay over snow-buried creek mouths once known intimately by *voyageurs*, and later by men who roamed these parts in the gold rush of the 1860s. The latter left the name's of creeks, such as: Carnes, Holdich, Mar, Big Eddy, and Eighteen Mile Rapid. These gravel flats had felt the pick and shovel of men who had arrived in an assortment of homemade vessels, from rowboats to rafts. For a brief period the sternwheeler *Forty-niner* travelled between Downie Creek and Arrow Lake.

In late afternoon Eastward Ho rounded the last bend of the day and pulled into Downie Creek. A small cabin was available near a cafe and gas station operated by Ed Wallis and his mother. Later in the evening we chatted with Ed who was interested in local history. He recounted:

"Once in my wanderings I came across some notations incised onto a tree trunk. A person of authority examined it and stated that it was an inscription by David Thompson done in 1812. The tree was cut down, and the slab containing the notations was sent to the B.C. Provincial Museum."

In a critique of this book, W. Kaye Lamb had said: "I can tell you a story about the slab that your informant Ed Wallis described. I'd vouch that it was the same slab brought into my Victoria office some years ago. At first I couldn't make out what was on it, but one morning with the sunlight streaming through my window, as I walked by at a certain angle, I saw clearly incised in the wood, a date, a position and the letters P.K. I feel sure that it wasn't Thompson's inscription but rather that of Paul Kane, an early painter of the Canadian West. He had journeyed westward through Boat Encampment in November of 1846 and returned in October two years later. He crossed the Rockies both times through Athabasca Pass."

Mr. Kane's journal was examined and this is what *observer* Kane had written:

I waited in Boat Encampment for the HBC's horse brigade to come and transport their supplies eastward across the mountains. The voyageurs prepared a 'lob-stick'. A high tree with thick branches at the top was chosen. All the lower limbs are then removed. A smooth surface is cut on one side of the tree on which the person, in whose honour it has been trimmed, is invited to cut his name. Upon completion, three rounds of blank charges are fired, three cheers given, and the spot afterwards bears the name of his encampment. On this occasion I had the honour of carving my name on the 'lob-stick'. Afterwards, of course, I supplied the expected tot of rum.

The next morning, stresses engendered by the past few days affected two crew members. My subconscious brain, chewing over problems connected with the Rocky Mountain Trench, roused me from a tired sleep. I wrote up the log, but insomnia remained. When others stirred, making motions toward breakfast, I couldn't will myself out of bed.

That same night Don's back was acting up, loading him with pain. Those muscles pulled in the Black Canyon of Thompson River were contracting in severe spasms and requiring frequent medication.

After sizing up his companions, Dave suggested a day off.

In mid-afternoon the sound of an American-accented voice brought everyone to life. A stocky figure clad in a red plaid jacket stood in the doorway, orange hard-hat tipped back on his head, a corncob pipe clenched in his mouth.

"I'm Bob Jackson, manager of the Hydro project at Mica Creek," he announced. "Everything has been laid on for your arrival. When can we expect you?"

Then the news that was music to our ears, "We have arranged for the 'bombardier' to carry your gear from Boat Encampment to Kinbasket Lake. We believe the upper half of the lake is ice free."

Well, that was the best medicine anyone could ask for. Lethargy vanished. Everyone jumped out of bed to shake hands with the bearer of such glad tidings. After consulting a map, the crew estimated Mica could be reached in one day's travel. To Bob Jackson, "We'll be off early tomorrow. Look for us before nightfall."

Saturday morning was cool but refreshingly clear. The mists and clouds of previous days were rising from the steep Columbia Valley. Unveiled snow clad mountains soared above heavily treed slopes.

Death Rapids, or as the *voyageurs* called them, *Les Dalles des Morts*, provided the next difficulty. The ugly, steep chute bottomed out with a series of high standing waves at the ankle of a dog-leg. David Thompson surveyed this menacing stretch of water on his first ascent of Columbia River in September of 1811. Six years later, Ross Cox, a Nor'Wester returning to Montreal with a canoe brigade, wrote of them in his book 'The Columbia River'. His story was responsible for this spot achieving its morbid title.

When Cox's party reached Boat Encampment and made ready to ascend the Rocky Mountains over Athabasca Pass, a few of the *voyageurs* were so worn out, ('knocked-up' as the author described them), that the leader, Angus Bethune, declared them unfit to make the crossing. He sent six *voyageurs*, plus Holmes, the English tailor stationed at the NWC's Fort George, back down to Fort Spokane in one of the canoes. Cox heard of their horrible fate.

In trying to lower the fully laden canoe down the topmost series of rapids, a line attached to the canoe, parted. Away went their entire stock of provisions and guns. Thoroughly exhausted, the now frightened men made a desperate bid for survival by trying to fight their way to Upper Arrow Lake through a hundred mile stand of densely forested Douglas fir and hemlock. The terrain was very steep. The trees pressed together so tightly that animals and natives completely shunned this portion of the Columbia Valley.

On the third day of their travail, *voyageur* Macon died. His remains were divided equally between six starving men. The next to expire was Holmes, whose emaciated body was served up to the remaining five. The party continued to struggle on through dense forests, the dead supplying fuel for survivors. Only two, Dubois and La Pierre reached Arrow Lake.

They put together a makeshift raft and cruised around the shore of the lake to find help. Nothing. The inevitable happened. A death-struggle took place between the two, La Pierre emerging as victor. Eventually natives found the lone survivor, and took him to Fort Spokane where he recounted an unbelievable tale of killing in self-defense. He was transported to Montreal; tried for murder, but acquitted for lack of evidence.

Eastward Ho's uphill battle continued. After Death Rapids, a series of shallow channels diminished our propeller supply. Dusk descended before the outskirts of Mica Creek were sighted. Shadowy figures on the bank waved us in.

The next morning we continued upriver to Boat Encampment where a hotel and coffee shop catered to loggers and truckers. The original Boat Encampment had been on the north, or right hand side of the Columbia, between Canoe and Wood rivers. (Left or righthand side of a river is determined by looking downstream.) There, eastbound travellers exchanged canoes and riverboats for snowshoes and horses in readiness for the 70-mile trek over the Athabasca Pass.

Both east and west valleys of the Big Bend Highway are history now. Enchanting names such as Canoe River, Kinbasket Lake, Boat Encampment, and exciting places like Death, Priest and Gordon rapids, have all been well and truly drowned by the hand of man.

Above the confluence of the Wood and Canoe Rivers, the Columbia was smaller, but more vigorous. A stout steel bridge crossed to the east bank. Gordon Tanner informed us: "The road stays on that side all the way to the Trans-Canada Highway near Donald Station, but the Highway's Department has yet to plow it out."

We turned north toward the Wood River. Upon arrival, being a sentimentalist, and wearing hip waders, I felt compelled to step into the stream that had brought David Thompson down from Athabaska Pass to the Columbia River.

Mr. Thompson: *Our residence was Boat Encampment where we camped to make a canoe. The climate is too mild to promote growth of thick birch-rind so we turned to Cedar of which there was plenty. We split thin boards, six inches in width, constructing a canoe 25 feet by 4 feet. Without nails, we split roots from pine trees, producing a canoe as light as birch bark, but stronger. We made camp near a junction of two rivers from the mountains which come together to run into Columbia River.*

Our guide, Thomas the Iroquois, had crossed the pass in the mountains before, but I believe I am the first white man to. On this alluvial are trees of enormous size; cedars up to 12 feet across and pines up to 14 feet. The stream we descended from the mountains I named Flat Heart, (now Wood River) because my men became frightened by the depth of snow. The other river I named Canoe.

Looking across the valley at the line of 10,000-foot mountains crowding the eastern skyline, one could picture Thompson's small group winding down the valley of the Wood, making toward the Columbia River. By crossing Athabasca Pass Thompson had breached the Rocky Mountains a second time. His first breakthrough was Howse Pass, the one Eastward Ho was headed for. But it was the Athabasca Pass that became part of the official road to and from Canada. It was used annually until the mid-19th century and guaranteed the safety of travellers from the Piegans who roamed the Howse Pass area. They remained a force to be reckoned with for several decades.

There is not space enough to talk about Athabasca Pass in detail. As the main corridor through the Rockies in Canada's first transcontinental highway, it is a subject that warrants a full-blown book of its own. A few years after rising waters behind Mica dam had obliterated Boat Encampment, three of the Eastward Ho crew made a summertime trek through Athabasca Pass. On the Alberta side, Dinty Moore and friends met us with canoes in which we all paddled down the Athabasca River to near old Fort Assiniboine.

Several well known people have recorded crossings of the Athabasca Pass, such as Sir George Simpson, Paul Kane, and Thompson of course. Others were Capt. Warre of the Royal Engineers. He came to investigate the feasibility of sending an army unit for the protection of British interests in the Oregon Territory. David Douglas, the botanist who supplied the name *douglas fir* to one of our native species, came through in 1827. Gabriel Franchère, an Astorian and part of a large contingent who returned to Montreal by canoe in 1814, journeyed through here, as did Ross Cox, the fur trader who provided the story of the naming of Death Rapids.

Before leaving, there should be a word from *observer* George Simpson, Governor of the HBC. He made three crossings over this steep mountain pass: *At the very top of the pass a small circular lake empties itself in opposite directions and is said to be a source of the Columbia and Athabasca Rivers, both of which empty into separate oceans. This circumstance being remarkable I thought it should be honoured by a distinguishing title and it was forthwith named 'The Committee's Punch Bowl'.*

The 'Committee' Simpson made reference to were the directors of the HBC who met regularly in London, England, to review all activities of the HBC. In Canada, Simpson was often referred to as the "Little Dictator", but as far as the London Committee was concerned, he was an appointed employee. He reported directly to the Committee, and carried out their recommendations with dispatch. His position could be likened to that of a President who is hired and fired by a Board of Directors. Even after receiving his knighthood in 1841, Sir George continued to regard his 'Committee' with deference and respect.

After proving Athabasca Pass a practical route for light goods and personnel, Thompson had intended canoeing down the Columbia River, but he was forced to change that plan.

I only had three men, Pierre Pareille, Joseph Côté and René Valade, with courage to risk the voyage. We were too few to find our way through the numerous Indians we had to pass. To strengthen my number I elected to proceed up-river to my first crossing of the Rockies, then continue south to my established trading posts, (in present day Idaho). *I knew I could hire free hunters there for the Pacific voyage.*

The term 'free hunter' was used to indicate individual fur traders who operated on their own. The established firms tolerated them and sometimes hired them on short-term contracts, but they never allowed them to combine into competitive positions.

Early in the morning of April 18th, exactly 156 years after Thompson, Eastward Ho started on skis to follow Thompson's upriver track. Just before our departure, Gordon Tanner and George Meyer left with the canoe on top of their bombardier. Their first drop, consisting of tent, sleeping bags and some food, would be a day's ski journey for us. A second load, of canoe, motor, gas and food, would be taken to open water, a distance, hopefully, no further removed than another day on skis.

Don was on trial. Dave had doped him with sufficient painkiller to make carrying a pack more bearable. If the spasms started again, Don knew he would be asked to return to Mica with the bombardier. He was determined to carry on. Shouldering his pack and gritting his teeth, he set off at a pace that made the three of us step out.

Our packs were relatively light, containing canoe mail, lunch and sweater. It was a perfect day for cross-country skiing. Bright blue skies arched over a canopy of trees bordering the sunlit roadway. Heavy breathing from the skiers sent white puffs of moisture twinkling upward into the dry air to mix with flashes of brilliance from the frozen snow crystals hanging on droopy evergreens. This valley, the southern extension of Rocky Mountain Trench, is colder and dryer than the Mica Creek side. There is less snow, but winter temperatures hold sway a few weeks longer.

Occasionally the road took us near the rim of the canyon. The sound of muffled blows could be heard emanating from the river as it churned over boulders and crashed onto slate-like ledges. The back-breaking, leg-numbing chore Thompson faced in dragging a canoe up through that canyon made Eastward Ho appreciate their jaunt on skis.

Mr. Thompson: *With provisions, baggage and snowshoes, we embarked on April 17th. The strong current was beset with many rapids. Two had to walk in water beside the canoe while two on snowshoes tracked with a line. At sunset, having come nine miles, we sat all night on a few bare rocks in the mouth of a creek.*

When the returning bombardier crew stopped to talk, they reported reaching the upper, or southern end of Kinbasket Lake where Sullivan River enters.

"I guess the movement of the Sullivan has freed the lake of ice from there south. You should reach your canoe by tomorrow afternoon.

We've dropped your sleeping gear at a likely looking campsite a mile on from here."

Night had almost enshrouded the valley by the time Gordon and George had drawn up for a hasty farewell. It meant they would be doing much of their homeward journey in darkness. The canoe crew shook hands with a couple of very generous guys, then watched the bombardier snort a line of blue smoke as it plunged down the road and around the bend.

Silence reigned. The only sounds were the scraping of skis and the rasping of poles breaking through the crust. We found our camping gear on a little promontory outside a circle of spruce and poplar. Close by, a mountain stream searching for the lake gurgled its way between snowbanks to supply water for the campsite.

Next day, at the end of Kinbasket Lake, tracks of the bombardier led toward the water and our big red canoe. Underway again, no obstacles presented themselves for the first thirty miles, but then the banks steepened dramatically into a vertical rock-walled canyon. Progress came to a sudden halt. The bow of the canoe bobbed on the bottom step of an impenetrable series of cataracts extending completely across the narrowly confined river.

Little information about this canyon had been gleaned beforehand, nor had we been able to procure large-scale contour maps dealing with this segment of the river.

This appeared to be the bottom end of Surprise Rapids, which one writer had described as necessitating a quarter-mile portage. The river looked absolutely impassable, at least at this particular water level. A series of jagged ridges cut obliquely across the bed of the canyon forming one waterfall after another. There was no beach or shelf from which to line the canoe, and the water was too deep and boisterous between the rock ridges to permit wading.

The cliffs were scanned on both sides of the river for any sign of a track or tree blaze that might indicate a way out. Nothing! There was no place to hoist half a ton of gear up this perpendicular wall soaring to the height of a six story building. One could only conjecture as to how Thompson managed through here. He did not mention it specifically.

The shelf on which the canoe had landed was too close to water level for camping. A slight overnight rise in the river could float our tent away. We hurried downstream to take advantage of the little light remaining, finally locating a mound of snow broad enough for a campsite.

After a morning conference, it was decided the only way out of this mess was to hoist everything up the bank to the snow-covered road, then try dragging a fully loaded canoe over the snow. A map showed the main road leaving the river at the canyon, not returning until Donald Station, thirty miles away. We had to gamble on finding an access road to the Columbia before that, or we could become mighty hungry boys before seeing Golden. By the tightly packed contour lines on the map the canyon appeared to be three miles in extent.

Two men scrambled up a snow-clad bank with a rope. A plastic tarp was used as a sling to haul everything to the roadway. With much grunting and straining the canoe was brought up.

The four haulers paused to catch their breath, looking dubiously at the mountain of stuff piled around. Motor, gas, oil, spare parts, food, canoe mail, skis and camping equipment, all to be dragged for perhaps six miles. "This better work," said Don, "or we're in deep trouble."

We placed all our possessions in the canoe. Tying four ropes to a thwart, we looped and slipped the free end around our waists. When everyone was in harness, someone yelled "Mush!".

We leaned into the ropes. The canoe inched forward. Gradually overcoming inertia, it gained momentum, sliding along behind at a slow, steady snail's pace.

At first there was concern that the snow would grind off the protective coating of paint and score the canvas, but after an hour's tugging there was no sign of wear. The first two miles consisted of a continuous rise, steep in places, leading to high bluffs overlooking the canyon.

Around one of the bends, a recent mud slide had wiped out a fifty yard section of roadway. There was no apparent movement of the slide right then, but the surface was thawing, and the whole mass could shift without warning. Equipment and canoe mail were carried over in several rabbit-hopping trips.

The empty canoe was next. Muscles taut, bent knees trembling with tension, we edged warily out across the slide, ready to run at any sign of ground movement. Two or three pebbles rolled and bounced off the canoe, startling us, but that was all. With some relief we deposited the heavy bundle on the far side.

Harnessed up again, Eastward Ho's struggle continued. By midday the sun had burnt off all cloud cover, warming the air and taking the starch out of the once frozen surface. We began to sink deeper and deeper into the road of snow.

Mud slide beside Columbia R. takes out the road

Stripped to the waist, four sweating bodies lurched along, trying to maintain an even strain on all the ropes, alternatively cursing and laughing at ourselves.

Jim blurted out: "I know how the Egyptian slaves felt pulling those two-ton blocks to the pyramids."

Later in the day a side road pointed in the direction of the river. Jim skied off to inspect it.

Half an hour passed before Jim came shuffling over the rise on his mushy outbound track. His pals waited anxiously. As he approached we could see a big grin lighting up his countenance. With excitement in his voice, he described the road to the promised river.

"The track led upwards for about a mile. At the top of a hill I looked down the other side. There was the river without a sign of white water. I didn't think it necessary to take the time to investigate further." Following Jim's turnoff, the pulling began with renewed spirit.

As the afternoon wore on, warming temperatures penetrated more deeply into the snow making it a struggle to walk, even without the drag of a half-ton toboggan. At each step we sank over our knees.

Surmounting the brow of a long hill, we all gazed thankfully at the river flowing serenely along. Stumbling down, with my last step I collapsed in the canoe's track. I was literally shaking with fatigue, unable to summon enough energy to undo the rope around my waist. Don was tired too, but not those young guys, Jim and Dave. In three minutes they were hopping about and chirping like birds, ready to start again. Don and I could only shake our heads and marvel at the difference twenty years can make in energy levels.

In the canoe again, filaments of the Bush River entered on the east side. In the shallows of its delta, a young bull moose tossed his head with a snort and went churning off through the snow. A few more bends of the Columbia and a trapper's cabin came into view. It was found habitable after removing a family of pack rats, and a carpet of mouse droppings from the table. With a red hot fire blazing merrily in the stove to heat dinner, we settled into surroundings most cozy.

Next day the mouth of Beaver River appeared where we had hoped to meet Bill Gifford. We were a day late, but there he was in his plaid shirt, waving enthusiastically from the bank. We left the canoe in the bushes and drove into Golden to check on the state of the Kitchen Rapids and Redgrave Canyon. We also had to prepare for our trek across the Rocky Mountains.

In no time at all it was a hurry-up day like the one in Revelstoke; people coming and going with information; radio and newspaper interviews, phone calls to the back-home media, working with Edo on film-making, lining up food and equipment, preparing a speech for another civic luncheon; a hundred and one things.

At first the only response concerning the river, all negative, came from non-canoeists, people who had seen the rapids from a passing train. This was rather like asking a non-skier to describe the difficulty of a particular ski slope. There had to be someone in Golden who had actually been on the river. We kept looking.

Late in the evening we came across Otto, a former riverboat man who had once worked this particular stretch of river at this time of year.

"In view of what you have come through already, with caution and a little luck, you should make it to the Blaeberry River all right," was Otto's verdict.

Satisfied with his assessment, we headed off for the canoe early next morning. Kitchen Rapids, which the maps and everyone, except Otto, had said were dangerous, was a pussycat. There was a spate of white water below Redgrave Canyon, but Otto's accurate description took the sting out of it. At low water, the canyon itself was very accommodating.

British Columbia river troubles were practically over, and a relaxed crew joked and laughed with the abandonment of schoolboys on vacation. What a wonderful feeling it is to tackle a difficult task and emerge victorious. We had completed a 650-mile canoe route never covered in its entirety before. By following three river systems we had climbed 2,500 feet from sea level, and would soon be in position to hike over the world-famous Canadian Rockies.

By midday the sun had warmed the spruce-scented air. As far as the eye could see the snow-clad Rocky Mountains marched south abreast the white-capped Selkirks. Dark-green carpets of coniferous trees swept down to a silvery belt of poplars lining a pale green waterway.

Still clad in hip-waders, we disembarked at the mouth of Blaeberry Creek to stand knee-deep in the Columbia River. We bowed our heads, then bent over and immersed them in homage to the propitious river gods who had allowed us to forge this new link in the Trans-Canada Waterway.

There is always an element of doubt with most endeavours, but from this point on, barring a catastrophe, water problems should be surmountable. Once on the North Saskatchewan River, the road to Montreal will follow a proven route. And the further east we go, the longer the highway will have been in use. From now on, if sickness or accident should befall anyone, two members could carry on in the spare 18-foot canoe that is carried on the roof of the camper.

Eastward Ho completed the Columbia River on April 22nd, five days from Boat Encampment. *Fifth man* David Thompson, held up by deeper snows and more ice, had to endure three weeks under much more rigorous travelling conditions.

At the mouth of the Blaeberry on May 8, 1811, Mr. Thompson:
After a day of strong rapids, we arrived at a Hut we had built on this river, which I originally called Kootenay River, but later corrected to Columbia River. It was here, four years ago, having crossed the defile of the Rocky Mountains from the headwaters of Saskatchewan River that I first saw this great river which would eventually lead me to the Pacific Ocean.

To utilize these high mountain passes, early explorers relied upon the knowledge of First Nations people who had been hunting in them for centuries. The chase consisted of deer, elk, caribou, goat, bear, moose, and buffalo. In many places the first non-natives to penetrate the Rockies were the independent free traders who played a role similar to the *coureur de bois* of the 17th century. Such men had crossed these remote mountains some time before the Lewis and Clark expedition. Thompson speaks highly of this hardy breed of men who had done much original investigative work.

Mr. Thompson: *The roving disposition of French Canadians is well known. They once numbered 350 men and hunted in the Illinois area. But a precarious way of life, sometimes involved in Indian wars, reduced their numbers to 150 men. The United States insisted they either become settlers on the land or move elsewhere. They chose the latter, taking up rifles and crossing the Missouri with their women. They continually advanced westward towards the mountains where I met them in the Pend Oreille area* [of present day Idaho].

The same fate still attended them, as all the natives of this fine country are often in a state of petty warfare. Many of the men camped with Indians who would acknowledge no neutrals. They had to fight for the party with whom they were found. Enemy Indians, dreading them as good marksmen, consistently aimed at them in battle. When I first became acquainted with them in 1809, they were reduced to 25 men.

Without exception, the Indians, both friends and enemies, spoke of them as a brave race of men whose conduct was always proud and manly. Yet even these few were reduced to two, Michel Bordeaux and Michel Kinville, often companions of mine. They were brave and faithful, on whose word for life or death I would depend. In the summer of 1812, on the side of the Salish Indians, they were both killed by Piegan warriors.

We ran out of food and were forced
to kill and eat several of our pack horses.
David Thompson

Chapter Nine

Across the Shining Mountains

Like Thompson, Eastward Ho made ready to ascend the western flank of the Rocky Mountains through Howse Pass. It is a sixty-mile land bridge between the Columbia River of B.C. and the North Saskatchewan River of Alberta. We expect it to be a five-day overland journey, most of it on skis. Our land party will take the canoe around and meet us at the Saskatchewan River. An ascent to the summit of the Pass from the Columbia River side will entail a half-mile vertical climb.

Jim sorted out the camping equipment. Dave apportioned the food and rearranged his medical kit. As 'postie' he assigned four parcels of canoe mail, one for each man to stuff into his pack. Don scouted the town for a couple of ski-doos to transport Bill and Edo twenty-miles up the mountain to shoot some film.

It seemed the lights had barely been turned out when the alarm clock jarred us awake at the voyageur's hour of three a.m. The sky was filling with light when we turned our backs on the orange-tipped Selkirks on the west side of the valley. Our boots grated on a frozen crust as we swung easily along on the untrammeled snow. An even blanket of snow softened by the sun, but re-frozen by a night's frost, is a delight to walk on. Dry ice crystals cushion your tread and provide a non-slip surface as well.

A steady pace was maintained during the cool morning hours, but the sun's rays peeking over the rim of the Rockies gradually flooded into the valley, warming the air within. Dave and Jim, dazzled by all the beauty and light, were trigger-happy with their cameras.

The Blaeberry had to be crossed many times. Thompson referred to this stream as *Portage River.* A crystal-clear rivulet, it sparkled and spun its way toward the Pacific Ocean. Brightly hued pebbles on its floor formed a colorful mosaic.

Coming to yet another stream crossing, we scrambled down a snowbank to eat lunch on an exposed gravel bar, then catnapped in the still, warm air. We were roused by the distant drone of a ski-doo. The sound changed to a roar as two vehicles came bucking and slithering around the bend above our siesta patch. Bill drove the lead machine. Edo hung precariously on behind, one hand gripping Bill's jacket, the other his precious Bolex camera. By the grin on his face he was enjoying the wild ride. Barry, a telephone lineman commandeered by Don, drove a larger vehicle and trailer.

The sight of four near-naked bodies sunbathing in the snow provided a laugh for the ski-dooers, but after dropping down into the bowl, they too were amazed to feel the tremendous amount of radiant heat generated by the sun shining into the bowl of snow.

Camp was made on the edge of a snow covered gravel plain spewed out by the Blaeberry's annual spring flood. The treeless area was a mile wide and extended northward four miles, narrowing to an apex at the base of a high cliff. The Rockies generally lie in a north-west, south-east direction, but up ahead a twenty mile section of the mighty cordillera had been scrunched into a solid east-west lineup. To cross over Howse Pass itself, the course would be due north rather than north-east.

From the western base of this imposing convolution, Eastward Ho gazed upward at a chain of rocky, snow encrusted mountain tops. To the left lay the wrinkled front of Mummery Glacier, with Mt. Mummery itself soaring out of the ice to 11,000 feet. In line with Mummery were the glaciers of Mt. Cairnes, Lamb, and Conway. Mount Conway and Howse Peak stood as silent sentinels over the Howse Pass.

Passing Mummery Glacier heading into Howse Pass

Around the fire that night, with the stars twinkling on one after another, Dave discovered an acoustical effect of the high valley. The surrounding mountains formed a natural amphitheatre. A shout, a pause, and a booming echo would mock back with remarkable clarity. Eventually a bone chilling wind off the glaciers chased us into our down-filled sleeping bags.

An interesting discovery was made that night. The three who slept in the tent woke before dawn complaining about being cold. The others who slept outside under a lean-to were quite comfortable. We concluded that down sleeping bags, or down anything else for that matter, operate most efficiently when surrounded by an envelope of air. In a confined alpine tent, bodies expire so much moisture that the air becomes damp and clammy, negating the insulating effect of down. After crossing the Rockies we switched to an open-faced tent which enhanced our night-time comfort.

With filming completed, the ski-dooers headed back to Golden and Eastward Ho's ascent continued. A cloud cover rolled in, making us anxious to finish the steepest part of the climb before a possible snowstorm arrived.

The first problem presented itself immediately after starting. The snow was rock hard and skis slithered uncontrollably in all directions. Frustrated by the lack of progress we slung them over our shoulders. Our skis were the metal downhill types, equipped for mountaineering with adjustable boot cables. They were fine for touring through open country, but a weighty encumbrance when carried. Light weight cross-country skis would have been better.

The Blaeberry exited from a cleft in the mountain that Thompson had termed the *defile*. He mentioned the landmark several times.

The defile hides the Blaeberry River

What a thrill it was to see it as Thompson had, so many years ago. Directly in front, a sheer rock wall, the base of Howse peak, soared straight up for a thousand feet. Behind it, Mt. Cairnes came abruptly down. The clue to passage of the Blaeberry was a tell-tale line of trees bordering the watercourse. The stream exited between two massive gates of sedimentary rock.

We followed a blazed trail which zig-zagged up the left hand slope of the valley, but an avalanche spilling down the mountainside obliterated the trail and forced us to drop down to the creek-bed again. Following the course of the stream entailed a steep ascent between vertical canyon walls, jumping from one ice-sheathed boulder to another. On one of his leaps into space, Dave missed his footing and plunged waist deep into the numbing water. He didn't complain about being wet, but he was fuming when he discovered his camera had been soaked. It would be weeks before it could be repaired.

Don's back was giving him a bad time, although he insisted upon carrying a full pack. Dave administered a pain-killer. Looking part mountain goat, Don kept forging ahead, across steep slopes that dropped almost perpendicularly into walled gorges. The three of us were afraid he might slide off his precarious perch. One slip would mean a hundred foot drop to the rocks below.

"I'm sorry," he said afterwards. "I was afraid to stop. The pain was driving me crazy. I felt I had to keep moving or I'd never make it. Guess I was punchy and desperate."

After lunch a light snowfall began. Skis were strapped back on. Thickening clouds obliterated the distant peaks, then darkened, as if preparing to unleash a storm. Slightly past the draw of Parapet Creek, on a flat bluff overlooking the Blaeberry, a map showed Doubt Hill, the last steep rise before the height of land. It was still a few miles away, and not reachable before dark. Camp was made in the remaining light.

On one of his later crossings of the Howse Pass, our *fifth man* Thompson wrote: *After our return to the Rocky Mountains with trade goods for our Kootenay and Salish Indian friends, and well into the defile of Portage River, I arranged to have the two kegs of alcohol tied onto the back of the most vicious horse in the brigade. The wild creature soon made short work of his cargo by bucking and rubbing it against the rocks, the contents discharging into the stream.*

It has been my constant policy to resist the use of spirituous liquors in my territory west of the mountains. It causes nothing but harm to a primitive people unaware of its evil affects. I objected at putting the 90 lb. kegs in my canoe when at our supply depot on Rainy Lake, but was overruled there by my senior partner John MacDonald. I made my point, however, as no further attempt was made to carry liquor over the Rocky Mountains into the Columbia Department while I was in charge.

Thompson had his way, but his stubborn stance worked to his disadvantage subsequently.

It had long been my desire to establish the proper height above sea level of the Rocky Mountain massive and to ascertain heights of varying peaks within the cordillera. Consequently I penned my request for a mountain barometer from the Hon. William McGillivray, Agent and senior partner of the North-West Company. He acceded to my request placing it in the hands of Mr. John McDonald to send on to me. My brother-in-law, for he was married to my wife's sister, did not take care to have it properly packed. It arrived full of water and broken into pieces.

I requested another. This request was granted but it too met the same fate. Thus I was never able to obtain an accurate measurement above the level of the ocean for all our interior lakes, streams and mountains. I tried rough and inaccurate methods such as the temperature of boiling water, or measuring descents and ascents over long distances, but I needed a barometer to know the truth.

Thompson's failure to obtain proper scientific equipment adversely affected his altitude measurements of mountain peaks. They were often overestimated by as much as 50%. His figures alone might not have been given credence, but a few years after him, botanist David Douglas, picked his way past the 'Committee's Punch Bowl'. The 'bowl' was the mountain tarn in the centre of the Athabasca Pass first surveyed by David Thompson in 1811.

Like Thompson, Douglas also passed under the shadow of two high peaks guarding the pass. He named them Mt. Hooker and Mt. Brown after two distinguished scientists in botanical matters, who, like Douglas himself, were members of the Royal Horticultural Society.

When Douglas' journal came to light, published posthumously, [he was trampled to death by an enraged bull after falling into an animal trap on a mountain trail in the Hawaiian Islands] it too stated that the mountain peaks of Hooker and Brown soared to 16,000 feet. Douglas was part of the scientific establishment, so when he made an observation, people nodded and said, "Hmmm", not withstanding the fact that he was a botanist, not an experienced mountaineer.

These wildly inaccurate figures by Thompson and Douglas caused quite a furor in the alpine community. Members of various climbing organizations throughout Europe kept making frequent forays into the Canadian Rockies in search of those two elusive peaks that dwarfed anything the Alps had to offer. It took the investigations of Walter Moberly, the railroad surveyor, to put the matter to rest. From an accurate base line he calculated that the peaks were a little less than 11,000 feet high.

The trouble wasn't that Thompson, or any other surveyor, couldn't measure heights properly. By triangulation and knowing the length of one side of a triangle, a reasonably accurate vertical rise could be obtained from any base point. Thompson's and Douglas' error stemmed from the fact that neither of them had any idea how far the foot of the mountain was above sea level. They erred considerably in their baseline estimate.

A precision barometer with a properly recorded sea-level reading would have straightened the matter out. Lest you should think Thompson and Douglas rather stupid, imagine yourself travelling across the country for a thousand miles, then estimating your vertical ascension.

The threatened snow storm failed to materialize that night. Only a few inches fell on the knoll overlooking the diminished Blaeberry. By morning, fresh westerlies were blowing the spiralling snowflakes to other parts of the Rockies. Sleeping in a damp tent on a cold mattress would not seem the best of conditions for anyone with a back injury, but Don began to improve from that day on. It was a testimony to both Dave's care and Don's own determination.

That morning fresh cougar tracks led from our tent across the new fallen snow and up the draw. Other than commenting on the fact that the mountain lion must have been searching for food around the campsite, little heed was paid at first to the continuous row of pawmarks.

At several places we crossed the snow-filled Blaeberry by choosing a suitable snow bridge. Eventually, after a few crossovers, someone noticed that in every instance of crawling underneath and rejecting unsafe ones, the bridge picked would be the same one the lion chose, as indicated by his tracks. To save the time spent examining each bridge, from then on we simply followed the cougar's course.

We could have thrown away the map. Our local expert invariably took the easiest and safest route and guided us to the summit of Howse Pass itself. To crown it all, he took us right past a yellow sign nailed to a spruce tree which announced in heavy black letters: *Banff-National Park Boundary.*

Jim brought a laugh with: "This cougar must be an Alberta Chamber of Commerce member in disguise."

The party paused on the height-of-land, skis straddling the B.C.- Alberta border. We threw snowballs down the slope of the Pacific watershed, others onto the eastern side of the Rocky Mountains. The latter would melt and flow down to Hudson Bay.

Our feline guide leads us to the BC — Alta border

Our *fifth man* had this to say of his first crossing of the Rockies, which was from east to west on the 25th of June, 1807:

From the upper reaches of the Saskatchewan, where we cached the canoes, we proceeded on horses to the height of land, accompanied by my wife and children. The snowflakes melt and flow to the Pacific Ocean. I was over-joyed at the sight. May God in his mercy give me to see where these waters enter the ocean, and return safely.

Our cougar guide preceded us down the tilt of land, crossing from one side of Conway Creek to another. Pawmarks led to the broad valley of Howse River, then disappeared over a wind encrusted plain that stretched eastward for a dozen miles.

The next day we were to rendezvous with our land party at the Saskatchewan River Crossing of the Banff-Jasper Highway. Don pointed out a coyote some distance off. Seeing skiers, it lopped away, bushy tail pluming out behind.

A strong head wind forced a stop in the lee of a gravel mound. It must blow incessantly up this valley. Thompson remarked on the frequency of gales sweeping through the flat, open terrain. After a brief wait we stepped out to face the piercing blast again. A ridge of snow entering the north side of the valley indicated the North Saskatchewan coming down from the Columbia Icefield. Through pre-arrangement with the Park's Branch, we spent the night in a Ranger's cabin.

In the morning a series of undulating snowdrifts had to be crossed. They turned out to be puffed up with air, and were without substance. Even with skis on we sank to our hips. We could neither wade through the snow nor lift our skis high enough to clear it. The situation was ridiculous and frustrating. Removed skis and packs. Tried dragging the load. Nothing worked.

What a sight it must have been; four harassed figures, so near their goal, flailing madly through that sea of white fluff. We spent an agonizing hour plunging, crawling and swimming toward the highway.

By late afternoon, beyond the trees we caught a glimpse of a bridge across the North Saskatchewan. Two small figures were on it, keeping cold vigil. To our right the Mistaya River entered the Saskatchewan. It was too deep to cross here, so we turned upstream a few hundred yards to reach a ford. Bill Gifford met us on the other side, and we greeted each other warmly.

"Edo is waiting on the bridge of the Saskatchewan where you turned to come up here. He's set to photograph you coming in."

"To heck with picture making," we chorused. "We're dead! Been going since dawn! We want to dump these loads of misery from our backs as soon as possible."

The thought of traipsing back down the disordered boulders was just too much. We were in no mood for detours. Bill's 'sweet persuasion' prevailed, however, "Just a bloomin' minute!" he declaimed, "Either you S.O.B.'s go down to Edo, who's been waiting in this cold wind for you bums for hours, or you can damn well walk the two miles up the highway to your night's lodging!"

The revolt subsided. We stumbled back down the highway side of the Mistaya to the Saskatchewan, grumbling into five-day beards. With sour faces we made toward the camera where Edo, peering through his lens, ground merrily away. If it was realism of mood he sought, it was achieved here.

One final effort up the steep embankment and it was over the guard rail to Bill's station wagon. Another difficult segment of the trans-Canada canoe journey had been completed. Once the strain of backpacking was removed, distress soon disappeared. Bill said: "Dwayne, the assistant Park Ranger, has cleaned out a cabin for you."

Dwayne's wife Donna invited the crew over for coffee and cinnamon buns. And were they ever delicious! Donna must have been brought up in a family of four brothers. How else could she have known to bake such prodigious quantities? An assembly line of hot cinnamon rolls, straight out of the oven and dripping with melted butter, went from baking pan to mouth for some time.

Eastward Ho was soon busy preparing for another phase of canoe travel, a long, downhill one. This was to be a 1200-mile run of the North Saskatchewan River, out of the Rockies, across three Prairie Provinces and into Lake Winnipeg. The river's turquoise-tinted sheen, distilled from the surrounding glacier-hung valleys, would change into a clay saturated river. But right here its clarity and sparkling brightness was breathtaking.

The greatest vertical drop occurs in its upper 120 miles between Saskatchewan River Crossing and Rocky Mountain House.

Someone had told Eastward Ho that the river, having flushed itself out, was open all the way. Again, second hand information proved to be incorrect. Due to a recent cold snap the water was extremely low, with newly formed ice flows clinging tenaciously to the riverbank. Our fear was that ice might cover the river completely as we proceeded out of the mountains.

On the last day of April the crew slipped their canoe off an ice flow into the blue-green waters of the river. Except for the asphalt ribbon of the Banff-Jasper Highway threading its way between Mt. Murchison and Mt. Serbach, the setting would have looked just the same to explorer David Thompson.

Mid-channel the river ran to a depth of six feet, but around each bend it would shoal to a few inches, necessitating a leap overboard by all four paddlers in order to clear the ever-present gravel bar. One hesitated to sully the purity of these crystal-clear waters, but the maneuver had to be repeated many times.

The Saskatchewan flowed east for fifteen miles, then north through the broad, dry Kootenay Plains. This area was once a favourite campsite of the Kootenays before the Blackfeet drove them westward across the Rockies.

This untrammeled wilderness, as pristine as Thompson found it, was slated for a rude change. Progress was at work again. Survey crews were laying out markers for another dam. This one will destroy the most exciting part of a beautiful canoeing river.

Travelling light, without motor, tent or sleeping bags, we planned to meet the land party later in the day where the road paralled the river in the valley of the Kootenay Plains. Toward supper time Don raised Bill Gifford on the walkie-talkie. Bill's voice came through loud and clear, but he wasn't saying what anyone wanted to hear.

"I'm stuck in the mud. Been shovelling from pothole to pothole all afternoon. Edo's somewhere ahead. How far I'm not sure. The road seems to be getting worse. It's my bet the camper is stuck too."

We couldn't see the highway so it was hard to judge exactly where he was. Don called into his mike, "Try beeping your horn and we'll see if we can figure out how far away you are by sound."

Immediately a blast came out of our walkie-talkie. We counted up to ten before a softened tone came echoing along the valley, indicating about two miles. Further beeps came first from the south, then from the north, or whichever way a breeze happened to be moving. A line of tall timbers flanking the highway obscured our view of it.

"You'll just have to get along without us tonight," Don retorted. A bit of a laugh since Bill had all the sleeping bags and food in his station wagon. The only 'extras' the canoeists had was the mail, a comfortless burden. Don signed off with, "We'll try you tomorrow."

With the canoe tilted onto its side to afford protection from the searing wind, the night was spent beside a blazing fire. Like hot-dogs on a spit, we roasted on one side while turning blue with cold on the other. Scrounging for firewood in the dark and rotating in front of the fire all night wasn't conducive to sleep. Gleaming white stars accented the cold.

The light of morning saw us heading through brush for the highway, breaking into a dogtrot to restore circulation in legs which felt like bent icicles. A steep bank signaled the edge of an older river bed and the David Thompson Highway just beyond. On the road we turned south, spotting the camper at the bottom of a deeply rutted hill. It was down to its axles in frozen mud. Bill was there too, having left his mired vehicle a mile away.

We set off for Bill's car immediately, wanting to free both units while the ground remained frozen. The station wagon looked like an amphibious vehicle floating in a river of mush. It took a couple of hours of digging, rock-filling and log-laying to free both vehicles.

Back on the river, the downhill journey continued, gaining entrance to the Ram mountain range. After the entry of the Big Horn River, the Saskatchewan became more boisterous as it began to worm its way down the Gap, a rugged canyon that had been gouged by the North Saskatchewan River through the Brazeau Range of mountains. A herd of elk stood nearby. Frightened by the canoe, they wheeled in unison and went clattering up the gravel bed of a contributing stream, a large bull in the lead. A strong smell of sulphur hung in the air but a search for the tell-tale plume of steam from hot-springs was in vain.

Camp was set at the base of a cliff, and a fire lit between ourselves and the river. Midnight temperatures dropped well below freezing, but the fire-warmed rock wall at our back made a great heat reflector, in spite of a light snowfall.

Our position was mid-way through the Gap where Gap Creek enters. It was here, in October of 1810, that four tents of Piegans set up a blockade to prevent Thompson from proceeding westward through Howse Pass, an action that prompted Thompson to search for Athabasca Pass.

Thompson and two companions had come on horseback to wait above the Gap for the loaded canoes that were coming up the Saskatchewan River. The canoes were laden with trade goods to be back-packed over Howse Pass, then carried down the Kootenay River to Thompson's trading posts in today's northern Idaho.

Mr. Thompson: *Becoming worried by the non-appearance of the canoes, I sent my two men downstream to look for them. They returned after dark and said they had encountered a camp of Peeagans at the Gap, circumvented them, then located a hastily erected rampart of stones built for defense. Some of the stones had blood on them. They rode down along the river for a ways, then, against my instructions, fired off a gun into the air. They had hoped to elicit a response from our canoemen, but heard nothing.*

I told them they had acted foolishly, and their action would bring the Peeagan warriors, excellent trackers all, down upon us at any moment. We must mount and ride for our lives. We rode all night. Luckily for us a snowstorm blew down from the mountain peaks to bury our tracks and we made our way to an abandoned trading post known as Boggy Hall.

Thanks to the efforts of Mr. Alexander Henry Jr., who had re-opened Rocky Mountain House, the canoes and men were safe, but unable to proceed. Mr. Henry found me in our hide-away and informed me that the Peeagans had put a price on my head for taking guns and ammunition to the Kootenay tribe, their main competitors for the far-ranging plains bison.

I decided to change our route to the defiles of the Athabasca River which would place our people out of the reach of the Peeagans. With winter coming on, a search would be attended with great inconvenience, fatigue and privation, but there was no satisfactory alternative.

That night, Eastward Ho's tent must have been close to where the Piegans had placed their barricade, for here the canyon floor is very narrow, leaving few choices for camping. With no enemy afoot, our sleep was undisturbed.

The Rocky Mountains gradually came into view.
As we proceeded they rose in height, with immense masses
of snow appearing above the clouds, forming an impassable
barrier even to the Eagle. We did not believe our guide
who said: "As we ascend the mountains of snow,
the weather will become more mild." But it was so.

David Thompson

Chapter Ten
Ice

In coastal mountains the temperature generally drops as one ascends to higher elevation. On the eastern side of the Rockies the opposite holds true. This is why with the onslaught of the bitter winds of winter, migrating animals and native people left the treeless plains and moved up into the hills for three or four months of the year.

Running the rest of the Gap, Eastward Ho gradually drew out of the mountains. Rock cliffs of solid shale gave way to high banks of conglomerate followed by alternating layers of gravel, sand, or clay. Spruce and pine changed to aspen and poplar. At Shunda Creek, the Saskatchewan swung from north-east to east.

The uneven bed of the Saskatchewan River was unsuitable for horses so First Nations people established a horse trail along Shunda Creek. This route served as a bypass for riders entering and leaving the mountains from the foothills, and it was the way Thompson's small party had come prior to their flight from the Piegans. Today, the David Thompson Highway follows the centuries old trail that meets the North Saskatchewan River again near the mouth of the Big Horn River.

A map showed several coal mines in the surrounding area, indicating a geological phenomena for our *fifth man*.

Mr. Thompson: *In the spring at freshet time, coal is deposited along the sands of certain branches of Saskatchewan River. When the water lowers sufficiently, several bushels of good quality coal were collected within the vicinity of Rocky Mountain House. My blacksmith thought its quality better than any brought from England. This coalbed extends beyond 56 degrees of north latitude. Smoke River, a branch of Peace River, is named because of the fires which have been burning and smoking on its banks since the memory of the oldest Indian on that river.*

Unfortunately for Thompson's heirs, he did not stake a claim around any of his geological discoveries.

Canoe sledding on the North Saskatchewan River

On the eastern side of the Brazeau Range, through which Eastward Ho had been proceeding, ice shelves jutting out from the banks of the North Saskatchewan River began creeping closer and closer to one another. The inevitable happened. At a certain bend, the river completely disappeared under a sheet of ice stretching from shore to shore. There was no end in sight, so the crew had to repeat their husky-dog performance initiated on the Columbia River.

The canoe slid with surprising ease over the smooth river ice and a good walking pace was maintained until patches of open water intervened. If the opening was extensive, rather than haul around it, time was saved by sliding the canoe into the water and paddling with the current until the river disappeared under the ice.

When approaching open water, the technique employed was to throw the traces into the canoe and position ourselves, two to a side in a staggered line, each man holding on to a section of gunwale. With a "one, two, three, Go!", we'd charge toward the river as fast as hip waders would allow. When the lead man felt the ice bending beneath his feet he would dive into the canoe, followed by each person in turn. The fourth man came in over the stern.

Getting the canoe out of the swiftly moving river and onto the ice called for a different technique. Bulled along by a strong current, it was impossible to bring the canoe to a complete stop. The following method was devised for landings.

With a closure looming, a light-footed crewman like Dave or Jim stood at the bow, a rope in one hand and a paddle in the other. When close enough, he would leap out of the canoe, landing with all fours on the ice to distribute his weight, and immediately head shoreward, pulling the canoe as far onto the ice as possible. The paddle was supposed to be a form of insurance should the jumper break through the ice. In theory, the paddle would keep a person's head above water until someone fished him out. Fortunately, it was never put to the test.

In a well coordinated maneuver, half the canoe could be slid onto the ice, enabling the paddlers to step briskly out with hauling traces tied around their waists, ready to move quickly off. This method worked tolerably well, and the exertion kept us warm.

This method of travel was not possible with birchbark canoes. *Voyageurs* had to wait beside the river until it opened.

Camp that night was opposite the entry of Ram River. The air was exquisitely clear and hoar-frost glistened across a white expanse of snow. Aurora Borealis, with its colourful display in the northern sky, and the mournful call of wolves far up the Ram Valley, lulled us to sleep.

Alexander Henry Jr., a fellow partner in the NWC, took over management of Rocky Mtn House from David Thompson. He was returning from a dog team run up the North Saskatchewan in Feb. of 1811 when he noted in his log: *At sunrise we passed Ram River; the cold so severe, and the wind so piercing, it was only with great exertion we could keep from freezing. I have always observed when travelling in this country in winter, we feel the cold most between daybreak and sunrise.*

Eastward Ho spent the next day alternately sliding and paddling the canoe. A map showed a settlement called Garth which perhaps took its name from John MacDonald of Garth who was born in Garth Castle in the highlands of Scotland. He was a brother-in-law of our *fifth man,* David Thompson.

By late afternoon the map indicated we were near Pangman's Tree. Peter Pangman was one of the early Montreal men of the post-La Vérendrye period, and is said to have been the first trader to enter the fastness of the Rocky Mountains. Thompson mentioned the location of the pine tree on which Pangman had carved his name.

Further downstream two solitary chimneys stand on the north bank of the river. They are remnants of the original Rocky Mountain House when it was a gateway to the Rockies. Erected by MacDonald of Garth in 1802, it served as headquarters for David Thompson until the winter of 1810. It is a popular name. There were at least three other Rocky Mtn. Houses on the east side of the Rockies. They could be found on the Athabasca, Peace, and Mackenzie Rivers.

Eastward Ho had intended to stop below the chimneys and look around the site of this old establishment, but a troublesome rapid opposite the old fort forced a change of plans. Flying down a crescent of foaming waves, we were well past the site of the original Rocky Mountain House before we could check our headlong rush.

Observer Alexander Henry Jr. had this to say:

Our establishment stands on a high bank on the N. side of the river, its situation well adapted for defense. The channel of the N. Saskatchewan when we arrived in the fall of 1810 is only 30 yards wide and interrupted by a strong rapid, where the water rushed among some large stones, forming a cascade whose perpetual moaning makes it a dismal neighbour. This is the first rapid of note when ascending from Fort Edmonton.

Below the falls, the Clearwater River, *La Rivière à L'Eau Claire* to the *voyageurs,* entered on the right. It is part of a geographical oddity formed by itself and three other rivers, the Bow, Red Deer, and North Saskatchewan. In a cradle of the Rockies between Sunwapta Pass and Bow Pass, these four streams originate within a few miles of one another. The N. Saskatchewan and Clearwater rivers sweep north-east while the Bow and Red Deer ramble south-east. The latter join at Empress to form the South Saskatchewan River. By the time all four have united into one Saskatchewan River at Prince Albert, they will have circumscribed a vast pear-shaped figure across the prairie portions of the Provinces of Alberta and Saskatchewan.

Bill Gifford was waiting at a bridge crossing the N. Saskatchewan and drove the crew into Rocky Mountain House. We went in search of Vic Maxwell, captain of the Alberta Voyageurs. The latter were participants in the Canadian Canoe Pageant that was to leave Rocky Mountain House on May 23rd to paddle 3,200 miles to Montreal. The brigade of six-man canoes was made up of ten competing teams, each one representing a Province of Canada. The Yukon and the North West Territories took the place of Prince Edward Island and Newfoundland.

News travels quickly in a small community and Vic found us in the barber shop. His handshake was enough to tell you he was one of the best. His was a grip of steel, with palms callused as hard as the paddles he stroked with. A square-set jaw, dancing blue eyes, wavy blond hair, and wind-brushed ruddy skin, made him a handsome voyageur.

Rumour had it that the North Saskatchewan was plugged with several ice jams so Vic arranged an aerial inspection in a friend's plane for Dave and myself. Early the following morning we were humming north over the river, here a turgid, mud-colored stream discolored by the clay and humus of the foothills. Twenty-five miles downstream, just below the mouth of the Baptiste River coming in from the west, the first blockade became visible. The river was plugged by a mile-long jumble of dirt-stained ice.

Beyond, more blockages could be seen, interspersed with bits of open, begrimed river. North of those obstacles, the real catastrophe appeared; a grey, snakelike, stationary mass of ragged ice trenching to the far horizon. From 2,000 feet there was no end to it. Our worst fears were confirmed.

We returned to discuss the bad news. Few access roads appeared on the map. Tenting in a desolate spot somewhere along the riverbank in near winter conditions to out wait the ice wasn't too appealing, but that was the course of action decided upon after listening to Vic Maxwell, who said, "Every oil rig dotting the landscape has a road leading to it. The roads might not show on your map but in fact they touch the river in several places. You can't predict these kind of conditions accurately, a slight rise in temperature or a warming wind can set the whole frozen mass on its way. It can disappear in two days."

"We expect to finish tomorrow's training session where a road from Alder Flats meets the river," Vic continued. "Why not meet us there for lunch. Its about 50 miles north of here. If you start an hour earlier, we'll probably catch up to you around the Baptiste River, which is half way. Your land party can drive to the rendezvous, and if conditions look bad, take you off the river."

Vic's suggestion made sense, and it cleared Eastward Ho's impasse, if not the river's. The decision was made to shove off the next morning.

On May 6th Eastward Ho slid their canoe back into the sluggish stream. The river had slowed considerably in the last few miles. We were using the spare five h.p. motor, thinking it would be an advantage in the broad, shallow, river, but we soon regretted the decision. With the motor bracketed to a high-transom V-stern, it was difficult to keep the propeller in the water. Following a slowdown by the helmsman, two men would have to shift their weight toward the stern to bring it down so the propeller could bite the water. Every bend of the river, with its inevitable gravel or sandbar, prompted a repeat performance of two ballasts clambering back and forth over food boxes and packs.

In spite of its inconvenience, the five h.p. pushed us faster than paddles only. This canoe, with its flared sides, wasn't designed for efficient paddling; it was primarily a freight canoe, broad of beam and stable.

Initially the NWC employed only *north* canoes west of Lake Superior, but they began to copy the HBC's use of York boats, as *observer* Henry Jr. notes at Terre Blanche River on May 24, 1810: *My people arrived with the four new bateaux, not quite finished for want of nails; 3600 were not sufficient for four boats forty feet long; they require at least 400 more.*

Making good on his estimate, Vic and his voyageurs caught Eastward Ho near the Baptiste River. Both canoes stopped for a chat and a breather, then resumed travelling. Eastward Ho with its five h.p. motor, was no match for those six stalwart paddlers. With our kicker firing at maximum revs and three paddling as hard as we could, Eastward Ho couldn't keep up with the Alberta team. While paddling, Vic called stroke from astern.

At Alder Flats, the ice jams viewed from the air had moved on. Eastward Ho decided to chance the run to Drayton Valley. Throwing in some food and gear for an extra couple of days and clamping on the 20 h.p. motor, we wished Vic and his crew good luck for the upcoming contest, and waved goodbye to all.

The Brazeau River came in on the left. Thompson called it *North Branch River.* A good head of water could be observed in its outflow, which meant a fair volume was being released from the upstream dam. In our ignorance, we expected the rise in water level would flush out the ice. In fact, it merely swept more icebergs off the riverbank into an already ice-saturated Saskatchewan, thus compounding the trouble.

Beyond the forks the river began to pick up speed. There were still numerous shoals and islands, but the faster moving water was easier to read. The countryside was dreary looking, with no signs of spring. Poplar and alder trees waved brittle fingers in the wind. The bank was high in places, sometimes 300 feet when the river cut along the base of a hill.

No game was observed, but there were many species of birds; Buffleheads, Loons, Grebes, and Franklin's gulls with their compact white bodies, black heads and black-tipped wings. There were the high-flying formations of Canada geese and the larger Snow geese heading south. Lots of colorful Teal, Mallard and Pintail took off and landed on the river's edge.

Seven miles below Brazeau River, a low-lying flat area on the left side of the North Saskatchewan was the site of Boggy Hall, an old NWC trading post built for the Cree and Assiniboine trade. Our *fifth man,* David Thompson, had put up at Boggy Hall in the late fall of 1810, when on the run from the Piegans who had prevented him from using Howse Pass. It was there he came to the decision to seek another crossing of the Rockies.

Near Washout Creek the river started to swing northward again and we began congratulating ourselves on reaching Drayton Valley that afternoon. No sooner had we entertained this thought, however, when progress came to an emphatic halt. A large ox-bow had slowed the river down enough to ensnare all the ice.

Hoping the blockage might be short lived we clambered out onto some high ground for a view. The ice pack continued on as far as the eye could see. We camped right there, hoisting the canoe up the sheer wall of ice that lined the river.

In the morning, the jam had added another few hundred yards to itself. Had we not removed the canoe from the river, it would have been smashed beyond repair. Now it had to be dragged back upstream to get around the newly added ice. We scuttled across to the west side where a road wound over a bluff.

After storing the canoe well above the river's icy grasp, we started walking northward to Drayton Valley. A truck gave us a lift into town. Don spotted the camper-truck in a garage having its oil pan replaced. Too many gumbo roads!

The N. Saskatchewan River remained immobilized at the bridge south of Drayton Valley. To utilize the delay, a return trip was made to our cache on the river in order to hike out the mail. Bill Gifford brought the canoe on top of his station wagon.

A Mr. and Mrs. Morris of Drayton Valley were very hospitable, putting Eastward Ho up in their home during a frustrating two-day wait beside the river.

Some shifting of ice on the second day indicated things might move any time, prompting a vigilant watch beside the bridge. Sure enough, by about five o'clock, water pressure had built up to such an extent that the whole river-wide conglomeration of ice slowly began to rise like dough in a pan. At a hidden signal, the grinding mass started to move.

To capture this sight of inexorable power, Edo had set his camera on the edge of the river, directly beneath the plug holding back the mile-long build-up of ice. Looking through his lens, he was unaware the river level had actually elevated and now hovered menacingly several feet above himself. The rest of us, a hundred yards away, could see the ice monster swelling upwards. Edo appeared not to hear our yells and whistles, and seemed oblivious to arm signals. He would merely wave back, continuing to grind away in the spirit of a professional cameraman, heedless of danger.

Bill Gifford finally ceased his futile calling and dashed across the shore-ice. He dragged Edo off, protesting, and still clenching his tripod and camera. Moments later the slab Edo had been filming from was whirled away and crushed under a mountain of debris.

What a spectacle it was to witness two such gargantuan forces of nature in conflict. Ice blocks the size of a garage, and weighing hundreds of tons, would rise up, then plunge beneath the surface of the boiling river, only to be spewn out further down like ice cubes popped from a tray. Eventually, after throwing off its winter's yoke, the river became the final victor.

The last jostling blocks of ice ground against the steel girders of the bridge and passed out of sight around the bend. Looking at the placid waters now flowing so quietly, it was hard to believe it had been capable of such destructive power only minutes before.

The canoe crew bedded down under the bridge to depart at first light. The morning run was excellent, but at noon yet another ice jam intervened. No passage could be found, on the right side, the left side, or down the middle. We scouted the woods along the river for a road. Nothing!

It took seven back-breaking, dangerous hours, and four repeat trips, to move everything over the rough and tumble bottleneck. The ice had pushed right up to the base of a thickly wooded scrub of trees. Although we could worm through the brush, we couldn't take the canoe through without cutting a four foot wide swath. We had no axe. The only alternative was to drag the canoe across the jumbled up slabs of river ice tilted at every angle imaginable.

The tricky operation was agonizingly slow. We had to lift and pull and shove the canvas-covered craft up, down and over an interminable number of awkwardly placed ice cakes. The sight of that ice jam surging under the bridge at Drayton Valley was very much on our minds. We didn't venture far out on the river, but kept a ready eye open in case a quick dash to shore was in order.

Many times we would jump down onto a solid looking slab of ice, only to have it disintegrate underfoot. That misstep often resulted in a bone chilling plunge into the river. Only a firm grip on the gunwale of the canoe kept the unfortunate one from vanishing under the ice.

Don was feeling quite smug for a time, having managed to stay dry while the other three had received an immersion. Finally he too took the plunge. When he 'came a cropper', a chorus of gleeful cheers burst forth from his three pals.

One pleasant happening occurred that tortuous day. While scouting fruitlessly through the woods for a road, we came across an exquisite example of Nature's planning; a small bit of magic not yet destroyed by the rude hands of man. Breaking through a thicket of brambles we entered a natural parkland. A quiet pond, dyked beside the river by a filled-in stream bed, shimmered along the bottom of a bank of aspen trees. Beaver mounds rose out of the pond, while holes in the bank and mud-slicked slides bespoke the presence of the fun loving river otter.

The approach by humans, and a subsequent sharp smack of a beaver tail, brought complete silence. We sat without moving. In a few minutes action began again. Squirrels appeared, chattering and scolding their way from limb to limb. Woodpeckers and jays flittered overhead, lending flashes of color to the faded shades of winter vegetation. Finally the skittish beavers emerged to gather a tasty morsel of aspen branch for the hungry kits at home. Eastward Ho left the sanctuary feeling more at peace with the world.

Hard work on the North Saskatchewan River

After a day of hauling the canoe up and down the staggered ice jams, we finally reached open water. By nightfall, the outline of Genesee bridge and the headlights of Bill's station wagon could be seen. Numbed with cold and fatigue, we trailed stiffly up the bank into the welcome warmth of the camper, and a steaming mug of hot rum. Having broken through the last of the Albertan ice jams, we reached Edmonton the next day .

Edmontonians made Eastward Ho welcome. The Gyro Club, forewarned of our coming entertained royally and saw to the storage of equipment. The Y.M.C.A. arranged accommodation at their downtown hostel. We then made ready for the long slide across the northern prairie.

The next chapter contains a brief outline of the disposition of Canada's First Nations people of the open prairie, as recorded by David Thompson. He observes the lifestyle of the nomadic *Meadow Indians* prior to the breakdown of their society by the mass immigration of New Canadians.

They called him 'Koo-Koo-Sint'.
"He who looks at the stars".
How First Nations people
saw David Thompson

Chapter Eleven
People of the Prairie

Before Europeans appeared on the scene in the early 18th century, First Nations people of the prairies had achieved an ecological and ethnological balance well suited to a nomadic existence. We can acquaint ourselves with that environment by examining David Thompson's 'Narrative'.

A distinctly Canadian anomaly was the fact that a large group of people, with a common mother-tongue, had spread across the land from the Atlantic to the Rocky Mountains. They were the Cree Nation and they spoke an Algonquian language. This was of great benefit to traders who could make verbal contact with relative ease wherever the Cree roamed. The Churchill River prescribed their northern border, while the North Saskatchewan, Saskatchewan and the Winnipeg rivers marked the southern one.

Northward of the Cree, from tree-line to barren land, the Athapaskan speaking Chipewayens followed the caribou from the Mackenzie River to Hudson Bay. On the Cree's southern flank the Assiniboine or Stonies, who spoke the same language as the Sioux, roamed the prairie from Lake Winnipeg west to the Alberta border.

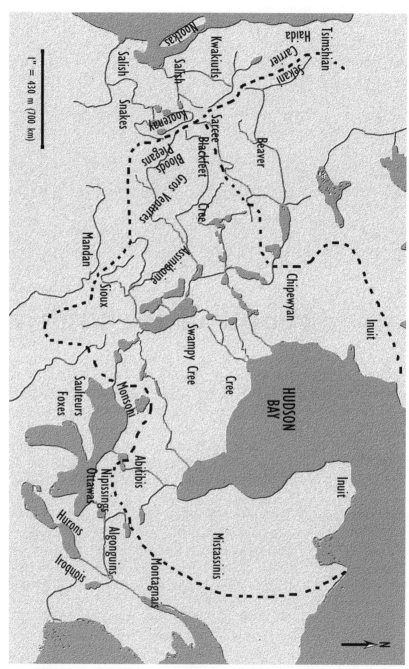

Disposition of First Nations – circa 1800

The Blackfeet, Bloods and Piegans, known collectively as the Blackfeet Confederacy, moved in seasonal circles between present Edmonton and Montana. They were the frontier people and generally led a more precarious life than other tribes.

The Kootenays dwelt along the eastern foothills of Alberta and into the spine of the Rockies. South of them were the Interior Salish, then came the Snakes or Shoshonees, sworn enemies of the Blackfeet.

In a rough way this was the disposition of the people of the mid section of Canada when fur traders, such as our *fifth man* Pierre La Vérendrye, first appeared on the eastern horizon, in the 1730's. He found a certain amount of accommodation between the people living on contiguous borders. Although martial arts were encouraged by peer groups, and scalps were a trophy to bring prestige and a bevy of maidens to the tent of any young warrior, full scale battles seldom took place and loss of life was fairly minimal.

Without the destructive power of guns, or the mobility of horses, conflict was usually confined to a rush in the night against one or two families. It takes a great deal of incentive to meet rivals face to face and engage them in mortal hand to hand contact. Only the warrior class dared that sort of action.

This relatively non-confrontational atmosphere was about to change drastically, and forever, with four *gifts* from the white man. The gifts were *guns, horses, disease* and *alcohol.* Thompson has already spoken to us about the devastating effects of alcohol, but guns and horses first upset the long-standing intertribal equilibrium. Both arrived about the same time, although they came from different sources.

Guns began arriving in large quantities with the NWC traders operating out from Montreal, affording a temporary benefit for the first ones who received them, an advantage that was short-lived. Guns soon became indispensable for both hunting and for warfare.

The Great Plains proved a natural feeding and breeding ground for the horses imported from Spain. These grazing animals gradually infiltrated northward from tribe to tribe, spreading in large numbers throughout the prairies after the middle of the 18th century. David Thompson records an interview held with an elderly warrior of the plains whose name was Saukamappee, a Cree adopted by Blackfeet when he was a young man. He could recount events going back to the time of La Vérendrye:

Our enemies the Snake Indians now had horses on which they rode swift as the deer. They could dash at the Peeagans with their stone 'pukamoggan' and knock them fatally on the head. We had no idea of horses and could not make out what they were. At last, as the leaves were falling, we heard that a horse had been killed by an arrow shot into his belly. A number of us went to see him, and we all admired him. He put us in mind of a stag without horns; and we did not know what name to give him. But as he was a slave to man, like the dog which carried our things, we named him 'Big Dog'.

Saukamappee continued his discourse with an account of his first encounter with the dreaded smallpox, against which his people were defenseless:

Our wars have since been carried by ambuscade and surprise of small camps in which we have greatly the advantage, from the guns, arrow shods of iron, long knives, flat bayonets and axes from the traders. While we have these weapons, the Snake Indians have none. We thus continued to advance through the fine plains to the Stag River, (Red Deer River), when death came over us all, and swept away more than half of us by the Smallpox, of which we knew nothing until it brought death among us.

We caught the sickness from the Snake Indians in the following manner: Our scouts alerted us to a large camp of the enemy which we attacked next morning at the dawn of day. With our sharp flat daggers we cut through the leather tents and entered for the fight. Our war-whoops instantly stopped, our eyes were appalled with terror; there was no one to fight with but the dead and dying, each a mass of corruption. We all thought the Bad Spirit had made himself master of the camp and destroyed them. It was agreed to take some of the best of the tents, and any plunder that was clean and good, which we did. We also took away the few horses they had.

The second day after, this dreadful disease broke out in our camp. We had no belief that one man could give it to another, any more than a wounded man could give his wound to another. We did not suffer so much as those that were near the river, into which they rushed and died. We had only a little brook, and about one third of us died, but in some of the other camps there were tents in which every one died. When at length it left us, and we moved about to find our people, it was no longer with the song and the dance; but with tears, shrieks, and howlings of despair of those who would never return to us. The Bison and Red Deer were also gone, whither we could not tell.

We believed the Good Spirit had forsaken us, and allowed the Bad Spirit to become our master. What little we could spare, we offered to the Bad Spirit to let us alone and go to our enemies. To the Good Spirit we offered feathers, branches of trees, and sweet smelling grasses. Our hearts were low and dejected. We shall never again be the same people. We thought of War no more.

We'll let our *fifth man* David Thompson continue with some of his own observations:

The Indians of the Plains make no use of canoes, frequently stay many days in one place, and when they remove, have horses and dogs, both in summer and winter. They have no hard labour, but have powerful enemies which keep them constantly on the watch and are never secure except in large camps.

The manners and customs of all these tribes of the Plains are much alike, and in giving those of the Peeagans, it may serve for all the others. Being the frontier tribe, they lead a more precarious and watchful life than other tribes, and from their boyhood are taught the use of arms, and to be good warriors, they become more martial and more moral than others, and many of them have a chivalrous bearing, ready for any enterprise. They have a civil and a military Chief.

The War Chief was Kootanae Appe. His stature was six feet, six inches. Tall and erect, he appeared to be of Bone and Sinew with no more flesh than absolutely required; his countenance manly but not stern, his features prominent, nose somewhat aquiline, his manners kind and mild; his word was sacred. He was both loved and respected, and his people often wished him to take a more active part in their affairs, but he confined himself to war.

Kootanae Appe by his five wives had 22 sons and four daughters. His grown up sons were as tall as himself. He was friendly to the White Men, and in his speeches reminded his people of the great benefit of which the traders were to them. He had acquired his present station and influence from his conduct in war. He seldom took the field with less than 200 warriors, but frequently with many more; his policy was to get as many of the allies to join him as possible, by which all might have a share of the honour and plunder, and thus avoid those jealousies and envying so common amongst the Chiefs. He praised every Chief that in the least deserved it, but never appeared to regard fame as worth his notice. Yet always took care to deserve it, for all his expeditions were successful.

From infancy they are exposed to the weather and have not that softness of expression which can be so pleasing. But they are a fine race of men, tall and muscular, with manly features, and intelligent countenances, the eyes large, black and piercing, the nose full and generally straight, the teeth regular and white, the hair long, straight and black; their beards would be equal to those of white men, did they not continually attempt to eradicate it. Their colour is something like that of a Spaniard from the south of Spain, and some like that of the French of the south of France, and this comparison is drawn from seeing them when bathing together.

The Indians are noticed for their apathy, but this is more assumed than real. In public he wishes to appear that nothing can affect him, but in private he feels and expresses himself sensible to everything that happens to him or to his family. After all his endeavours to obtain some object in hunting, or other matters, and he cannot do it, he says "the Great Spirit will have it so", in the same manner as we say "It is the will of Providence". Civilized men have many things to engage their attention and to take up their time, but the Indian is very different; hunting is his business, not his amusement, and even in this he is limited for want of ammunition. Hence his whole life is in the enjoyments of his passions, desires and affections contracted within a small circle, and in which it is often intense.

The men are proud of being noticed and praised as good hunters, warriors, or any other masculine accomplishment. Many of the young men make fine dandies of themselves by painting their faces with White, Red, Green, Blue and Yellow, or part of those colours. When married all this painting is at an end.

The young men seldom marry before they are fully grown, about the age of 22 years or more, and the women about 16 to 18. The older women who are related to them are generally the match makers, and the parties come together without any ceremony. Polygamy is allowed and practised, and the Wife more often than the husband is the cause of it.

When a family comes, a single wife can no longer do the duties and labour required, unless she, or her husband, have two widowed relations in their tent, and which is frequently not the case. So a second wife is necessary, for they have to cook, take care of the meat, split and dry it; procure all the wood for fuel, dress the skins into soft leather for robes and clothing; which they have also to make and mend, and other duties which leaves scarce any part of the day to be idle. In removing from place to place, the taking down of the tents and putting them up are all performed by women. Some of the Chiefs have from three to six wives, for until a woman is near fifty years of age, she is sure to find a husband.

The Indians of the Plains all punish adultery with death to both parties. This law does not appear to be founded on either religious or moral principles, but upon a high right of property as the best gift that Providence has given to them to be their wives and the mothers of their families; and without who they cannot live. Every year there are some runaway matches between the young men and women; these are almost wholly from the hatred of the young women to polygamy.

When a fine young woman, proud of herself, finds that instead of being given to her lover, she is to be the 4th or 5th wife to some Man advanced in years, where she is to be the slave of the family, and bear all the bondage of the wife, without any of its rights and privileges, she readily consents to quit the camp with her lover, and go to some other camp where they have friends. In this case the affair is often made up; and the parents of the young woman are more pleased, than otherwise; yet it sometimes ends fatally. If the young couple can escape a few months, the affair is sometimes settled by a present of one or two horses; but if the young man is considered a worthless character, which is often the case, his life pays the forfeit of his crime. If the woman shares the same fate, her nose is cut off as a mark of infamy, and some of these unfortunate women have been known to prefer death to this disgrace. Some cases are very hard.

The character of all these people appears to be brave, steady and deliberate, but on becoming acquainted with them there is no want of individual character, and almost every character in civilized society can be traced among them, from the gravity of a judge to a merry jester, and from open hearted generosity to the avaricious miser. This last trait is more detested by them, than by us, from their precarious manner of life, requiring assistance from each other. Especially in provisions is great attention paid to those that are unfortunate in the chase, and the tent of a sick man is well supplied.

They have a haughtiness of character, that let their wants be what they will, they will not ask assistance from each other, it must be given voluntarily. Disgrace they cannot bear, especially in public. Upon some business I was at one of their camps with five of my men. An Indian passed us on foot, apparently irritated at something that had happened in hunting. He had let his horse loose and his little horse whip was at his wrist. His wife was outside the door of her tent listening to the general conversation. When he came to her he said something and struck her gently with his whip. She entered the tent immediately. In an instant she came out, passed her husband, turned and faced him, then spoke:

"You have before all these disgraced me. You shall never do it again."

With that she drew a sharp, pointed knife from its scabbard, and before anyone could realize her intent, plunged it into her own heart. The whole camp was in an instant uproar, and all seemed to regret her death, blaming the husband for the tragedy. Not a word was spoken against her suicide, for a blow, especially in public, is a high disgrace. She was carefully buried, and what belonged to her, broken or killed.

Her husband was fond of her. He sat quietly in his tent all day, but at night went to some distance, and there would call upon and lament her death. Before her death he was an active and successful hunter, but since then never went hunting and lived upon any thing that was given him. The affections of an Indian are deep, for he has nothing to turn them to other things.

The Natives of all these countries are fond of their children. They have faults like other children, but are not corrected by being beaten. Contempt and ridicule are the correctives employed. These shame them without breaking their spirit. As they are all brought up in the open camp, other children help the punishment.

It sometimes happens that Husbands and Wives separate. If they have children, the boys are taken by the Fathers and the Mothers bring up the girls.

David Thompson sympathized with the plight of the native people. He was well aware that the flood of land-hungry immigrants from Europe was an inexorable force driving the First People from their traditional homeland. In spite of several sincere attempts to stem the tide by Great Britain, with proclamations of containment such as the 'Quebec Act', the situation was hopeless, and unstoppable. Although his line of work was part of the problem, Thompson attempted to lessen friction between the two competing cultures whenever possible.

The fur traders from Canada had extended
their trading posts so as to almost cut off all trade
from the Bay.

David Thompson

Chapter Twelve
Edmonton to the Pas

"Gateway to the North!", say Edmonton boosters. They are not far out in their arc of hyperbole, but Edmonton, now the Capital of Alberta, once had a problem making up its mind where to begin. Over a period of seventeen years HBC men hustled Fort Edmonton back and forth to four locations on the Saskatchewan River, before allowing it to settle permanently at the present site in 1812. Part of the reason for so much shifting about was that the two competing fur organizations covered each other's moves like chess players. If the NWC erected its Fort Augustus, the HBC would quickly erect a Fort Edmonton in the same neighbourhood. When one moved, so did the other.

One of Edmonton's foremost City Fathers, and a long-term manager of old Fort Edmonton, was John Rowand. A former Nor-Wester, he was in charge of the various Fort Augustus' before the 1821 amalgamation of the NWC and the HBC. He proved such a reliable person that even *observer* Sir George Simpson, with his distinct bias against all North-West Co. hands, recognized Rowand's obvious abilities.

Returning from the west coast through Edmonton on May 2, 1825 he wrote:

I found Mr. Rowand up to his ears in business, as usual. Without exception he is the most active man and the best qualified person of any to be found in the Indian country.

Under Rowand's tenure Edmonton became a true transportation centre. Trade goods and pemmican came up the Saskatchewan to be stored with the bales of sorted furs readied to be reshipped downriver for Montreal and thence to Europe. After 1821, York Factory on Hudson Bay handled most of the furs exported to Hudson Bay House in London, England.

From Fort Edmonton horse brigades ranged south along the Rocky Mountain foothills to present day Montana, or snaked westward to Fort Assiniboine on the Athabasca River. From Fort Assiniboine canoes were paddled or dragged up river so parties could cross the Rockies at Athabasca Pass, or they might be run 'down north' to Fort Chipewyan on Lake Athabasca, or to Great Slave Lake, and even beyond.

Paul Kane was a distinguished Canadian artist of native lifestyles. He told us the story of the "*lob-stick*" back on the Columbia River near Boat Encampment. In his Wanderings of an Artist, 1846-48, *observer* Kane describes a wind-up to the celebration of Christmas at Fort Edmonton, when it was but an outpost on the Saskatchewan River, three thousand miles from civilization.

By evening the hall was ready for the banquet and the dance to follow. Indians with heavily painted faces, voyageurs with red sashes and beaded moccasins, half-breeds glittering with ornaments; all laughed and jabbered in as many different tongues as there were styles of dress. English was little used. Only those at the dinner table could speak it.

The dancing was picturesque, all joining in. Occasionally I led forth a young Cree woman, sporting enough beads to make a pedlar's fortune. In the centre of the room I danced round her with all the agility I could exhibit, to a highland reel tune played by a vigorous fiddler. My grave-faced partner would jump straight up and down, on her toes, as only an Indian can dance. Shining-faced ladies and children, squatting on the floor, applauded mightily.

The morning before Eastward Ho's departure from Edmonton, the crew were fortunate to have coffee and a chat with J.C. MacGregor, chairman of Alberta Hydro. Possessing a humorous and engaging manner, Mr. MacGregor not only administered a large corporation, but was an author of note, and a keen student of Canadiana.

He has written several books on the Canadian West, including "Blankets and Beads", which was much studied for details of the Saskatchewan River.

Later the Eastward Ho contingent drove to Father Lacombe's Mission in St. Albert. The worthy Father, a young priest in the later days of John Rowand, had been a powerful figure on the side of compassion and social justice. He championed the weak and down trodden and his mission became a haven for many a bruised soul. At the time of the North West Rebellion, his strength and wisdom saved countless lives of natives and whites. The Blackfeet and Cree who frequented Fort Edmonton trusted Father Lacombe and obeyed his plea to refrain from violence.

Eastward Ho left Edmonton on May 13th, happy to be on the move again toward an objective. We had fallen behind schedule because of the unexpected ice conditions of the North Saskatchewan River.

Fort Saskatchewan, twenty miles north-east of Edmonton, was the next location of interest. On the south or right-hand side of the river, it is one of the few forts not established by the fur trade. Inspector Jarvis of the North West Mounted Police supervised its construction in 1875.

Across the North Saskatchewan from the fort, the Sturgeon River enters. Its mouth marks the site of the first Fort Edmonton, erected by the HBC in 1795 and where the Saskatchewan ceases its winding ways to run steadily north eastward.

In its sweep across the top of the prairie, the North Saskatchewan became a busy fur trade artery for traders from both Hudson Bay and from Montreal, which is to say the HBC and the NWC. Between La Vérendrye and Thompson's time, over 50 trading posts were erected along its 1,000 miles of canoeable water. A century of Canadian history took place at those tiny outposts of commerce, strung out like beads on a string. When fur was king, each of them was a centre for storage and exchange.

A handful of forts continued to grow as urban centers for expanding farming activity, but most only lasted as long as the fur bearing animals remained within the radius of a particular post. Places with fine names, Bourbon, Acton, Buckingham, and Chesterfield; and others less prestigious, Boggy Hall, Hungry Hall, Quagmire House and White Mud, passed into oblivion; their activities erased by time and nature.

It was a search and destroy economy. Some of the older and wiser members of First Nations people, and perhaps a handful of fur traders, such as David Thompson and Daniel Harmon, understood the long term effects of raping the land. Most were after the short-term gain. The prevailing attitude during the hey-day of the NWC was, "Its here for the taking. Get what you can, when you can."

White Earth Creek entered on the north side of the river. It was the most easterly site for Forts Augustus and Edmonton, and it also marked the most northerly position of the trans-Canada waterway. *Observer* Henry Jr. called it *Terre Blanche House* when in command there. He cited it as: *Too cold for comfort when the chilling north-west winds sweep down the valley.*

Air temperature was important to post managers who were expected to grow vegetables to supplement their men's diet of fish and meat. A grey-white mud surrounding a nearby lake was the source of the term 'White Earth'. It was a popular place for First Nations people to collect the mud used for daubing onto their bodies. Builders of the fort applied this whitewash to the walls of their structures.

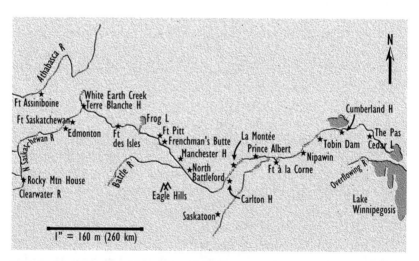

North Saskatchewan River: Edmonton to The Pas

Eastward Ho's first night after Edmonton was on the south bank of the river, confined by the Snake Hills and the Snipe Hills. This was north of the town of Brosseau which originally began as St. Paul de Cris.

Chris is French for the Christenaux or Cree Indians. Father Lacombe established a mission here in 1866. The higher elevations on Snipe Hills afforded an expansive view of the lower prairie, and caused our *observer*, Paul Kane, to note: *We had much difficulty that evening in finding a place to camp away from the immense number of buffalo that surrounded us, finding it necessary to fire off our guns during the night to keep them away.*

Observer Henry Jr. wrote of a buffalo hunting method called *pounding*, popular with the Assiniboine people in this area.

The Assiniboine are the most expert nation of the plains in constructing pounds. They vary in size but average 100 yards in circumference and are five feet high. Trees are cut down, laid one upon another and interwoven with green branches. The enclosure is generally between two hillocks at the foot of rising ground. The entrance is 10 yards wide and always fronts the plains.

On each side of the entrance commences a range of fascines, (stout sticks laced together), the two rows spreading asunder as they extend to about 100 yards, beyond which openings are left at intervals up to a distance of 300 yards from the pound. From then on cross-sticks are placed at intervals in imitation of a dog or other animal [sometimes called dead men.] These extend for about two miles. Double rows of them are planted in several directions.

Young men are sent out to collect the buffalo – a tedious task which requires patience, for the herd must be started by slow degrees. This is done by setting fire to dung or grass. Three men will bring in a herd of several hundred from a great distance.

Coming in sight of the ranges, the drovers excite the herd to go faster. At the entrance a swift footed person has been stationed, covered with a buffalo robe and trophy to imitate that animal. When the buffalo appear to be following he sets off at full speed, imitating the cantering animals as well as he can.

Every available man, woman and child have laid themselves down between the fascines and cross-sticks to shout and wave their robes to head off an errant animal.

"With the stampeding buffalo successfully directed to the entrance, the decoy rushes into the pound and out through a hole on the far side. The buffalo tumble in pell mell, many breaking their legs and necks as the descent is generally six to eight feet, and tree stumps are purposely left in the ground. The entrance is closed, then the men assemble around the inclosure and let fly with their bows and arrows until the whole herd has been slaughtered.

Commonly, there is a master of the pound who divides the carcasses, rendering each tent an equal share. It is in his tent that the numerous pound ceremonies are observed. There the young men are always welcome to feast and smoke, and no women are allowed to enter, as that tent is set aside for the affairs of the pound.

The river highway turns south to flow under the Duvernay-Brosseau bridge where a Catholic church sits atop a hillock, keeping watch over the silvery road rolling down to Lake Winnipeg.

On this portion of the Saskatchewan, small car and passenger ferries cross the river at ten mile intervals. A mild altercation took place at one of them. On our approach, a strange boil-up of water could be seen a few feet ahead of the ferry's prow. The skipper was gesturing from his wheelhouse and obviously trying to draw our attention to something. He kept pointing towards the water at the stern of his vessel. When we got close to the ferry's track, Don cut our motor in order to appraise the ferryman's concern.

We were glad of Don's caution. Two large, ugly hooks, partially submerged, protruded from bow and stern of the ferry. A continuous underwater cable spanning the entire river, ran through them. Occasionally, the cable would slash upward above the surface of the water with enough whip in it to cut our canoe in half. After that episode the helmsman waited until the ferry was safely onshore with its threatening coils inert, before passing over the hidden menace.

Voyageurs did not have to contend with this menace, but our *fifth man* describes a similar hazard:

Mr. Thompson: *We embarked on the sinuous stream of the N. Saskatchewan below the Kootenay Plains when a large sawyer of 18 inches diameter sprang from the river within four inches of our canoe. A blow from it would have dashed the canoe to pieces. A 'sawyer' for want of a Greek name is a large tree torn from the banks by the current, whose roots lodge in the shallows, but whose trunk is pushed underwater by the swift moving river. The elasticity and buoyancy of the tree causes it to rise like the spring of a bow. I once saw a Bison Bull across a sawyer that had come up to take him under his belly. The bull was swimming with all his might, his fore legs on one side, his hind legs on the other, but he went nowhere, only as the sawyer dodged him up and down. We all had a hearty laugh.*

In mid-May on the N. Saskatchewan, birds were the only wildlife in evidence. At one point a feathery owl wheeled and dove at a slower moving bald eagle, shooing the larger predator away from its nest. A flight of black male scoters flapped their way into the air, while their sooty brown females were busy building nests in the nearby reed-filled back-waters.

Some difficulty was experienced in finding a channel around two-mile long Fort des Isles, a well known stopping place for *voyageurs*. Three large fur trading competitors, the HBC, the NWC and Alexander Mackenzie's short lived XYC, all placed trading posts on Fort des Isles in 1800. One can envision the hub-bub of activity that must have taken place long ago on this now deserted island. First Nations people, born bargainers themselves, welcomed this competitive environment. It drove fur prices up and the costs of muskets and fire-water down.

The river turned north east, holding that course to the bridge at Elk Point. The north shore marked the site of two trading posts; HBC's Buckingham House built in 1792 and the NWC's Fort George. This bridge marked an ancient crossing of the Saskatchewan by the Cree. Fur traders once fattened their horses in the rich pastures that grace this broad valley.

Nearby Frog Lake was a source for tasty whitefish prized by men of the fur trade. It was also the scene of a senseless massacre of civilian whites during the brief but bloody outbreak of the North-West Rebellion of 1885. In March of that year a seventy man contingent of North-West Mounted Police, together with thirty Prince Albert Volunteers, moved out to dislodge 350 armed Métis who had looted and burned stores and habitations at Duck Lake.

The Métis, practiced riflemen and professional buffalo hunters under the leadership of Gabriel Dumont, routed the approaching soldiery. News of the defeat spread like a prairie fire across lands of Assiniboine, Cree, and Blackfeet. Embittered and helpless under the inexorable takeover of their domain, and well aware of how thinly spread the newcomers were throughout their traditional hunting and trading territory, some warriors rose up to smite the white men who they considered interlopers on their land.

It was a blow of frustration. Inspector Dickens, son of the famous author Charles Dickens, was stationed at Fort Pitt. He sent a warning to the dozen or so white people at Frog Lake, fifty miles to the north-west, urging them to abandon their homes and seek his protection.

Unfortunately the settlers and two Roman Catholic priests, acting on the advice of Native Agent Quinn, declined the invitation.

Having in the past dwelt mostly with Wood Crees, a group less warlike and volatile than their relatives of the Plains, the small band of settlers thought they could deal with the situation. They even sent away six policemen stationed there, feeling that the presence of authority would arouse a smoldering resentment on the part of native people. They learned too late that unbridled force can be contained only by a greater force.

In early April of 1885, the day after the police departed, a band of Plain Crees entered the village, ransacked the HBC store, then burst in and disrupted the church service. Not wishing a confrontation within the sanctity of their Church, the priests asked the parishioners, a mix of Christianized natives and whites, to disperse. The congregation rose in a body and left the building.

This act of unity seemed symbolic somehow to the overwrought Crees. They went mad. A volley of shots rang out. In an instant all but one of the males lay on the ground outside the picket fence of their churchyard, writhing in death's agony.

Two women, along with HBC trader W.B. Cameron, were trussed up and imprisoned. The three survived to tell of their torment. Cameron wrote a gripping account of the whole affair in his book, "Blood Red the Sun".

A few miles beyond Frog Creek, the Vermilion River enters on the right. Opposite, on the Saskatchewan's north shore, both the NWC and HBC had establishments. Each called their sites Fort Vermilion.

Twenty miles further, on the boundary line between the provinces of Alberta and Saskatchewan, another ferry crossing indicated the location of Fort Pitt, established by the HBC in 1830. It was a way station for horses on the overland trail from Fort Carlton to Edmonton. It was burned to the ground during the height of the North-West rebellion.

Like nearly all trading forts, Pitt was on the north side of the Saskatchewan River. There was a strategic reason for this. The Saskatchewan served as a dividing line between nomadic prairie peoples who were continuously skirmishing with each other. The Blackfeet and Cree were two such groups, although they did entertain temporary alliances periodically. Traditionally, Blackfeet hunted on the south side of Saskatchewan River, Cree on the north. Traders supported this geographical separation. It helped keep the peace. Fighting was bad for trade.

That night Eastward Ho camped on the south side, across from Frenchman's Butte. Thompson and Alexander Henry Jr., fellow partners in the NWC passed this way many times. Henry wrote:

The canoe brigade arrived, the men unloading and carrying the baggage into the fort. Blackfeet hunters returned with 10 cows. Cows are preferred to bulls for tenderness. We had a dance lasting till daybreak. Our HBC neighbors were invited to the party. All was mirth, our men as smart and active as if they had rested a month.

One can imagine the screeching of the fiddle and the whoops of dancers plying their well deserved revelry throughout those tiny outposts. A modicum of European culture, albeit rough-hewn, was on display within that vast wilderness. Similar festivities would take place at dozens of trading fortifications when canoe brigades arrived in from Fort William or Fort York with their annual supply of trade goods.

On Dave's week in charge of meals he promised breakfast 'en canoe' to see if some time could be shaved from the usual two hours it took to break camp. Crouching under a specially arranged tarp with the coleman, he proceeded to make 'mush'. Steam emanating from an orange tent and streaming out behind the canoe, must have presented a strange sight to any observers on shore.

Eventually bowls of gruel emerged at the end of a hand, and worked down the line until all had a dish on his lap. The cold morning air rushing past quickly congealed steaming porridge into thick slabs of cold oat-cake. Nary a complaint was aired, however. None were eager to stand in *cook's shoes*.

Numerous beaver swam by, and several families of Great Blue Heron stood stilt-legged in large bramble nests high atop the leafless aspen trees.

An island on the left was pinpointed as the site of Manchester House, which Tomison of the HBC built in 1785. David Thompson was stationed here and suffered a broken leg in this vicinity.

In his book "Blankets and Beads", J. C. MacGregor explains that here in 1788, the HBC built and launched the first York boats constructed on the Saskatchewan. Used to freight pemmican down river to Cumberland House and beyond, they could carry three times the freight of a fully loaded *north* canoe. Orkneymen from Scotland, employed in large numbers by the HBC, probably preferred a stable rowing boat to the strange, wobbly birch-bark canoe.

The Nor'Westers, from their large emporium at Ft. William on Lake Superior, had to travel 300 miles further to reach the Saskatchewan than did their HBC rivals stationed at York Factory on Hudson Bay. To compete over this greater distance, with its numerous portages on the Rainy and Winnipeg Rivers, the NWC had to stay with lighter and faster, but smaller capacity vessels. As well, they had to ship everything an additional 1,000 miles between Montreal and Fort William. This discrepancy in transportation costs eventually broke the aggressive North-West Company, when the market for beaver and other furs inevitably declined.

Around noon a bridge signaled the approach to North Battleford. An earlier built Buckingham House, erected in 1779 by Mitchell Oman of the HBC, once serviced this area for both Cree and Blackfeet. Many First Nations people were present, coming in from three large reserves surrounding the confluence of the Battle and Saskatchewan Rivers. The men, with large physiques, were well set up and handsome. They struck one as looking remarkably like old portraits of pure Hawaiians. Battle River is said to have received its name from the frequent skirmishes between Blackfeet and Cree which took place along its lower reaches.

This centuries old gathering place was the setting for at least four trading houses. The earliest was probably that of William Holmes, one of the signatories of the first NWC agreement of 1780. An independent fiery man, he operated in and out of the partnership for several years, ultimately doing well on the Saskatchewan. Returning to Montreal, he bought a seigniory in the countryside, equipped it with fine furniture and silver to retire on the banks of the St. Lawrence River.

Below Battleford travel was slow and frustrating, the river full of innumerable islands and unseen sand bars which put a shiny, knife-sharp edge on Eastward Ho's propeller. Scudding along at full bore, the first notice of something amiss would be a change in the tune of the motor from a high pitched whine to a deep throaty gurgle. Astern, a darkened trail of muddy water could be seen bubbling to the surface. An easing of the throttle would level the canoe, allowing the prop to rotate more freely. A moderate speed would hold until the helmsman's impatience returned. Fortunately for transom and motor the skeg never struck a heavy object, in spite of all its dredging.

Five miles below the mouth of Battle River a line of bluffs rise to a height of 500 feet above the level of the plains. Labelled Montagne d'Aigle by *voyageurs*, Thompson first saw these Eagle Mountains on his trading journey to the Blackfeet encampment in 1787-88. His small party of six had started on horseback from Buckingham House.

Mr. Thompson: *We passed on the west side of Eagle Hills which rise from the river in undulating grassy ascents. Thermal winds eddy over the conical shaped hill, providing perfect soaring grounds for predatory golden eagles. The application of the name was not directly from those magnificent birds, however, but rather from the bizarre and risky hunting methods used by local Cree Indians in the early days.*

To garner his prey, an Indian would lay flat on his back in a shallow pit dug into an exposed knoll, twigs and leaves covering his body. Placing a fist-sized piece of raw buffalo meat on his camouflaged chest, the dusky hunter would wait with absolute stillness. A sharp-eyed eagle on the alert for edibles might eventually sight the blood-dripping delicacy. Approaching upwind, curved talons at the ready, the monarch of the air would swoop in to seize the tempting bait. The instant it hovered within reach, the hunter would thrust his arms upward and grasp the extended legs of the marauder. In a flurry of dust and broken feathers he then slammed the screaming, wing-thrashing bird to the ground, swinging it violently from side to side, until death had eased its awful agony.

The mouth of Eagle Creek marked the most southerly point of the N. Saskatchewan at latitude 52 degrees 21 minutes. Ten miles further on, the bridge at Borden Crossing was sighted. It was eight p.m., not quite dark. On the south bank, where the river narrows, Dave Chisholm's parents waited patiently along with several friends. The canoe crew were whisked into Saskatoon to the warmth of a cozy hearth, hot bath and a home cooked meal.

With access to a phone Don checked The Pas airport, 300 river-miles further east, for a reading on the condition of Lake Winnipeg. It was now the middle of May, and Eastward Ho had become wary of the fact that 'old man winter' is often slow in retreating from the prairie. Don's report confirmed our worst fear. "The big lake is still frozen and likely to remain so for several weeks."

This was an added blow to an ever-tightening schedule. Lake Winnipeg, itself a 270-mile leg of the journey, called for a minimum three-day crossing. We were aware of the inherent danger from sudden storms and high-standing waves of that relatively shallow body of water, but planning had not taken into account all the delays created by ice.

Back on the North Saskatchewan, the crew stowed two new propellers in the canoe, before setting off for Prince Albert 100 miles NNE. The river was still sluggish and shallow which meant more propeller dredging throughout the day. By noon, the map indicated the site of old Fort Carlton on the south side of the river.

Before the North-West Rebellion, Fort Carlton had been a busy northern terminus for horsemen riding to and from the South Saskatchewan. The latter was also called South Branch River. An easy days ride on an ancient track led between the North and South Saskatchewans, through Batoche and Duck Lake, names made famous by the Métis uprising of 1885. Established in 1798 by the HBC, Carlton was once as large and important as Forts Garry and Edmonton. Reduced to a blackened ruin in that 1885 summer of discontent, the fort never performed the phoenix-like trick of rising from its ashes.

Across the N. Saskatchewan the NWC had established Fort La Montée; literally, 'the mounting place'. Stables were provided so traders coming up river with canoe brigades could mount horses and ride westward over open grassland between the Thickwood Hills and Turtleford, avoiding the long southern loop of the Saskatchewan.

This respite from canoes was only available to traders and hunters. The *voyageurs* had to sweat it out on the river below, laboriously paddling or poling their way upstream between hundreds of sandy islets.

In fur trade parlance Carlton was considered to be like other *forts des prairies* Eastward Ho had passed, such as Vermilion, George, and Edmonton. They were not only gathering posts for fur, but also provisioning centres.

Our *fifth man* Mr. Thompson stated: *Carlton served as a depot for Pemican, a product of the flesh of Bison; dried, smoked and pounded fine. In that state it is called Beat Meat. Melted fat is then added. Depending upon the area, local berries may also be put in for flavouring. The mixture is then tightly packed into bags made from bull-bison hides called Taureaux. When full they measure two and a half feet by one and a half feet and weigh 90 lbs. Voyageurs who can eat eight pounds of fresh meat a day are content with a pound and a half. Pemican would suit the Army and Navy admirably.*

Just west of Prince Albert, Sturgeon River entered on the left, its name an indication that the mighty sturgeon once migrated up the sandy Saskatchewan from Hudson Bay. The name was also applied to several Sturgeon Forts in this area, the most noted one was established by Peter Pond, two miles above the present-day bridge. He built and wintered there in 1776.

Pond was a force in the fur trade. Semi-illiterate and somewhat of a brute, he was suspected of killing two men in separate incidents in the fierce competition for furs. Yet he helped to open up the Northwest and subsequently pointed the way to the Pacific Ocean for Alexander Mackenzie.

The night was spent in Prince Albert at the behest of Mayor Barski, and many residents gathered on the bank of the river to greet Eastward Ho. People generally, including the media who stopped long enough to hear the history involved, were fascinated to learn about the connecting streams that link Canadians together.

Our 'twenty-horse' had been heating up, necessitating an inspection by an Outboard Marine agent. The problem proved to be a worn-out impeller. Constant friction from gritty grains of sand drawn into the water intake tube had scored the hard rubber flanges of the impeller down to its brass nub. The motor wasn't designed to drive through river bottom all day long, but with a new impeller installed it was soon humming its old tune.

There was little to attract attention for a few miles. The current was slack. To escape incessant wind and spray, all but the driver had retired under the tarp.

The normal routine was to rotate the helmsman's position every hour. Before calling Dave for his turn, Jim, without saying a word, had gradually turned the canoe around 180 degrees so that her prow pointed westward. Then he had yelled, "Time"!

On the changeover nothing was said. Under the canvas Jim divulged his little joke to the rest of the crew, who, feigning lack of fresh air, threw back the tarp to await Dave's reaction and witness the inevitable sparks. Nothing happened. The sky was overcast so Dave couldn't notice that the sun was now at his back; nor were there any distinctive hills to provide landmarks. One bend of the river looked much like another.

Not wanting to be back in Prince Albert again, Don eventually yelled, "Hey Dave, you're going the wrong way. We're headed for New Westminster"!

Dave looked at him as much as to say, "Yeah, yeah; very funny," but held his course.

It took a lot of persuasion before Dave could be prevailed upon to cut the motor and let the canoe come to a halt. Slowly it began to drift backwards, toward the east. The crew rolled in the bottom of the canoe, doubled up with laughter.

Grimly, Dave restarted the motor, banked the canoe in a tight turn and roared off down river again. He was not amused.

Not long after Jim's 'joke' the river began pulsing with new vigor. A shearline was now visible along the gravelled shore. At the top of this incline, *voyageurs* who had been struggling up from Cumberland House with line and with pole were able to resort to paddles again. Their gut-twisting, shoulder-straining work of lining had begun at Squaw or Tobins Rapids, 130 miles downstream.

Near the exchange from poles to paddles, Eastward Ho's canoe started to bounce down through Cole Rapids, named after a fractious trader killed by the Crees in 1779. Here they passed the ruins of a partially built hydro-electric dam which had been destroyed by the power of the river before its completion .

Another hour brought the crew to the junction of the North and South Saskatchewan Rivers. The term 'Saskatchewan' comes from a Cree word meaning 'fast water'. Originally applied to swiftly moving portions of the river, it was spelt in many ways. Our *fifth man* David Thompson preferred: *Kisiskatchewan.*

The fork of the two Saskatchewans, about mid-point in the Province of Saskatchewan, is believed to be the westernmost position in Canada explored by sons of Pierre La Vérendrye. Below the union the Saskatchewan becomes serpentine, coiling back on itself into ox-bow loops, yet increasing speed as if to make up time over these detours. Then, in a sudden change of mood, it runs straight on towards Nipawin.

When France was in control of Canada, Canadian traders following La Vérendrye were active on this section of river. Chevalier de la Corne, noted soldier in the colonial forces of New France, established a trading post called St. Louis along the lowest ox-bow. Later traders referred to it as Fort La Corne. Alexander Henry Jr. *observed* its location:

We camped where the French formerly had an establishment. Some years ago remains of agricultural implements and carriage wheels could be seen. Their road to the plains is still visible, winding up a valley on the south side.

It was a surprise to learn that draft vehicles had rotated their wheels 2,000 miles west of Montreal as early as the mid 18th century. Perhaps they were forerunners of 'made-on-site' Red River carts that squealed their way from Fort Garry across the broad prairie to Edmonton.

The river twists again a few miles above Nipawin, producing some mild rapids noted as *cadotte*. Perhaps they were named after J.B.

Cadotte who wintered here in 1775-76. He was a partner of Alexander Henry Sr., uncle to Alexander Henry Jr.

After the Cadottes came the Nipawin rapids. This is near an old French fort called 'Nepawee' by Henry Jr. In his edition of "Henry and Thompson", Elliott Coues mentions the name and provides spelling variations; Nipawi, Nepoway, etc. He suggests one meaning of the word is 'wet place', which certainly suited the marshy area along this section of river. This location also demarcates the encroachment of the great forest land that stretches from Edmonton to Hudson Bay. Here it engulfs the south side of the Saskatchewan River.

Nipawin has been given a more romantic connotation. To the Cree it meant 'a lying down place'; and applied to the high bluff on the south side of the Saskatchewan, it came to mean 'where the people wait':

Each spring, 600 miles upriver from here in the vicinity of present-day Edmonton, men of the Cree tribe would depart by canoe to take the winter's accumulation of furs down to Hudson Bay. The families left behind, women, children and old folk, under the care of a few hunters, would leisurely make their way down the north side of the river, picking and preserving all manner of summer berries en route.

Opposite Nipawin, with a commanding view downstream, the Cree would camp to await the arrival of their men. For the young particularly, the anticipation of reunion would be like waiting for Santa Clause. When the men arrived they would bring all sorts of European goodies; King George tobacco for the old men, awls and needles for the wives, beads and pretty ribbons for the young girls. It was an exciting time for young and old.

At sundown our canoe landed under the bridge spanning two high bluffs outside the town of Nipawin. Bill Gifford was there, waiting with Henri Andre and John Vail, interested businessmen from Nipawin who had come to render assistance.

Henri was a man of the fur trade, having been a furrier for twenty years. He put Eastward Ho in touch with Joe Brown, supervisor of the Squaw Rapids dam, who warned them of a possible ice problem on the lake created by the dam. After listening to the litany of delays we had already experienced, Mr. Brown took pity on us and arranged an inspection flight for Jim and Dave.

At dawn Friday morning they were airborne in a three-seater Cessna, and within minutes were witnessing what they didn't want to see. "Not again!," Dave yelled. A white sheet stretched completely across Tobin Lake.

It appeared from the air that a spit of land on the south west corner of the man-made lake could be reached by canoe. It was marked Anklevitch Point on the map. A long, tedious walking detour lay in store after that.

We left our new friends in Nipawin, and by noon began to see the unmistakable signs of a drowned landscape where the receding waters of a draw-down had left its indelible mark. The path of despair entering the lake was ugly and depressing. Lowering of the water level turns a once green and lovely landscape into an embattled war zone. Dead and dying trees lift broken limbs above the surface of the water, appealing soundlessly to mother nature for salvation.

No insect-chasing birds flit from tree to tree. Gone are the resting, nesting places for vireos and warblers. All is silence; a moonscape. A quick glance at a few remaining traces of greenery might lead one to think some trees were adjusting to an everglades environment, but a close examination showed otherwise. It was but a last gasp for life. The dismal reality was the slow, inexorable drowning of a forest.

Submerged trees create a navigational hazard near the shoreline. Unless a broad swath has been cut around the perimeter of a newly created reservoir, any border of a man-made lake will be impenetrable from the mass of brittle, interlaced branches. Boat access to a new marine environment is jeopardized.

British Columbia has many such eyesores as a result of years of neglect in instituting proper land-clearing policies for its hydro-electric dams. Alberta, fortunately, has not. The government of that province long ago decreed that standing timber in all reservoirs must be completely cleared to the uppermost level of flooding.

Anklevitch Point was formerly high-ground farm property which managed to keep its head above water. Landing on its grassy shore our crew started hiking toward Squaw Rapids dam. Scudding clouds dropped enough rain to soften up the good old prairie gumbo, adding pounds of gooey mud to each step. My misreading of the map put us on the wrong road, adding a few extra miles. The unnecessary distance was a real drag, as my plodding companions were quick to mention. It took a day and a half to cover the unexpected thirty-six mile walk.

At the dam, the shore below the spillway was lined with fishermen casting out their lines and pulling in pike by the dozen.

Thanks to Joe Brown, Saskatchewan Hydro turned the crew loose in their executive suite, complete with kitchen and running hot water. Had we been of the 'protest' generation we might have refused accommodation and tented beside a drowned tree.

That evening Superintendent Brown showed us through the generating plant with its humming dynamos. He was asked about water levels in the Saskatchewan River below the dam.

"The gauges indicate a below normal flow." he stated. "I intended to let more water out this week-end so we might as well do it now. We'll release 4,000 cu. feet immediately and another 4,000 tomorrow to bring the total to 34,000 cu. feet per minute. That should keep you off the bottom. Come over here Don and pull this switch, by tomorrow you'll be riding high."

Don reached up and drew down the lever, saying, "I feel like King Canute in reverse".

The Saskatchewan leaves the hills at Squaw Rapids, slowing down to a meander. Eastward Ho soon had to make a choice of New or Old Channel. Fortunately we chose the latter. The map indicated it to be a slightly shorter and more convenient route to Cumberland Lake.

Beaver had been seen in several tiny rivulets off the main river, and now muskrat homes were in evidence along the banks of Old Channel. This low-lying country with hundreds of miles of streams and ponds coursing through a soft clay-like mud, is ideal for burrowing animals, and a perfect setting for muskrat which are very prolific here.

Muskrat are cousins to beaver. Cree residents make a good living trapping the soft-skinned rodent, as did their forefathers of past generations. A larger member of the 'rat' family, it derives its name from a musk-like odor exuded from a plump, foot-long body. This local, reddish-brown species, has an eight inch hairless tail. Like beaver, muskrat are at home in water, propelling their way with webbed hind feet. Their houses may consist of a cavern dug in the bank of a stream or, alternatively, a dome-shaped sod and twig structure held together with mud. Entrances are underwater. They often take over beaver dens if the original owners have departed.

Muskrats are a source of food as well, and sold in the market as 'marsh rabbit'. Hunters trap them in late fall when pelts reach prime condition. The fur is often dyed to imitate sable, seal, or mink. Its natural colours are brown, red-brown and silver-grey. 'Rat' pelts when made up into coats or jackets have longer wearing qualities than many luxury furs. In the seventies, from over twenty species of wildlife pelts, including coastal sealskins, muskrat and beaver pelts accounted for over 50% of Canada's total fur crop.

The next objective was Cumberland House, a few hundred yards removed from the south shore of Cumberland Lake. The modern trading post sits on a pancake-like island formed by the Bigstone River on its west side and Tearing River on its east side. Both rivers, each about two miles in length, drain Cumberland Lake, running south past the island into Old Channel. After Cumberland Lake, Old Channel swells into a full Saskatchewan River.

Motor car access to Cumberland House is by ferry over the Saskatchewan to a paved road in the village. The road follows a well-beaten trail known as the *pemmican portage*. Here, tons of preserved buffalo meat, rations for the *voyageurs*, would be off-loaded from canoes or York boats and carried overland along the trail to NWC and HBC provisioning posts.

Intending to enter Cumberland Lake by turning up Bigstone Cutoff River, it was found – Surprise! Surprise! – that the river was clogged with ice. Eastward Ho pitched their tent beside the river and proceeded to wait for the land party. Had we chosen New channel, we would have ended up on the far side of frozen Cumberland Lake, with no access to Cumberland House.

Cumberland House is the oldest, permanently established community in western Canada. A pleasant place in the sunshine, it had an up-to-date HBC store and churches, curling rink, school, hospital, pub, and pool hall. Many inhabitants are Cree and Métis. One delightful old gal we met was Sally. Over a 100, she had been a teenager during the Riel Rebellion of 1885.

Cumberland House today does not loom large in the important scheme of things, but in its time, 1775 – 1821, it was the centre for North America's canoe highways. As Elliott Coues, editor of Alexander Henry Jr.'s journal wrote:

– we are here in the focus of a vast network of waters whose strands radiate in every direction. A canoe could start from this house and, with no portage more than a day's length, be launched on the Arctic Ocean, Hudson's Bay, Gulf of St. Lawrence or Gulf of Mexico; and without much greater interruption, could be floated on to the Pacific.

Henry Kelsey of the HBC was probably the first white person to visit this marshy land. In 1690, from York Factory on Hudson Bay, he accompanied a party of Crees returning to the prairies and wintered with them in this area. Half a century later La Vérendrye's sons came by here, after establishing a post further downstream at The Pas. In the early 1770's the Frobishers camped and traded on Cumberland Lake. A year later, Samuel Hearne, the famous HBC Arctic explorer, established his Cumberland House near its present site. Hearne chose this location because it was already the crossroads of trading Indians and because the lake provided an excellent food source of whitefish, sturgeon and pike. In season, ducks and geese abounded.

Just prior to Hearne establishing Cumberland House, the Frobisher brothers had intercepted Chipewyans bound for Hudson Bay from Lake Athabasca, thus discovering Cumberland Lake to be a vital link in the Athabasca trade. A centuries-old native canoe route led from Cumberland Lake's north east corner into Namew Lake, then across Amisk Lake into swiftly flowing Sturgeon-Weir River, which in turn connected to the Churchill River. In Cree language, *namew* means sturgeon, *amisk* equals beaver.

The Churchill River provided the main avenue to beaver-rich Lake Athabasca. It also served as an artery into the north and the north-west via the Mackenzie and Peace Rivers. It was the main east-west corridor for canoe traffic until Thompson began using the Saskatchewan for his frequent forays to the Rocky Mountains. A few years later, after comparing travel time on the two rivers, Gov. George Simpson concluded that Thompson was right. From then on the Saskatchewan was deemed a superior artery for water-borne traffic.

Athabasca-bound *voyageurs* referred to Sturgeon-Weir River as Rivière Maligne. Its four feet per mile drop was an almost continuous rapid. Working a canoe up this lively stream involved a dozen portages, entailing much unloading, dragging, and poling. It was a different story going in the reverse direction. A downstream run could be sheer delight with skilled paddlers in control.

The clear water of Sturgeon-Weir heads in a small, still pond from which a 300-yard portage trail leads into the Churchill River system. This portage was first named by Frobisher and Henry Sr. as *Portage de Traite*. They had stopped a band of Chipewyans on their way from Lake Athabasca to Fort Churchill. The natives traded away all their furs to the men from Montreal, hence the name *Trade Portage*.

Early Monday morning Eastward Ho broke camp on the bank of Saskatchewan River which was running clear again, but unfortunately they didn't leave early enough. Just as they were ready to push off into the slow moving current, masses of ice from the previously frozen Bigstone River began to pour into the channel. Within minutes the route was strewn from bank to bank with jostling ice cubes of gigantic size. The sudden outpouring of ice also broke the cross-river ferry cable, leaving Edo, Lorna, Bill, and their vehicles, stranded on the Cumberland House side of the river. There was nothing the canoe crew could do but twiddle their thumbs until the slabs of ice thinned out.

Later we tried again and discovered that by travelling at the same speed as the river, some progress could be made. All four kept busy with paddles, pushing the canoe away from the sharp, jagged slabs that could crush the canvas-covered craft. It wasn't long before a bright sun and hustling river dispersed the ice, enabling the resumption of motorized speed to The Pas.

The earliest description of The Pas is from Anthony Henday of the HBC. After visiting the Blackfeet Nation and sighting the snow-capped Rocky Mountains, he stopped here in May, 1755, when returning to Hudson's Bay with his Cree friends. The Frenchman in charge of the post at The Pas when Henday came calling is believed to have been Sieur de La Corne. *Observer* Henday:

We paddled 60 miles, coming to a French House passed last Autumn, with a Master and 9 men. Upon arrival they gave our Natives 10 Gallons of adulterated Brandy and they are now drunk. The master invited me in to sup with him. He was very hospitable and dressed very genteelly, but the men wear thin drawers and stripped cotton shirts ruffled at the hands and breast. This house has long been a place of Trade belonging to the French and named Basquea.

Carrot River entered on the right just above The Pas. Like the Saskatchewan, it too provided an entry into the prairie for nomadic Crees. Two miles further on by the mouth of Pasquia River, which drains the Pasquia Hills, they spotted the bridge that crosses the Saskatchewan River at The Pas. Thanks to the good offices of the mayor we were able to set up camp in a civic park which ran down to the river.

A couple of after-dark visitors were troublesome. The bridge deck spanning the river afforded protection from the weather and served as a hangout for young toughs not 'oriented toward purposeful pursuits'. They proved harmless, but their attitude was reminiscent of the reception given to *observer* Alexander Henry Sr. when he was visiting in 1775. He wrote in his journal:

On arrival, the chief named Chatique, meaning The Pelican, came to the beach in front of thirty followers, all armed with bows and arrowspears. Chatique was over six feet and with a large, powerful frame. He invited us to his tent and was particularly anxious to bestow his hospitalities on those who were the owners of goods. We suspected an evil design, but judged it best to play along with treachery rather than display fear. Entering the lodge, armed men surrounded us.

    Chatique welcomed our arrival, adding that everyone of the village had long been in want of many things of which we were possessed in abundance; that we must be well aware of his power to prevent us from going further, as if we passed now, he could put us all to death on our return. Under these circumstances, he expected us to be exceedingly liberal in our presents. To avoid misunderstanding he would inform us what he must have. He went on to say he was well acquainted with white men and knew they promised more than they gave; that with his number of men he could take the whole of our property without consent, therefore his demands ought to be regarded as very reasonable. He desired us to signify our assent to his proposition before we quitted our places.

    After a short consultation we promised to comply. ... We bestowed the presents, or rather yielded them up, and hastened away from the plunderers.

Eastward Ho's land party arrived, and all seven assembled on the green grass of the park, making a colourful caravan along the south bank of the Saskatchewan River. The camper, with the spare red canoe perched on top and appendage-like trailer behind; Bill's green station wagon; the twenty foot red canoe; all encircled the crew's white, Egyptian-cotton tent. The ensemble looked like a small military unit out on field maneuvers.

The pause at The Pas was too long for our liking. We were not mentally prepared for the long delay. The last week of May was a complete write-off, and the low point of the trip. Everyone came down with colds.

Advantage will be taken of this delay to speak about the Beaver, the furry little animal with the flat tail that enticed traders and explorers out into Canada's wilderness.

In this new-found age of 'conservation' one might make a case for inserting the homely, brown Castor Canadensis on our national flag, in place of the red Maple Leaf which sunlight pales so quickly. For over two centuries, Canadians pursued the luckless beaver with relentless fury. The energy generated by this pursuit was the main driving force of the economy. It was well, perhaps, that we were not aware of environmental issues in the 17th and 18th centuries. For without the two hundred year long chase for *beaver*, the first Trans-Continental highway would not have been a 'Canadian affair', nor would Canada have become a nation 'from sea to shining sea'.

A species of rodent that sports a fine set of buck-teeth, the North American beaver averages two feet in body length and has a twelve inch, flat, scaly tail. Beaver in the St. Lawrence, the Mississippi, the Missouri and Saskatchewan River valleys ran about forty to fifty pounds. The Athabasca country produced whoppers of seventy pounds.

Everyone knows that beaver are eager to fall trees. What is not so well known perhaps is that, in spite of all their practice, they will occasionally drop a tree on themselves. Its comforting to realize even beaver aren't perfect.

Trees and their limbs are a food source as well as a basic ingredient in house and dam construction. For beaver, gnawing on tree trunks is necessary for yet another reason. Their opposing pair of front teeth in upper and lower jaw never cease growing. When the animal becomes old and too feeble to embark on a hard day's gouging, their ever-growing chisel-like incisors eventually make it impossible for the poor beast to chew its food, whereupon it dies of starvation.

Our rodent's fur is made up of two kinds of hair. A long course guard hair protects a soft downy inner hair. The inner one is finely barbed and was discovered long ago by European manufacturers to provide an excellent material for felt making. Furriers preferred pelts that had been worn as garments. Motion and perspiration removed the guard hairs, leaving the choice inner lining intact. Thus it was that the primary producers of the product were, quite literally, asked to trade beaver robes off their backs. Used clothing received a bonus. No wonder native people used to laugh at the white man.

When 18th century fashion decreed the beaver hat to be a mark of distinction and so treasured that it was passed on from father to son, the hatters of France and England and the trappers and traders in Canada enjoyed a new high. The industrious, intelligent, prolific little animal, the only one other than man that landscapes and performs major construction work, became a carrot to draw men across a continent. Fashion sent men to drown a sailor's death and to perish in scurvy-ridden Canadian winters. Fashion sowed new seeds of discord amongst First Nations people.

Beaver pelts varied in quality, yet they managed to become the standard for all goods and services along the far flung wilderness frontier. Its inherent value was such that the HBC issued brass coins entitled *made beaver* which became currency in the fur trade.

David Thompson, an early environmentalist, wrote: *A worn out field may be manured and again made fertile; but the Beaver, once destroyed, cannot be replaced. They were the gold coin of the country, with which the necessities of life were purchased.*

Eastward Ho is poised on the western edge of three great prairie reservoirs; Lakes Winnipegosis, Manitoba and Winnipeg. The next stage will be through the heart of La Vérendrye Country, the lands between The Pas and Lake Superior. Prepare to welcome aboard our third *fifth man*, Pierre La Vérendrye senior. We should have need of a larger canoe because there were five exploring La Vérendryes. Pierre senior had four sons and a nephew, all of whom served with him in the *pays d'en haut*.

He 'suffered the slings and arrows of outrageous fortune'.
Credits to W. Shakespeare: La Vérendrye, 1685-1749

Chapter Thirteen
fifth man **Pierre La Vérendrye**

C anadian explorer, Pierre Gaultier de Boumois, Sieur de Varennes de La Vérendrye, was born in Trois Rivière, Canada. In spite of twenty years dedicated to searching for a canoe passage across the continent, La Vérendrye's lifetime rewards were neither financially gratifying nor socially prestigious. He and his four adventuring sons left this world as poor and publicly unrecognized as on the day of their births. It took the belated eye of history to rescue the La Vérendryes from obscurity, and grant posthumously, the attention they deserved.

Pierre the future explorer, like his father and two of his older brothers, chose a military career, signing on as a cadet in the colonial army at the tender age of eleven. Embroiled in several North American engagements, he saw action in the French-Indian raids on Deerfield, Mass., and in landings on Newfoundland. He received his ensigncy at twenty-one.

An older brother, Louis Gaultier, had returned to France to become an officer in the Regiment de Bretagne. When news reached Quebec of brother Louis' death, Pierre decided to hie himself over to

France, apply for a commission in Louis' regiment and adopt his brother's titular name of La Vérendrye. He was successful in both counts, but he returned to Canada a severely wounded veteran of the murderous Battle of Malplaquet.

Waiting for Pierre La Vérendrye with outstretched arms was his faithful fiancée and childhood sweetheart, Marie-Anne Dandonneau. Married shortly after his return, La Vérendrye took up farming on land obtained as part of his wife's dowry.

After fifteen back-breaking years, Pierre was eking out a bare existence augmented by a stipend from reserve army pay, while he and Marie-Anne were raising a family of four boys and two girls. In winter, Pierre also operated a small fur trade post on the St. Maurice River on property left to him by his father.

La Vérendrye's possessions were neither large nor productive enough to sustain him in the role of Grand Seigneur. He was often in debt, borrowing to cover sudden emergencies and selling bits of property to release his indenture. One gets the impression it was Madame who kept the financial house in order, having inherited her father's common sense in money matters.

Fed up with farming, La Vérendrye, through his brother Jacques René, accepted an army posting as military manager of two trading posts on the Nipigon and Kaministiqua Rivers of Lake Superior. Like many Frenchmen before him, La Vérendrye became obsessed with the idea of developing a canoe route across the continent; a North-west passage to the riches of the Orient.

La Vérendrye had an easy way with people and he began interviewing the Chippewa who hunted to the north and west of Lake Superior. He spoke to wandering Cree, who traded with the Assiniboine and Blackfeet of the Great Plains and the English down on the muddy margins of Hudson Bay. He put together a memorandum and a map based on information supplied by a Cree named Auchagah. On his return to Quebec he presented his plan of western exploration to Governor Beauharnois. The Governor was enthusiastic with La Vérendrye's scheme and forwarded it to the Court at Versailles with a recommendation for acceptance. He no doubt pointed out the advantages of finding the 'River of the West' that flowed into the sought for 'Western Sea'.

The burgeoning bureaucracy of Louis XV's Court, with more pressing calls on its state-run enterprises, turned the scheme down. The flint-hearted Minister of Marine, Comte de Maurepas, took a personal dislike to La Vérendrye and repeatedly squelched any thoughts of monetary assistance from France.

Governor Beauharnois remained supportive, however, and granted La Vérendrye a license to control the fur resources contained by the Lake-of-the-Woods watershed and all lands westward from there. This enabled La Vérendrye to enter into a series of partnerships with Montreal merchants to finance the procurement of men, equipment and trade goods, as well as a small military contingent.

He and Beauharnois realized that a pay-as-you-go scheme would retard westward penetration, but circumstance left no practical alternative. The central problem of travelling over immense distances, through territory containing many nations of differing tongues and competing cultures, guaranteed a high-cost, time-consuming operation. The highly mobile native population was in a continual hub-bub of wars and temporary alliances which only large-scale, self-sufficient military expeditions could solve quickly, a solution which Louis' Court would not countenance.

It is difficult today to fully understand all the problems that confronted western penetration, and why men such as Maurepas, far removed from the scene of the action, would become so scathing of La Vérendrye's slow progress. There were of course the inevitable petty jealousies aroused by any hint of favouritism on the part of government largesse such as the issuance of monopolistic favours to La Vérendrye. Whispers of evil intent would soon be relayed by mischief makers to the large ears of department heads across the ocean in France.

In spite of his tenuous beginning, La Vérendrye entered into the new venture with hope and enthusiasm. Early one morning in June, 1731, excitement hovered over the docks at Lachine as La Vérendrye's canoe brigade made ready to leave for the *pays d'en haut*. Leadership was a family affair. La Vérendrye's number one I.C. was his nephew, Christophe La Jemeraye, an experienced frontiersman at age twenty-three. In the canoes, waiting to shove off, were the three older La Vérendrye boys, Jean-Baptiste eighteen, Pierre Jr. seventeen and François sixteen. The youngest, Louis-Joseph, fourteen, could only bite his lip in envy and await the day he too could join his older brothers in adventure-land.

The La Vérendrye expedition had personnel problems from day one. Because of their late start in organizing an expedition they had to take second-best choices from the available pool of non-indentured *voyageurs*. The best ones had been signed up at the end of the previous season at the completion of summer contracts. When conditions at Grand Portage on the western shore of Lake Superior became difficult, La Vérendrye's canoemen mutinied. The result was the loss of an entire winter season of fur collection for the expedition. From that time on Vérendrye was beset with the difficulty of playing catch-up with his financial affairs.

There isn't space to go into detail of all the adversities and hardships which ambushed the La Vérendrye Expedition. Suffice to say the leader toiled for thirteen heart-breaking years to lay out a string of trading posts and fortifications from Ft. Pierre on Rainy Lake to Ft. Bourbon on the Saskatchewan River.

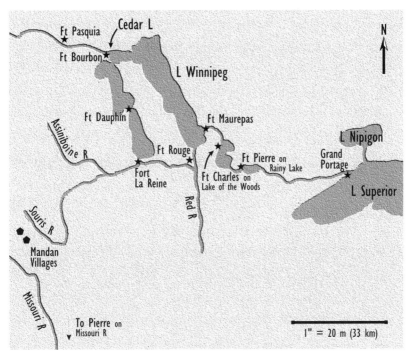

Nine trading posts established by the La Vérendrye Family

La Vérendrye also led a platoon of soldiers and Assiniboine warriors across the Souris River to villages of the Mandans. A sedentary people, the Mandans lived in semi-permanent earth lodges close by the Missouri River in western North Dakota.

We know that two of La Vérendrye's sons ranged southwest to the Black Hills and into the vicinity of present day Pierre, S. Dakota.

François La Vérendrye recorded depositing a lead tablet in March 1743 on a knoll of the Missouri Valley. Engraved on the plaque were the arms of Louis XV and the names of Gov. Beauharnois and Pierre La Vérendrye. One hundred and seventy years later a group of school children from the town of Pierre stumbled across it while playing in a farmer's field.

La Vérendrye had to cross half the breadth of Canada eight times in order to supervise the buildup of his western domain. The final canoe voyage was in the summer of 1744 when he returned to civilization. Worn out in body and soul he asked a reluctant Beauharnois to relieve him of his command. His sister's son had died from exhaustion, his eldest boy had been murdered by the Sioux, and at home, his tired wife had given up the ghost. Not a happy ending to fifteen years of effort and personal sacrifice. On top of it all he had to contend with a lawsuit and other monetary demands made against his person by dissatisfied financial partners.

Five years following La Vérendrye's departure from the scene, all the outposts so painfully established by him were abandoned by his successor. La Vérendrye was asked to come back and restore the organization. In 1749 he was in Montreal with two of his sons preparing an expedition to leave as soon as the ice had gone from the Lake of Two Mountains.

Number three son François, had explored the Saskatchewan River up to its forks and reported then:

It is the best way to reach the western sea. With the trading posts we have set up, one can canoe there from Montreal in a season, then obtain Cree guides who can lead an expedition across the prairies to the Rocky Mountains. Such is not the case by Missouri River.

Once more fate intervened between La Vérendrye and his aspirations. The grim reaper struck him down on Dec. 7, 1749. The man who had carved out a large wilderness area for New France was buried in Ste. Anne's chapel, in the church of Notre Dame, Montreal.

In 1794, all Montreal was agog at exciting news emanating from the west. A young Scot by the name of Mackenzie had become the first person to cross all of Canada in order to reach the Pacific Ocean. François, the longest surviving member of the Vérendrye family, may have read this news and thought: *That blessed Western Sea. A little bit of good luck, and we La Vérendryes might have turned over that page of history. Success was within our grasp.*

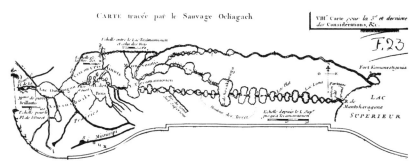

Map purportedly drawn by Auchagah to illustrate the canoe route from Lake Superior to the "River of the West".

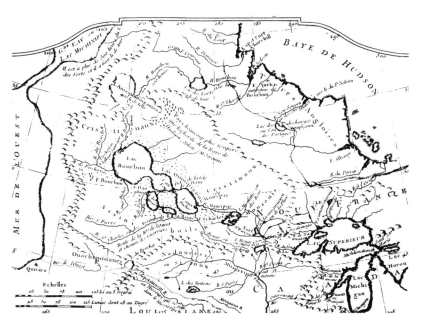

Map compiled by the exploring La Vérendryes to show, in part, the land through which they travelled. The juxtaposition of the "Sea of the West" is highly imaginative.

Du fort de la Reine,
il y a un portage de trois lieues au
Nord-Est pour tomber au lac des Prairies.
La Vérendrye

Chapter Fourteen
Lacs des Prairies

C rossing the provincial boundary of Manitoba put Eastward Ho into the next time zone, and an hour closer to their prime concern, the condition of Lake Winnipeg. The first large lake to be tackled by the expedition lay 150 canoe miles east of The Pas.

Lake Winnipeg had brought disaster to many a canoe brigade of yore. Although Canada's seventh largest lake, it is relatively shallow with depths averaging a mere sixty-feet. The distance from Norway House at the north end of the lake, to the marshy mouth of the Red River at the lake's southern extremity is 260 miles. Its maximum width of sixty-miles is at Grand Rapids, where the Saskatchewan River tumbles down into Lake Winnipeg. The *voyageurs* track across Lake Winnipeg, from Grand Rapids to the mouth of the Winnipeg River, was 200 miles.

The north wind on Lake Winnipeg can be violent, particularly at the change of seasons. On such occasions, it has been known to raise lake levels in the southern basin by as much as three feet. A sudden cessation of the north wind causes an immense body of water to rush northward. It then oscillates back and forth until its kinetic energy has been expended. A similar effect could be obtained by rocking a gigantic bathtub end to end. The observable motion was at first thought to be tidal. In fact David Thompson referred to the northern part of Lake Winnipeg as *Sea Lake*.

Auchagah, a far-ranging Cree, described it thus to La Vérendrye when the latter was in charge of the Kaministiqua trading post on the western edge of Lake Superior. This perhaps misunderstood information led La Vérendrye to hope that he was hearing about the 'Western Sea', which to the 18th century explorer meant the Pacific Ocean.

La Vérendrye may have been out two thousand miles in his search for the true Pacific Ocean, but he eventually got headed in the right direction. In his day no one knew how far west West really was. Chronometers for measuring longitudes at sea had not yet come into general use. The vastness of Canada was simply incomprehensible to Europeans.

La Vérendrye's first explorations across the prairie were south-west toward the Missouri River, but he ended up against an impenetrable wall of warring tribal factions that only a large military force could overcome. Then François La Vérendrye found his way to The Pas on the Saskatchewan River. *Le pas* in French means *the step*, and the La Vérendryes realized they were on the threshold of an approach to the Pacific.

From The Pas, Eastward Ho kept in daily touch with the airport at nearby Glace Lake. News from the pilots who regularly flew over Lake Winnipeg was not encouraging. The main ice sheet, although broken, was packed solidly into the northern half of the lake. It would need a strong north wind to shift the 5,000 square miles of ice enough to get it moving and breaking up.

The days slipped slowly by with nothing forwarding the expedition. "What can we do?", was the question asked a dozen times a day. The Pas, 2,000-miles from New Westminster was halfway, but almost three fifths of our allotted time was gone. We had to examine alternatives. Instead of ice-bound Lake Winnipeg, why not use La Vérendrye's first track to the Saskatchewan River, Lakes Manitoba and Winnipegosis?

In 1739 an Assiniboine party had guided François La Vérendrye northward from Fort La Reine, their post on the Assiniboine River near present day Portage La Prairie. François travelled over Lakes

Manitoba and Winnipegosis, collectively referred to as Lacs des Prairies, then over a two-mile portage into Lake Bourbon. This lake, which is now called Cedar Lake, is a final reservoir of the Saskatchewan River before its steep plunge down three-mile 'Grand Rapids' into Lake Winnipeg.

According to François' own account, he turned westward up the serpentine river to *la fourche de la rivière Poskoyac*, the forks of the Saskatchewan river.

A memorandum for La Vérendrye's map of the Saskatchewan states: *The Forks was a meeting place of the Cree of the Mountains, Prairies and Rivers for deliberation as to what they should do that year with the French or the English.*

The year after his younger brother's initiation of the Lac des Prairies route, the oldest surviving son, Pierre La Vérendrye Jr., with the guidance of Cree natives, opened up the more direct traverse across Lake Winnipeg. With the vagaries of weather, Lake Winnipeg entailed greater risk, but it was so much faster that it soon became the established route for canoe traffic.

Eastward Ho discussed the possibility of canoeing down the Saskatchewan to Cedar Lake, and portaging from there into Lake Winnipegosis. About that time they made contact with Bill and Irene MacLean, a friendly, hospitable couple living in The Pas. Bill had his own plane. After hearing their tale of woe, he arranged to take Dave up the following morning for a bird's-eye view.

On his return Dave reported: "Cedar Lake is solidly white and completely still. As far as the eye could see the whole northern portion of Lake Winnipeg is the same."

A Cedar Lake connection was out. Spirits plummeted.

Big conference that night. Discussion ranged from breaking the vow of 'shoe and canoe'; and driving, or even cycling south, until open water would allow entry of a canoe. For the first time we even spoke of quitting. There are more important things in this world than sitting around waiting for ice to melt. We had proved a point in canoeing by far the most difficult portion of The Forgotten Highway. The remainder was somewhat anticlimactic, having been done thousands of times before.

After many heated arguments we decided to carry on. What had begun as a small, personal venture had become, through all the publicity generated back home, a public commitment to the people of New Westminster. It would be humiliating to give up now and go back with tails between our legs. If the lower Saskatchewan River was closed, we would just have to start walking south from The Pas. Eventually, one must come to open water.

Although Dave had reported Cedar Lake frozen, only the northern quarter of Lake Winnipegosis contained ice flows. Our airborne observers said: "The ice sheet of Lake Winnipegosis appeared rather frazzled looking, suggesting some movement." A map showed Overflowing River entering the west side of the lake about sixty-miles south of The Pas. We decided to change course and follow François La Vérendrye.

The hike to Overflowing River took two days and a bit. The weather was sunny and clear the whole time, the nights warm, with few bugs flitting about. Summer's 'northern lights' were on display every night under the stars. As darkness crept in, a gleaming curtain would rise all around, like walls of a gigantic circus tent. A white iridescent glow, it was interspersed with streaks of soft reds, greens, and purples. Scientists say they are 'excited molecules of oxygen and nitrogen'. First Nations people who travelled with La Vérendrye thought of them as *ancestral spirits dancing*.

Eastward Ho started down the Overflowing River with a fully loaded canoe on May 31st. The run was enlivened by only one rapid, and within the hour the edge of Lake Winnipegosis was entered. And what did we find? Ice. Ice to the horizon filled Overflowing Bay. North and east, a solid sheet of white, to the south-east, a tantalizing glimpse of blue water shimmered in the distance. The hitch was the two miles of broken ice in between. There was no choice. We simply had to break through that ice.

We poked our nose into a mush resembling cream-of-wheat porridge. Three hours of tense helmsmanship, spent pushing and pulling with paddles to circumvent car-size ice cubes, brought the relief and freedom of open water. Cruising speed resumed.

Let it be stated for the record: The afternoon of May 31st, marked the end of Eastward Ho's month-long struggle with ice.

Out on Lake Winnipegosis the surrounding land was flat with few distinguishing landmarks on the horizon from which to take a bearing. By the use of map, compass, estimated speed, and a bit of luck, we reached Duck Bay in the evening.

As we eased into shore, a native lad came down to the beach, curious at the sight of a large red canoe with white lettering on its sides. The boy was all eyes and ears upon learning these men had come from the Pacific Ocean, and were on their way to Montreal in a craft like his father used for supervising his muskrat traps.

He left to return with Dad, who invited the crew to stay overnight in a vacant cabin. A pleasant evening was spent with the family. The father filled us in on the techniques of muskrat trapping.

Next day dawned bright and clear, but convection breezes rose as the sun warmed the air over the land. By mid morning the lake had became choppy, the wind whipping the canoe with spray to force a reduction in speed.

Lake Winnipegosis is 120-miles long, twenty-miles at its widest point and not over forty-feet in depth. From its eastern side, its waters discharge via the Waterhen River into Lake Manitoba. 'Winnipegosis' is derived from a Cree word, 'win-ipi', for 'murky waters', plus 'os-is', meaning 'little'. Like its sister Lac de Prairie, it was once embraced by an enlarged Lake Winnipeg.

The fifty or so miles to Meadow Portage took six hours. With the use of walkie-talkies we located Bill Gifford on the edge of a slough near the portage. The two mile link to Lake Manitoba was soon crossed. The eastern end of the portage was at the mouth of Waterhen River. Close by, a ferry landing had been built to supply farms established along the edge of the lake.

The location of La Vérendrye's Ft. Dauphin has long troubled historians. Some favour the northwest corner of Lake Manitoba at the mouth of Waterhen River. Comte de Bougainville stated in a memoir that: "Ft. Dauphin lay at the mouth of Troubled Water, 80 leagues, (approximately 160 miles), from Ft. La Reine."

Our *fifth man* M. La Vérendrye reported: *From La Reine* (Portage La Prairie) *there is a portage of three leagues to the north east to get into the Lake of the Prairies. You follow the south shore of the lake until you come to the mouth of a river coming from the great prairies, at the lower end of which is fort Dauphin, the fifth establishment, made at the request of the Cree of the Prairies and the Canoe Assiniboine. There is a 'trail' from there to Ft. Bourbon,* (old French post on Cedar Lake) *the sixth establishment, but the road is not good.*

In the English translation of Lawrence Burpee's "La Vérendrye", the word 'trail' is used, but the French version on the same page employed the word 'route'. 'Route' translates into 'way' and implies a 'waterway' or the commonly used expression of 'canoe road'. If this interpretation is valid, the 'route' would have been by water, probably with some portaging, from Ft. Dauphin on Lake Manitoba, through Waterhen River which is shallow and difficult, to Lake Winnipegosis. From the north end of the latter, canoe travellers would have a two-mile carry across one of two Mossy Portages to Fort Bourbon on Cedar Lake.

Early fur traders viewed the Saskatchewan River's entry into Lake Winnipeg differently than modern cartographers. To them the Saskatchewan River ended in Cedar Lake. Both natives and early whites referred to the wild run down Grand Rapids from Cedar Lake into Lake Winnipeg, as Rivière Blanche. Its white-water rapids caused it to be viewed as a separate river.

On the beach of Lake Manitoba's west side, Eastward Ho spent some time trying to tighten the canoe's keel which had worked itself loose. In the process Jim noticed four bolts were missing from the long-shafted attachment plate, the propeller and its linkages just dangling. "Its a miracle the whole apparatus didn't spin off into the bowels of Lake Winnipegosis," cried Jim. He robbed the spare 5 h.p. for parts, and managed a hurried repair so we could take advantage of the remaining daylight hours.

Lake Manitoba is the same length as Lake Winnipegosis. Its waters discharge from its northeast corner into Lake Winnipeg via the Dauphin River. 'Manitoba' comes from the Cree word *manitou*, meaning spirit or mysterious force. A beautiful word, it conjures up images of divinity.

The wind dropped with the sun, replaced by a gentle breeze bringing in a deliciously sweet smell of early summer. A myriad of flowers in bloom added their own rich aromas to the pungent odors of prairie grasses.

Morning brought an overcast sky and variable wind. The surface of the lake appeared lumpy, but no whitecaps crested the waves. We were away by six a.m., the wind blowing intermittently from the north-west onto our starboard quarter.

Once through Crane Narrows we turned south. The wind freshened and began to blow from the south-east. The lake's surface became quite confused, roiling from all directions at once. As we rounded the peninsula of 'Little Iceland' we were met by a gale-force wind that beat against our port side. It was becoming increasingly difficult to prevent waves from slopping over the gunwale. The helmsman wasn't liking the situation at all and we crept closer to the west side of the lake. Even under reduced speed, the canoe continued taking in water.

Finally the helmsman yelled out: "Look for a place on shore free of rocks; we're heading in before its too late!"

We were deluged by the angry waves hissing and boiling past the gunwale. Over the roar of sea and motor, Don's yell reached the stern. "There!", he shouted, pointing in the direction of a house and barn.

Helm was pushed to port. The canoe responded and swung 90 degrees to run before the wind. The beach was a quarter-mile away. We surfed madly down the crests of waves, their heights increasing as the lake shoaled toward land. Trying to prevent the craft from slewing around was strenuous work, as anyone who has surfed in a canoe can vouch for. You have to brace both feet, hang onto the steering arm with two hands, and pull with all your might to counteract the tremendous torque that wants to turn you broadside to the waves. It was an exciting run amidst roaring surf. Nose up, stern down, the canoe would be buried in foam one moment, then hurtling down the face of a wave the next. It was a strange sensation for the three men sitting in the bow floating two feet in the air.

Nearer shore, the combers began to run flat and slap in over the transom indicating there was little water under the hull. Afraid of hitting a sharp rock that could destroy the canoe, the helmsman closed the throttle and called out, "Everybody jump!"

We leapt overboard into knee-deep water and waded shoreward, stumbling through mud, pulling the water-laden craft onto the beach.

A line of dead and dying carp littered the water's edge in both directions. Although no explanation could be found for this scene of mass destruction, the seagulls and pelicans were having a ball feasting on the ugly, bloated carcasses. The carp, a course fish, had taken over the feeding areas of the once abundant white fish. Local people blamed unrestricted fishing.

At the gate of a picket fence, Mr. and Mrs. Bergson greeted our entry. "My gosh," Mr. Bergson said, "We thought you were goners. Saw you one minute, then you'd disappear. Had us worried for awhile. Sure glad I wasn't out there."

Mrs. Bergson was a real 'mom' type. She pushed us into the house, drips and all soiling her clean floor. "Get out of them wet clothes," she called, as she threw blankets at us.

She got busy rustling up a farmer's breakfast on the big wood-burning cookstove. "Scared the daylights out of us, you did. Thought you'd capsize right in front of our eyes. But we're used to the antics of young folk. Archie and I've raised eight kids here. They've all left the roost now but they come back often, with the next generation in tow."

After sampling Ma Bergson's cooking one could see why her offspring returned frequently. She had no running water, not even a hot-water tank, but it's a safe bet there were no delinquency problems in that family.

There wasn't another habitation to be seen on the flat farmland surrounding Bergson's, but they had a telephone. Through the ever helpful RCMP, Bill Gifford was contacted at Delta Beach, a resort area at the foot of Lake Manitoba. "Too windy to continue. Can you pick us up so we can do the hike from Portage La Prairie to the Assiniboine River?"

"Give me directions and I'm on my way," said Bill. "I've heard weather reports giving wind warnings of 65 k.p.h., and up."

Wind and ice were the two most common elements delaying canoe brigades. Perhaps it was just as well Eastward Ho hadn't tried crossing Lake Winnipeg. It had proved a graveyard for many *voyageurs*. With the trouble experienced on a relatively narrow lake such a Manitoba, what would the crossing of Lakes Superior and Huron be like, we wondered?

The station wagon arrived and the crew said goodbye to the Bergsons who assured us the canoe and equipment was safe with them. We slept in the car on the way to Delta Beach, and upon arrival were too groggy to appreciate the extensive bird sanctuary maintained there. Our trek south to the Assiniboine River began immediately. At 1:00 a.m., we were able to lay the canoe mail down beside one of its oxbow loops, where La Vérendrye had erected Fort La Reine in October of 1738.

It was from this point that La Vérendrye had marched south-west to the country of the Mandans on the upper Missouri River. His hope that they would provide a link between the Prairie People and the tribes of the Pacific slope proved futile.

The high winds of yesterday had dropped off. Not wishing to lose a minute of fair weather travel Bill drove us back to Bergson's farm. By four we were on the water. Dawn's grey light gave an eerie cast to the waves which still ran high out on the lake, but splashed harmlessly onto the port quarter.

Lake Manitoba is beamy at its southern extremity where it is twenty-five-miles across. We stayed within sight of the western shore in case a dash for land was necessary, and also kept our eyes skinned for ugly black rocks which showed occasionally. Often a swirl of water was the only indication that a dark menace lurked beneath the surface. We were continuously dodging fish nets, and islands of diving pelicans. The lake remained rough, hindering our speed.

It took six wearying hours to reach the strand in front of Delta Beach, but having already hiked to the Assiniboine River, it was now legitimate to drive across the portage.

Once underway toward Winnipeg, progress on the Assiniboine River was adequate, but like our *fifth man,* La Vérendrye, we found the meandering river tiresome. In 1738 he wrote:

This river comes from the west, winds a great deal, is wide, has a strong current and many shallows.

The 300-mile Assiniboine River originates in southern Saskatchewan, its twisting course doubling a straight line distance. It is named for the Assiniboine people who frequented the southern portion of Canada from Lake Manitoba to Lake of the Woods. The latter lake was for a time called Lac des Assiniboiles. The Assiniboines were related to the Sioux and spoke the same language. Just prior to the arrival of Europeans, however, the tribes had a falling out and they became implacable enemies.

As Eastward Ho approached Winnipeg at the forks of the Assiniboine and Red River, the city's Golden Boy could be seen atop the legislative building, gleaming in the rays of the sinking sun. Winnipeg was Jim's home town. Naturally he was called the 'Golden Boy' for a few days.

Arrangements had been made for the crew to sleep at the Winnipeg Canoe Club on the east bank of the Red River. Arriving at dusk, we stored our gear in a cavernous canoe shed. Dick Jones, president of the club was most helpful in locating an expert canoe builder to repair the damaged keel.

Underway again on June 5th, Eastward Ho passed old St. Boniface on the right, now amalgamated into the City of Winnipeg. There is a sensitive, symbolic memorial to La Vérendrye in St. Boniface which is well worth a stop.

The Red is aptly named, stained as it is by red clays of the surrounding countryside; an indication the soil is volcanic earth sloughed off by the once high mountains of the Canadian Shield.

Flood control gates below Winnipeg caused a slight delay. We passed Forts Garry and Selkirk, old settlements of the HBC.

Just before entering the labyrinth of channels that formed the delta, we slipped by the site of the original Ft. Maurepas, the first white settlement on the prairies. It was established in 1734 by Jean-Baptiste La Vérendrye.

To rush through Canada's history on a route that had taken 200 years to develop was a shame, but 4,000-miles was a long road for the limited time available. Eastward Ho had to concentrate on matters directly affecting progress.

Reed infested waters of the delta made excellent cover for thousands of nesting water birds. The reeds also made navigation difficult. Jean-Baptiste had problems finding his way through here in 1733, fortunately small river buoys now mark a channel through a maze of waterways. When ancient Lake Agassiz covered this land, the Red River drained south into the Missouri River.

Out on Lake Winnipeg, the winds of the previous few days had diminished, allowing Eastward Ho to speed past Victoria Beach, Winnipeg's favourite bathing area; then Elk Island, where we turned south-east into Traverse Bay and the broad estuary of the Winnipeg River. Again, time didn't allow investigation of old fur trade posts such as the second site chosen for Fort Maurepas, where *voyageurs* prepared for the dangerous traverse of Lake Winnipeg.

The Comte de Maurepas, Secretary of State for the Colonies under Louis XV, and living in the sophisticated environment of the Court at Versailles, probably recoiled in horror upon reading dispatches from New France which apprised him that a fur trader had named a rude fur trading post in his honour. No doubt the Count's peers would have jibed him unmercifully. Poor La Vérendrye, he just never got it right in addressing the haughty Maurepas who consistently displayed open hostility to every move La Vérendrye made.

In spite of death by starvation of a dedicated and much loved nephew, the sacrifice of an eldest son to internecine native warfare, and putting his old war-injured body at risk, La Vérendrye received nothing but abuse from the cynical Minister.

Count Maurepas received his come-uppance, however, when he tried to play a 'little nasty' on Madame Pompadour, the King's mistress. He met his match against that worldly woman about town. The Pompadour demanded, the King acquiesced, and Maurepas was tossed out of the Royal Court.

Opposite the site of old Fort Maurepas, on the south side of the river, the crossed spire of the Roman Catholic mission graced the sky-line. Next in line were the dazzling white buildings of Fort Alexander, bright red roofs, picture-like amidst trim picket fences and green fields. This is still an ongoing post of the HBC but much reduced in importance. In the heyday of canoe transport, Fort Alexander was one of the great provisioning-canoe manufacturing depots. The early Nor'westers first called it Le Sieur's post, then Bas de la Rivière. An Anglican mission flanks its upstream side.

The Winnipeg River has had a variety of names as well as sundry spelling variations. La Vérendrye, in a futile attempt to please the hypercritical Minister of Marine, first called it *Maurepas River,* then *Ouinipigon,* after the lake which it fed. Mackenzie referred to it as *Winipic.*

In a narrow neck of water opposite the town of Pine Falls, the *Manitou rapids* remind canoeists of the excitement once found here. A lively river used to dance down from Lake of the Woods in a series of gigantic steps, prompting *voyageurs* to call it *a noble stream.* Canoeing down it, nearly every bend contained the choice of a back breaking portage, or a dare to 'go for it'.

The Winnipeg River has had its share of victories over the years. It has claimed the lives of many challengers. The 140-mile river has a vertical fall of 330 feet, apparent by its dozen waterfalls and equal number of cascades. There were twenty-six to thirty-two carrying places, depending upon the height of water or the disposition of a particular canoe crew. If the *gouvernail* at the stern and the *avant* at the bow, each plying their elongated paddles, decided to risk one breathtaking rush in place of an hour-long sweaty portage, the *milieux* could be relied upon to paddle their hearts out for them.

Although the Winnipeg River has had its fangs removed, its remoteness and beauty still attract canoeists. Eight dams have taken the place of the falls and chutes, the portages and the décharges that once distinguished this formidable river. On the *voyageurs'* long road from Montreal, it ranked with the Ottawa in creating difficulties, triumphs, and griefs.

La Vérendrye, Fraser and Thompson went this way many times, but they did not leave particulars of the course of the Winnipeg River. The best eye witnesses for this portion are two men of renown in the fur trade, Alexander Mackenzie, who first saw this river in 1785, and Alexander Henry Jr. who travelled down it in the summer of 1800. Through the eyes of these two *observers* we can recreate the scene of what the river was like before the dam builders took over.

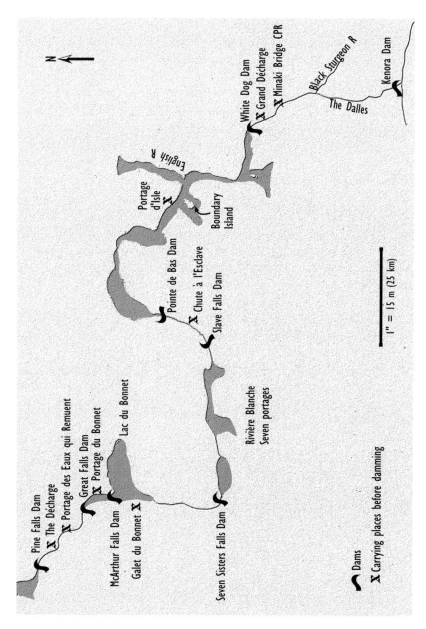

Winnipeg River

You will note that their descriptions are written with an east-to-west, or downstream direction. Going down is generally more dangerous and exciting than going upstream and thus makes better copy. Besides it was the way in which they first saw this 'noble stream'. We are also indebted to the late Eric Morse for his 1968 publication 'Fur Trade Canoe Routes of Canada'. It provided a comprehensive study of this and other well-used tracks of the *voyageurs*.

For west bound *voyageurs* terminating the exciting run down the Winnipeg River, Manitou Rapids forced a final portage. For Eastward Ho the only evidence was a slight acceleration of current. The high concrete walls of Pine Falls dam have obliterated three carrying places here; the *Décharge*, the *Portage des Eaux qui Remuent* and the *Portage des Chênes* (Oak Portage). In spite of flooding, some dancing waters remain as the Pine, Maskwa and Silver Falls rapids. The French names used by Mackenzie and Henry have a nice sound, particularly the *Eaux qui Remuent* which they described as 'waters that move up and down', or *boisterous waters.*

Great Falls dam provoked a second carry for us. It was once part of *Portage du Bonnet*, a long back-breaker for *voyageurs*, varying from one half to two miles, according to seasonal levels of the river.

The third obstruction, McArthur Falls dam, brought us to *Lac du Bonnet*. Prior to flooding from the dam, the gallic phrases of *Galet du Bonnet* and *Galet du lac Bonnet* were ascribed to this portion of the river by Mackenzie and Henry.

Dr. Kaye Lamb and Elliott Coues, respective editors of Mackenzie and Henry Jr. seem uncertain why their subjects use 'galet' instead of 'rocher', both words meaning 'stone' or 'rock'. One explanation could be that the *voyageurs* who bestowed their descriptive names, used 'roche' or 'rocher' to indicate massive stone objects ranging in size from large boulders to a high distant mountain. According to my French dictionary, 'galet', means a pebble in the singular use and a shingled beach in the plural form. Perhaps Mackenzie and Henry simply had 'gravel bars' in mind when writing 'galet'.

Observer Alexander Mackenzie mentions the *Portage du Bonnet: The Indians of this area had a custom of placing a circle of stones on the highest rock in the portage which they then 'crowned' with a wreathe of herbage and branches.* He then went on to say: *There have been examples of men taking seven packages of 90 pounds each, at one end of the portage and putting them down at the other without stopping.*

Is this an error in print or a monumental exaggeration? Seven times ninety equals 630 pounds. In one lift? Staggering!

The first three dams accounted for 125 feet of rise, over a third of the climb toward Lake of the Woods. Eric Morse tells us they eliminated seven portages. Above Lac du Bonnet the river current became apparent again. We headed south before swinging 90 degrees to the east. Around the corner was the Seven Sisters Falls dam. It marked the bottom end of a once eight mile stretch of continuously wild river, referred to as the *Rivière Blanche*. Mackenzie wrote: *... so called from its being ... a succession of falls and cataracts. Here are seven portages, in so short a space that the whole of them are discernible at the same moment.*

Blasting for the dam exposed a distinctive pink-hued granite which formed the base of the Pre-Cambrian Shield, the world's oldest known mountains. Natalie Lake, formed by the dam, now covers the notorious Seven Sisters.

The next upstream obstruction was Slave Falls dam. Number five in ascending order, its overflow cascaded down pink granite cliffs which glinted warmly in the afternoon sun. This carry was once *Chute à l'Esclave*, with a drop of thirty feet and a portage that consisted of 2,000 paces.

Pointe de Bois dam, which was next, was the first one built on the river. Further on a boundary marker advertised entry into the Province of Ontario. This is perfect recreation country, ideal for camping, swimming, canoeing and fishing.

Shortly after the provincial border a detour had been made for modern boaters around the west side of Boundary Island. The straight course still harbours the hazards of *Portage de L'Isle*. Both Mackenzie and Henry declared that this one fall had brought about more deaths and more lost merchandise than any other obstruction on the river. It was short, but deceptive, and the portage was troublesome. All but one of Henry's flotilla portaged there as our *observer* noted:

One of my canoes, to avoid the trouble of making this portage, passed down near the N. shore with a full load. I perceived the canoe coming off the side to Sault (i.e. to run the rapid). By some mismanagement of the avant, the current bore down her bow against a rock, upon which the fellow jumped. The canoe whirled around. Then the gouvernail jumped upon the rock, while one of the mid-men, not being sufficiently active, remained. The canoe was instantly carried out and lost to view amongst high waves. At length the canoe appeared, stood perpendicular for a moment, then sank down again. I perceived the man riding upon a bale of dry goods in the midst of the waves. We made every exertion to get near him. Alas, he sank under a heavy swell. The bale rose but the man appeared no more.

Eric Morse stated that the Minnesota Historical Society and the Royal Ontario Museum had scuba divers investigate this accident-prone area, bringing up the largest single haul of canoe-trade goods yet discovered.

A mile above the fateful *Portage de L'Isle*, English River enters the Winnipeg River. English River was another historic waterway. From it, native traders portaged across the height of land into Lake St. Joseph, headwaters of the Albany River which emptied into James Bay, the lower appendage of Hudson Bay. La Vérendrye complained that the Cree of the Winnipeg River often went that way to trade with the English on the Bay at Fort Albany, in operation since 1679.

An important connection led from Lac Seul through Sturgeon Lake into Lake Nipigon, and thence to Lake Superior. As Mackenzie said, ... *the country is so broken by lakes and rivers that people may find their way in canoes in any direction.*

We camped at White Dog dam. This site of Henry's *Grand Décharge* had a carry of 300 paces. Travelling downstream, *voyageurs* usually shot these rapids with partially laden canoes.

Satisfied with progress of the past few days, we recalculated our E.T.A. for Montreal. Judging by the time it had taken from The Pas, a mid-July arrival is conceivable if the winds on Lakes Superior and Huron cooperate.

It was ten miles to a railway crossing at Minaki Bridge. Another ten miles brought us to Black Sturgeon River. Here high granite walls ushered us through the Dalles. According to Morse, the digging of a side channel reduced river turbulence in this eight mile trough. At noon on the seventh of June we arrived at Kenora dam, the final upstream obstruction of the Winnipeg River.

Morse says there are three exits from Lake of the Woods, but Eastward Ho only located two, both flanking L-shaped Tunnel Island, and each containing a dam. By good luck Eastward Ho chose the one on the east side. The other, they learned later, belonged to a pulp mill and was choked with miles of peeler logs.

Voyageurs used to portage from Winnipeg River to the lake via Rat Portage, named for the large number of muskrats that habitually crossed there. KENORA is an amalgam of three older settlements, KEewatin, NOrman and RAt.

The river which falls into Lac des Bois
is very beautiful, bordered with groves of oak,
and the beaver are there in abundance.

La Vérendrye

Chapter Fifteen
Up the Rainy River

ake of the Woods is a high-water remnant of Lake Agassiz, that gigantic predecessor of all the Lacs des Prairies. The southern half of this multi-fingered lake is bordered by sandy beaches and loam covered headlands, quite different from its stony northern half which displays the granitic bedrock of the Canadian Shield. Its breadth is about sixty-miles; its longest axis of seventy-miles runs north-south. Those dimensions put it at 4,200 square miles, but only two thirds of that is water. The immense Aulneau Peninsula juts out from the lake's east side. The peninsula was named after Father Aulneau who, along with Jean-Baptiste La Vérendrye, was murdered by the Sioux on an island in Lake of the Woods.

The north and south-east portions of the lake are full of islands; 14,632 according to the Canadian Encyclopedia. It would be difficult to navigate through this labyrinth without a compass and a hydrographic chart, both of which we possessed. Under adverse weather conditions, with fog, snow or high waves distorting visibility, and with the lake subject to wild thunderstorms, many canoes foundered while crossing its wider reaches.

Several names have been recorded for this lake since Jacques de Noyon's discovery of it in 1688. He called it Lac des Assiniboiles. Coues tells us that other names were Lac des Sioux, Lac des Isles, and finally La Vérendrye's rendering, Lac des Bois. Most of the lake is in Ontario, but Manitoba and Minnesota also share it, with the latter having the largest section of open water.

The United States-Canada border follows the *voyageur's* track of the Rainy River. Where this river enters Lake of the Woods, the border turns sharply north toward the 49th parallel. Instead of stopping there, however, the *border* continues on an extra twenty-six miles. Twenty-three minutes north of the 49th parallel, it forms the Manitoba-Ontario border, then turns south back to the 49th parallel, in Lake of the Woods, and well offshore.

The reason for the peculiar looking jog lies deep within the tomes of treaty and survey commissions that marked a century-old border dispute between Britain and the United States. David Thompson was involved in the argument after his retirement from the fur trade. He spent three years with the joint British-U.S. Boundary Commission surveying from Lake Superior to what came to be called, the 'North West Angle' of Lake of the Woods. Ontario lost out on 600 square miles of territory, giving it up to the State of Minnesota.

Eastward Ho's course from Kenora squeezed through Devil's Gap, opened up for eight miles to run between Mather and Allie Islands, then swerved S.W. to French Portage Narrows. As the name implies, it was a canoe passage, and it went around the northwest end of Aulneau Peninsula. The Narrows is five miles long, terminating at French Portage. For Eastward Ho a portage was not necessary, but with a seasonal drop in water level *voyageurs* often had to carry here.

We tented on a grassy knoll of tiny Rubber Island. To the west lay Massacre Island, where the sleeping Jean-Baptiste La Vérendrye and his companions met their untimely end. For a description of this tragic affair read Lawrence Burpee's biography of Pierre La Vérendrye.

Further west lay the entrance to Angle Inlet and the site of old Fort St. Charles. This famous fortification, the anchor for La Vérendrye's penetration of the prairies, was burned down in 1769. It has since been located and restored.

Our *fifth man* La Vérendrye wrote:

There is a house for the missionary, a church, a house for the commandant, four main buildings with chimneys, a powder magazine and a storehouse. There are two gates on opposite sides, and a watch tower. The stakes (surrounding the enclosure to form a rectangle) are in a double row and are 15 feet out of the ground.

Fallen into disuse after the French period, Fort St. Charles was rediscovered by staff and student members of St. Boniface College, Manitoba. It had a strategic location chosen by a professional soldier with many years experience in guerrilla type warfare. He also heeded the advice of his allies, the Cree and Assiniboine people, in choosing the site. It stood at the mouth of a river in a small bay off the main lake. It had a good supply of drinking water and was protected from gale force winds that often raced across more exposed portions of the lake.

An important factor for canoe travellers was the abundance of wild rice in this area. As a source of fuel to feed the large combustion engine of a *voyageur*, it ranked in importance with corn from Detroit, dried peas from Montreal, or pemmican made in the prairies. In Cree territory, this post was also well placed for trading purposes with the Monsoni to the east and the Assiniboines to westward. Fort St. Charles was as far west as canoes from Montreal could travel, and still return in one season.

The next day was a wipeout for Eastward Ho. Awakened early by rain and wind under a heavy cloud cover, we launched the canoe into knee high combers, getting thoroughly soaked in the process. Jim took the helm, proceeding along under reduced speed.

Soon we were making no headway at all, merely courting disaster. In the lee of Bigsby Island we angled in behind a headland to close on the shingle beach of McCauley Bay. A high surf slewed us around, nearly broaching the canoe. A welcoming committee of zooming mosquitoes was on hand to greet us, proboscises at the ready. They too had sought shelter from the higher winds of the open lake.

The waves were pounding hard on the strand, so we dragged the canoe well out of the lake's reach, then headed for a deserted lighthouse and small detached building. The latter was completely bare. A single door swung crazily in the wind. In spite of oilskins we were wet through. Entering the cabin, we proceeded to warm up with calisthenics.

A little later, Don went outside, saying, "I'm going to fetch some food from the canoe."

In a few moments his muffled shouts brought us to our feet. We tore through the door and over the rise to the canoe to find Don, up to his waist in a pounding surf, struggling to keep his balance. He was trying to hang on to our canoe, now half full of water. Capping waves breaking high up the bank were producing a tremendous back-flow of water, sucking Don and the canoe out into the lake.

The rescuers jumped in to extricate their vessel from the lake's watery grip. Heavy rainfall and gale-force winds had combined to push an unusual amount of water into the unprotected bay, raising its level considerably. Had Don not appeared on the scene, all our possessions would have been swept out into Lake of the Woods.

By late afternoon, resigning ourselves to another lost day, we crawled into moist sleeping bags, hoping for a better tomorrow.

During the night Jim got up to commune with nature. On his return he woke the others with: "No wind, and no rain. I can see a streak of sky. Maybe we should move." After a brief confab, all agreed.

In open water, the sea ran high and in long folds, but there were no breaking waves to splash into the canoe. A pink sunrise glinted off the greasy backs of humping rollers spawned in the distant horizon. We made good time, and within the hour were behind the sand dunes of Sable Island. Wheeler Point was passed, then we entered the buoyed mouth of Rainy River.

The countryside along the Rainy River was open and pastoral. Cattle grazed along the river bank. Magpies flitted from one cow pad to another, black tails flicking as they hopped and pecked at the food supply of undigested seeds.

No problems were encountered on the 80-mile section of the Rainy River between Lake-of-the-Woods and the dam at Fort Frances. There are two minor swirls, remnants of the pre-dam rapids which David Thompson referred to as the Long Sault and the Manitou. When going downstream *voyageurs* always paddled through them, even with full loads .

The rise from Lake of the Woods to Rainy Lake is only 45 feet, with most of that occurring at Chaudière Falls, much reduced by dams of the pulp mills. Fort Frances was a bustling community of 9,000 whose raison d'être is pulp and paper and tourism. It has a feminine ending, named after Frances Simpson, wife of the HBC's Governor in Canada. Mayor John McVay and several others were most helpful in giving us contacts along the route ahead, and the Chamber of Commerce arranged a parade down mainstreet for us.

Bill Gifford met an old school chum from New Westminster here, George Walmsley. He owned the Rainy River Hotel and insisted on putting Eastward Ho up gratis. Along with its Minnesota twin, International Falls, Fort Frances serves as western gateway to one of the world's great recreational areas. A canoeing paradise stretches from here to Lake Superior.

Following La Vérendrye's tradition of establishing trading posts in the wilderness, the NWC built Lac la Pluie post in 1787 on the north side of Rainy River. Today it is encompassed by the western edge of Fort Frances. *Observer* Alexander Mackenzie said:

Here the people from Montreal come to meet those who arrive from the Athabaska Country. ... This is the residence of the first chief, or Sachem, of all the Algonquin tribes inhabiting this part of the country.

This was also where the NWC provided the special brigade to shuttle back and forth between Lake Superior and Rainy Lake. The *northerners* coming in from Lake Athabasca stopped here. They had a long way to travel in a short season that was often beset with delays from ice or wind, conditions to which Eastward Ho could relate.

For *voyageurs*, Chaudière Falls necessitated a 250 yard portage. Chaudière, or Kettle, received its descriptive French name from the quantities of mist, comparable to steam from a kettle, spraying upwards from the foot of a three tiered waterfall.

At all the stopping places on the route east from Lake Winnipeg, the French connection predated the English. De Noyon traded here in 1688. The La Vérendrye Expedition, specifically nephew La Jemeraye and eldest son Jean-Baptiste, built Ft. St. Pierre late in 1731. The location of this old fort is a mile and a quarter above the falls and on the north side of Rainy River. Nestling in a little bay under Pither's Point, it sat at the foot of rapids formed by water dropping out of the lake and rushing around the point.

It was necessary now for Eastward Ho to prepare for a different mode of travel. The 260 miles from Rainy Lake to Lake Superior would contain about half the portages made throughout the whole of our 4,000 mile journey. There would be 36 and they would entail 22 miles of walking. Since leaving the Pacific Ocean, Eastward Ho's course had been mainly on sizable rivers, suitable for a large canoe and motor.

Ahead, the terrain consisted of small lakes and ponds, connected by streams or intervening bits of land, the geography that forged the portable bark canoe. Quebec and Ontario contain thousands of square miles of just that kind of canoeing country. The ideal way to travel through it is in 17-foot, two-person canoes, using paddle-power instead of horsepower. For Eastward Ho, however, time was still the most precious commodity. A day gained by motoring had to take precedence over more pleasant prospects of paddling. We elected to stay with "Big Red" and its 20 h.p. voyageur.

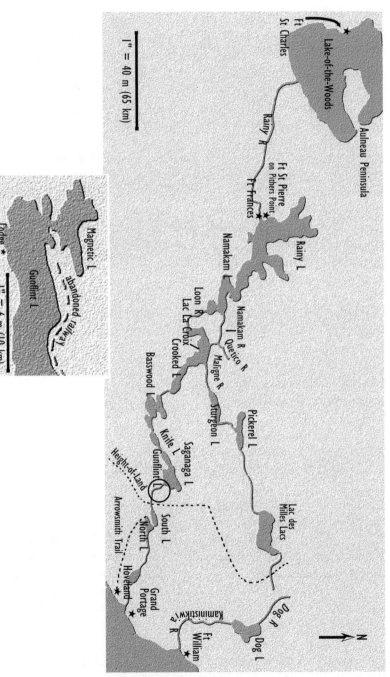

The Rainy River

Four mile-to-the-inch maps used elsewhere were totally inadequate for the intricate wanderings of the Rainy River east of Rainy Lake. The distance between Rainy Lake and Lake Superior is 180-air-miles, but the Rainy River meanders about so, it increases the ground distance by fifty percent. The expedition purchased large scale informative maps, designed specifically for canoeing. Put out by the W.A. Fisher Co., the paper used was parchment-like, durable and virtually waterproof. The maps carried notations for all the portages, which varied from a few yards to one and a half miles. They also labeled relevant locations and stated distances.

Eastward Ho would be following the Voyageur, or Border-Chain Canoe Route, laid down in 1732 by La Vérendrye, and followed by NWC men a few years later. Today it forms the boundary line between Canada and the United States; an example of international cooperation benefiting both countries.

Voyageurs or Border-Chain route – border post

There isn't space to record the detail of each portage but information is readily available for anyone wanting to canoe the Border-Chain route. We will pick out a few highlights from Eastward Ho's log, and record some historical data.

La Vérendrye's first trip over this long-established First Nations canoe route took five weeks, but with improvements in the trails and better staging of supplies and canoe crews, his brigades cut that time to two and a half weeks. Half a century later, in the highly organized days of the Nor'westers, travelling under payloads of a ton or so per canoe, brigades would take from ten to fourteen days for the journey. An express canoe, carrying important correspondence or company officials, could halve that time again.

In his entry for July 27, 1800, our *observer* Alexander Henry Jr. mentions meeting Roderick Mackenzie, cousin to Alexander Mackenzie and fellow partner in the NWC. Roderick was on his way east from Rainy Lake to Grand Portage, Henry was proceeding westward.

At eleven o'clock, four more canoes with Athabasca packs passed and at one o'clock Roderick Mackenzie arrived in a light canoe, two days from Lac La Pluie, expecting to reach Grand Portage early on the 29th; he left at 2 o'clock.

Roderick's rate of travel for the 260 miles in four days was over sixty miles per day. Amazing when one considers the number of times his men had to bring their canoe to shore, unload and carry, food, equipment, dispatches, etc., plus a 300 pound canoe, to the next body of water; there to reload and embark. Eastward Ho's speed on open water was more than double that of an express canoe, but we could not match the *voyageurs* through this kind of country.

Eastward Ho left Fort Frances on June 10th. Pither's Point, where Fort St. Pierre once stood, was soon rounded. The Fort had been built and named by La Vérendrye's advance party in 1731.

Eastward Ho had an easy crossing of forty-mile Rainy Lake, the largest body of water between it and Lake Superior. We zipped through the halfway mark of Brule Narrows and Soldiers Point and on to another 'Kettle Falls', with a portage at the eastern end of the lake.

Namakan River enters the eastern end of Rainy Lake, providing one of three accesses to Lac La Croix. *Observer* Alexander Mackenzie noted: *Lake Namaycan takes its name from a particular place at the foot of a fall where the natives spear sturgeon. ... The Cree say 'na may' for sturgeon.*

There is a portage by Loon Falls and another at the far end of Loon Lake called Beatty portage. Both are mechanical ones, privately run by owners who wouldn't take a nickel from the crew when told the whys and wherefores of Eastward Ho.

Observer Henry said of this portage: *"Petit Portage de la Croix of 200 paces"*.

In comparing accounts of these portages, one notes differences in lengths recorded by Mackenzie and Henry Jr. Probably the discrepancies were due to seasonal changes affecting weather and water levels. As to the standard 'pace', it was probably about two feet. The *voyageurs*, although tremendously strong men, barrel-chested and broad-shouldered, were relatively short in the legs. Long legs took up too much space in a canoe. Under heavy loads of 200 or more pounds the men moved with quick, running steps from one rest to another. In such circumstances, their strides were bound to be short.

Lac La Croix was an important crossroad in the annals of canoe travel and it certainly had a variety of name origins. *Observer* Mackenzie said: *It is due to its cross-like shape.*

Elliott Coues maintained: "It was first called Nequaquon and looks like a short ox-bow, not a cross."

Dr. Kaye Lamb: "It seems likely it was named after Sieur de la Croix who accompanied Jacques De Noyon to Rainy Lake in 1688, and was drowned in Lac La Croix on the return journey."

Dr. Lamb most likely has it right. Although Lac La Croix has two river entrances and exits, the name was pinned on it before the canoe routes were established. Furthermore, the shape is neither a cross nor an ox- bow. Together with Loon Lake, it forms three sides of a rectangle. The Border-chain route coursed through Loon Lake and the entire southern perimeter of Lac La Croix.

About the middle of the lake, on its north side, Namakan River leaves Lake La Croix, running north, then west into Namakan Lake. Sir George Simpson designated it as the preferred way for downstream or westbound traffic. Eric Morse agrees with Simpson and says that even today the Namakan is more wild and makes for a better canoe channel than the Loon Lake way of the border-chain route.

Namakan River receives the waters of Quetico River, which in turn opens up hundreds of miles of pristine wilderness. The river lends its name to Canada's extensive Quetico Park whose western boundary begins here. This gorgeous parkland stretching eastward to Saganaga Lake, takes in 2,400 square miles of natural beauty.

At this point in the journey, another way to Lake Superior is available. Instead of turning south around Coleman Island one can proceed directly east along the northern side of the rectangle to the Maligne River, which in turn ties in with the Kaministikwia River that flows down into Lake Superior at Thunder Bay. This route is fifty miles longer than the Grand Portage way which La Vérendrye pioneered in 1731. The latter remained the preferred route for *montrealers* until the turn of the 18th century, when the surveys of David Thompson put Grand Portage into American territory. As a result the NWC moved their western depot from Grand Portage to the mouth of the Kaministikwia River in 1803. It was named Fort William in honour of William McGillvray, head of the NWC.

On the south-east leg of Lac La Croix, on Irving Island, a stop was made to examine a historic landmark called Painted Rock. We first thought its designation came from the natural shades of greens and reds of the rock face itself, but on approaching, one saw quite clearly *painted* figures resembling moose. They looked like coloured petroglyphs or well-washed ancient graffiti. A note in 'Quetico Park Canoe Routes: *The scenes on these rocks were painted by Indians some 2,000 years ago.*

Next came Bottle Portage. Henry and Mackenzie used the French name of *Flacon Portage,* rating it "very difficult".

The first unassisted carry was at Curtain Falls, or *Rideau Falls* to the *voyageurs*. Next was Crooked Lake, an appropriate name for its snaking contours which Mackenzie refers to as *Lake Croche: ... it extends 18 miles, in a meandering form with a strong current.*

From Crooked Lake we had to portage several sets of rapids coming out of Basswood Lake. In this series of short runs we met a chap who had his transport system down pat. His six year old son travelled with him. In one lift, he carried their seventeen-foot canoe, a five HP motor, gas, food, tarp and camping gear. The boy managed his own sleeping bag. They were on the way to their home in Ely, Minn., via Basswood Lake. He was a most pleasant fellow, and being a frequent visitor, was able to pass on useful tips about this part of the world.

We also chatted with a portager who had two large packs slung fore and aft; one on his back, the other across his chest. It gave him an odd appearance to say the least, but he did look balanced.

Out on Basswood Lake we came across an overturned canoe, a motor still attached to its stern, and a gas tank floating nearby secured by a rubber umbilical cord. Pulling alongside, we anxiously checked the interior, relieved at not finding a body. Immediately we began circling in ever widening arcs on the lookout for floating objects or persons. Nothing. A motorboat appeared. The men aboard tied a line to the canoe, saying to Eastward Ho:

"Thanks for your help. Fortunately the three occupants of this canoe are all safe and drying out in a cabin down the lake. Most canoeing accidents come about through foolish behavior stemming from inexperience. People overload their canoe; when a wind whips up, waves slosh over the gunwales and they founder. These fellows were lucky to be picked up so quickly."

There are hundreds of canoe parties plying these waters, particularly in Basswood Lake which is near road access, and only 25 miles from Ely, Minn., a U.S. commercial centre for wilderness outfitting.

In the days of Alexander Mackenzie, this lake was known as Lac de Bois Blanc, perhaps a more accurate description than Basswood, which is an American lime tree. The white birch provides an abundant source of birch bark for native craftsmen. Our *observer* Mackenzie wrote:

The French have many establishments on the islands and banks of this lake. ... Before smallpox ravaged this country and completed what the Sioux in their warfare had gone far to accomplish, the destruction of its inhabitants, the population was very numerous; this was also a favourite place where they made their canoes.

It rained during the night rendering the air damp, but refreshing. The course was a mile across Carp Lake, then some rapids, followed by falls that required a portage into tiny Seed Lake. A dam had to be carried over, which put us onto Knife Lake.

As we skimmed across to the far end of Knife Lake, clouds began to dump their pent-up rain. This lake has a knife-like appearance, long and slim, but according to Coues the shape of the lake was not the basis for its name:

"The French used *couteaux* to describe the sharp stones and rocks both in the lake and over the portages."

Sharp stones would be agonizing to men carrying 200 pound loads, and clad only in moose-skin moccasins. Their feet must have suffered cruelly.

After Knife Lake, we discovered what we believed to be an error on our two maps. They both listed Monument portage, Swamp Lake, and Swamp portage, in that order. The 300-yard Monument portage was through black muck that oozed up past our ankles. The next, listed on the maps as Swamp p., we found both short and dry. Those names applied by cartographers to the two portages were qualitatively in reverse of the way Eastward Ho found the terrain. Both of our *observers,* Henry and Mackenzie, were in agreement with Eastward Ho's log.

Next in line was fourteen-mile Saganaga Lake, which is bisected by the eastern boundary of Quetico Park. Mackenzie said it took its name from the numerous islands contained therein. These same islands benefitted Eastward Ho. Out on the lake a blustery east wind and driving rain battered us. Advantage was taken of the islands, staying on their lee side as long as possible to avoid the worst of the waves. We island hopped down the centre of Saganaga Lake until the track turned south toward Canada Customs and the lodge of Jock Richardson.

Jock was interested in the historical aspect of our venture, having been involved with the National Geographic's scuba-diving expedition for fur trade artifacts. Following old journals, his group located the most perilous rapids where the greatest number of canoeing accidents had occurred. Divers resurrected implements of the trade dumped in various rapids by luckless *voyageurs*.

Maraboeuf Lake terminated in Devil's Elbow, one of the few instances where modern terminology is as imaginative as the names chronicled by Mackenzie and Henry. The current to work against was called Granite River. Full of twists and turns and small waterfalls, it necessitated several portages. One of the carries the U.S. map entitled as 'Blueberry Portage'. The Canadian map named it stiffly 'Wood Horse Portage'. Both choices missed the *voyageurs'* descriptive phrase of *Cheval de Bois* which translates into horses of a 'merry-go-round' or 'rocking-horse' variety. Henry said the carry was: *an ugly one of 400 paces.*

The portage footpath on the very edge of the river felt the shuffling feet of *voyageurs* two centuries ago. Then as now, white-water rapids wheeled like wild horses, tossing their manes in the air, and snorting as they pranced by. To *voyageurs* several months from home, the sight must have brought back childhood memories of exciting carousels or reckless rides on the family's rocking-horse. Whatever the origin, 'Cheval de Bois' has a nicer ring than 'Wood Horse' portage.

A mile further on, the last of this group of portages was a short one of forty yards. It circumvents a waterfall that drops twelve feet in a series of three equidistant steps. Labelled today with an unimaginative 'Little Rock Falls' the *voyageurs* knew it as *Escalier* or the 'Staircase'.

The Escalier portage put us on Magnetic Lake. A hurried exit from the latter, for Gunflint Lake, almost spelt disaster.

Night was falling. Anxious to reach a lodge on the far side of Gunflint Lake in order to advise Edo of our whereabouts, we pressed on, in spite of the dark. The course was up a narrow passage against a rush of water. A check of the map indicated neither rapids nor other impediments.

The helmsman gunned the motor to climb the incline. As we slipped through the gap the canoe gave a jerk, accompanied by an ominous r-r-r-ripping sound. Speed was checked for a split second, then the canoe continued on into the lake under full throttle. Jim and Don ran their hands down each side, as far under the bottom as they could reach, but felt nothing untoward.

A few minutes later Jim signalled to cut the motor. As we slowed he called out, "My arse is getting wet. I think we're taking on water."

Somebody grabbed a flashlight and shone it onto the ribs. Sure enough, in the middle of the canoe, water from the lake was bubbling through a break in the floor-boards. A pool two or three inches deep had already formed. No one had mentioned it sooner because there was always some water sloshing around in the canoe. The helmsman usually manned the hand pump, as water ran to the stern when underway, but he had been too intent on beating the oncoming darkness to notice.

This was a pickle. Well out into the lake by now, we could see lights across the way about three miles off. The tree-lined shore to our right was nearer, but would we be able to get off the water there? A low fog had encircled the perimeter of the lake. Debate was wasting valuable seconds.

The helmsman twisted the handle to full throttle and headed for the light peeping in and out of the mist over on the far shore. Don worked the pump. Jim baled out what he could with the 'pee-can'. Dave, up at the bow, hadn't yet felt any water.

We didn't dare slow down to check how things were doing. Survival lay in out-racing the rising water level in the canoe. When Dave began throwing up his arms in a scooping motion, everyone realized the safety margin was decreasing swiftly. Our speed lessened as the canoe became heavier, sinking lower into the lake.

It was a spine-tingling quarter hour. We won the race, but it was a close call. Half a foot of water had our craft resembling a bathtub again, reminiscent of our near swamping on the Thompson River, B.C., two months previous. We nudged it onto the beach in front of Gunflint Lodge.

In examining the canoe next day we found a five-foot tear of shredded canvas and two severed cedar planks. The cause of the accident was unknown until I consulted Alexander Henry's journal several months after completion of the Eastward Ho expedition.

Henry had written: *Thence we continued to Flint Lake, through which we passed.*

Henry's editor, Elliott Coues, then noted: "Flint Lake is more fully Gun Flint Lake, a term translating the French phrase *Lac des Pierres à Fusil.* ... near the west end the track turns N.W. through a narrow place of 6 yards wide for 15 yards. This constriction marks off a part of what was considered all of Gunflint Lake but is now distinguished by the name of Magnetic Lake, about a mile long N.N.W. *The Duluth, Port Arthur and Western Ry. crosses this narrow place to go to Gun Flint iron mine.*"

That last sentence of Coues' explanatory memo, written in 1897, provided the answer to the accident. The mine had long since folded and the railway line abandoned. In disrepair, the trestle over the narrows had collapsed. One rusty old spike, punched through a submerged railway tie, was sharp enough and long enough to perforate the skin of our wood-canvas canoe.

When four rum-looking men, dripping from all seams, squelched their way to the desk of the lodge, the young receptionist wasn't at all perturbed. She had become inured to the antics of canoeists. She listened to the story of their mishap, took pity on them and assigned a cabin away from the commodious lodge, at one dollar per head. A very reasonable offer.

On June 13th we were up early to see what could be done with the disabled craft. One of the lodge owners, Bruce Kerfoot, came down the beach to where the group stood inspecting their canoe.

"I may be able to help you," he said, after taking a look. Bruce knew how to patch a canoe skin all right. He attached small pieces of wood across the broken planking by screwing them from the outside, underneath the break in the canvas. With this base well prepared, he slipped a long strip of canvas underneath the tear. Cutting off the hanging bits, he proceeded to bond the two canvas layers together with amboid glue.

The canvas must not adhere directly to the hull. Properly installed, it provides a snug covering that envelopes the canoe, yet remains separate from it, allowing a certain resiliency. Thus one can break ribs, the fine inner hull, or the internal spine of the canoe, and still retain buoyancy, if the canvas remains sound.

In the days of birch-bark canoes, standard repair material was *bark, wattap, and gum.* No self-respecting canoe man left his post without a supply of these three items. All depots of the fur trade carried rolls of birch-bark for patching; bundles of split spruce tree roots, the wattap, for stitching; as well as pots of pine tree pitch, or gum, to stick it all together and render the shell waterproof. Nature provided an abundance of these substances throughout eastern Canada. The shell didn't have to be made of birch bark. It was the preferred staple, but barks such as basswood, elm, spruce, and others, were used.

By mid-afternoon the patch had dried sufficiently to allow placing the canoe in the lake, loading up and getting underway. Eastward Ho proceeded through Little Gunflint Lake and by the *Décharge des épingles* into North Lake, the uppermost reaches of Rainy River. After the quarter-mile portage into South Lake it would be downhill all of the 50 miles to Lake Superior.

Disembarking on the Rainy River side of the height-of-land, we had the reason, but not the means, to celebrate. *Observer* Henry's westward bound crews were better prepared, as he wrote:

We came to the Hauteur des Terres where the men generally finish their small kegs and fight many a battle.

In portaging from one drainage system to another, in this case 400 yards, one might expect a hill or at least a ridge. Such is not the case. The land looks absolutely flat. The track is wet in places, but only sensitive instruments could point out exactly where the water starts on its way to Hudson Bay, or trickled down to Lake Superior and the mighty St. Lawrence.

From South Lake, (Henry's Lake des Perches), we moved over the next portage into Rat Lake. Henry used the more dignified Marten Lake. From there, it was a short carry of a few yards into Rose Lake.

Rose was a shortened version for roseaux which meant reed-like or muddy. Some maps have it as Mud Lake. *Observer* Mackenzie had an interesting comment for paddlers on this lake:

In this part of the lake the bottom is mud and slime, with about three or four feet of water over it; and here I frequently struck a canoe pole of twelve feet, without meeting any obstruction. However it has a peculiar suction or attractive power so that it is difficult to paddle a canoe over it ...

Presently, on the south side of Rose Lake, Eastward Ho came to the big meany of the portages. Correctly entitled the Long Portage, it is almost two miles in length and leads to two small lakes called Rove and Watap, in that order. Perhaps Watap Lake was a source of *wattap*, the spruce tree roots used in the building or repair of canoes. We carried gear part way across, following an old railway bed until darkness settled, then tented on a grassy knoll in a swamp loaded with mosquitoes and burping bull frogs. Accommodation wouldn't have received a one-star rating from the Canadian Automobile Association.

Next morning Rove and Watap were soon done. Moose Lake was the next body of water; then Fowl Lake. We spent two hours searching the eastern end of Fowl Lake for the old portage trail that was supposed to parallel Pigeon River in its final run to Lake Superior. The map showed it as being on the Canadian side. We could make out a faintly discernible path but it was far too steep and overgrown to get the canoe through. We checked out the U.S. side, and it looked passable. Two fishermen, casting at the top of the river from their canoe, advised against going that way.

"That trail peters out. It goes to the top of a dam that's only a few hundred yards away. But if you locate the proper trail, it'll take you at least two days to drag that big canoe through them. There are only six miles of canoeable water between South Lake and Partridge Falls where you have to pull out for good. Then you still have a ten-mile hike to Grand Portage."

"If you're in the big hurry you say you are, we'd suggest you take a bypass and go into McFarland Lake. There is a lodge, and you can phone from there. A twenty-mile road leads to Lake Superior. You can send out your gear and hike yourselves."

They seemed well informed, so Eastward Ho heeded their advice, arriving at Wilderness Retreat Lodge on MacFarland Lake at dusk. It had rained off and on all day.

There must be something appealing about canoeists who are dripping wet. The owner, Margaret Brandt, pointed to a cabin, and with a grin said, "It's yours. Shower, then come for supper. It's all on the house."

Over breakfast next morning, Margaret said "Your land party will arrive around noon." She refused to take a cent for her hospitality.

Transport for the canoe appeared on the morning of June 15th. The crew started immediately down the romantic-sounding Arrowhead Trail, with the canoe mail. Twenty-miles later we arrived at night in Hoveland on Lake Superior, footsore and weary. The outstanding impression of the march was *monotony*.

Voyageurs faced many problems on the historic Pigeon River trail coming up from Grand Portage on Lake Superior. The work of the *northmen* with their twenty-five-foot *north* canoes began at Fort

Charlotte. The *montrealers* would have already carried the supplies for the interior up to the Fort over the muddy and steep nine-mile path from Lake Superior. This *grand portage* was quite the toughest of the many strenuous hurdles the *voyageurs* had to contend with. It caused La Vérendrye's men to mutiny on the shores of Lake Superior, in September, 1731.

Under the aegis of the NWC, the *montrealers* were lugging up to eight bundles, two at a time, over the slippery trail. They received one Spanish dollar for every package thereafter. The *northmen* sneeringly referred to them as *pork-eaters*, because their staple diet was pork and dried peas. Mackenzie wrote:

... so inured are they to this kind of labour, that I have known them to set off with two packages of ninety pounds each and return with two others of the same weight, in the course of six hours; being a distance of eighteen miles over hills and mountains.

That muscle-straining feat would mean the men moved at about three mph., carrying 180 lbs. on a path Henry describes as *'knee-deep in mud and clay'*. No wonder many died of strangulated hernias. As anyone who walks for exercise knows, three mph is a good clip on level ground, without a pack.

Observer Henry continues: *The canoes having been given out to the men, to gum and prepare, I found everything ready for our departure; and early this morning gave out to all their respective loading, which consisted of 28 packages per canoe, assorted for the Saulteur trade on Red river, namely:*

Merchandise, 90 pounds ea. – 5 bales; Canal tobacco – 1 bale; Kettles – 1 bale; Guns – 1 case; Iron works – 1 case; New twist tobacco – 2 rolls; Leaden balls – 2 bags; Leaden shot – 1 bag; Flour – 1 bag; Sugar – 1 keg; Gunpowder – 2 kegs; High wine, 9 gal. ea. – 10 kegs.

Plus equipage for the voyage: Provisions for four men to Red River: 4 bags of corn @ 1&1/2 bushels ea.; 1/2 keg grease (fat). 4 packages of 90 pounds each of private property, clothing, tobacco etc. for themselves and families for the year. When all hands were embarked, the canoes sunk to the gunnel.

The men would not paddle far. Within less than two miles they hauled everything out of the canoes for the first portage called Partridge or *Portage du Perdix*. It was about 400 yards around a high waterfall that raced over a seventy-foot precipice. Then all canoes were loaded for a two and a half mile paddle to the 'Prairie' where everyone camped for the night. Henry continued:

All were merry over their favourite regale which is always given on their departure and generally enjoyed at this spot. We have a delightful meadow to pitch our tents and plenty of elbow room for the men.

A *régale* was a treat dispensed to the hard-working *voyageurs*. It could consist of food or liquid, but on the trail, usually the latter.

The following day, canoes would proceed, some times with half-loads, to Big Rock, or Great Stone Portage of 500 yards. Then on with half-loads to Caribou portage of 550 yards. Three miles of paddling brought them to the mile-long Outarde, or Fowl portage, the ugliest but fortunately the last of the steep canoe carries. Its completion allowed them to lay down their burdens beside Fowl Lake, the waterway Eastward Ho detoured from to hike the Arrowhead.

Until 1803 Grand Portage was the great entrepot of the North West Co. The site is in American territory, south of the Pigeon River which marks the International Boundary. The Minnesota Historical Society has reconstructed and maintained a replica of the old palisaded fort.

Looking eastward, Hat Point can be seen to the left. On the right lies Grand Portage Island which afforded protection for the Otter, a seventy-five-ton sailing ship of the NWC that plied the waters of Lake Superior. Extensive shallows of the bay wouldn't permit building of a dock out from shore.

Observer Mackenzie left a description of the site, perhaps visited by Radisson and Groseilliers in 1662, but certainly established as a post by La Vérendrye in the 1730's:

The bottom of the bay, which forms an amphitheatre, is cleared of wood and inclosed; and on the left corner of it, beneath a hill, three or four hundred feet in height and crowned by others of a still greater altitude, is the fort, picketed in with cedar palisades and inclosing houses built with wood and covered with shingles. They are calculated for every convenience of the trade, as well as to accommodate the proprietors and clerks during their short residence there. The North men live under tents; but the more frugal pork-eaters camp beneath their canoes.

[Ed. note: thirty-five foot *montreal* canoes were larger and provided more protection from the weather than the twenty-five foot *north* canoes]

The mode of living at the Grande Portage is as follows: The proprietors, clerks and guides, and interpreters mess together, to the number of sometimes a hundred, at several tables, in one large hall. The provision consists of bread, salt pork, beef, hams, fish, venison, butter, peas, Indian corn, potatoes, tea, spirits, wine &c. and plenty of milk, for which purposes several milch cows are constantly kept.

The mechanics have rations of such provision but the canoe-men, from Montreal, have no other allowance here than Indian corn and melted fat. The corn for this purpose is prepared before it leaves Detroit, by boiling in a strong alkali which takes off the outer husks; it is then well washed and carefully dried upon stages, when it is fit for use. One quart of this is boiled for two hours, over a moderate fire, in a gallon of water; to which, when it has boiled a small time, are added two ounces of melted suet; this causes the corn to split, and in the time mentioned makes a pretty thick pudding. If to this is added a little salt, (but not before it is boiled as it would interrupt the operation), it makes a wholesome, palatable food, easy of digestion. This quantity is fully sufficient for a man's subsistence during twenty-four hours; though it is not sufficiently heartening to sustain the strength necessary for a state of active labour. The Americans call this dish 'hominee'.

The North men being arrived at Grand Portage, are regaled with bread, pork, butter, liquor and tobacco, and such as have not entered into agreements during the summer, which is customary, are contracted with; to return and perform the voyage for one, two or three years: their accounts are also settled and such as choose to send any of their earnings to Canada, receive drafts to transmit to their relations or friends: and as soon as they can be got ready, which is no more than a fortnight, they are again dispatched to their respective departments.

As difficult and dangerous as canoe work was, the survivors were a proud lot. Marjorie Wilkins Campbell in her book "The North West Company", tells of an old professional who was wont to boast:

"I could carry, paddle, walk and sing with any man I ever knew. I have been twenty-four years a canoeman, and forty-one in service; no portage was ever too long for me. Fifty songs could I sing. I have saved the lives of ten *voyageurs*. I've had twelve wives, six running dogs and spent all my money on pleasure. Were I young again, I would spend all my life the same way over. There is no life so happy as a *voyageur's*!"

We weare Caesars,
being nobody to contradict us.
Pierre Esprit Radisson

Chapter Sixteen
Two Great Lakes

Eastward Ho sat poised on the western shore of Lake Superior for a dash across the world's largest fresh-water inland sea. From Thunder Bay to Sault Ste. Marie lay 300 miles of open storm-swept water. A quick and easy trip, or a foul and time-consuming one, lay in the lap of Zephuros.

Under ordinary circumstances one would follow the *voyageur's* route along Superior's northern coastline in order to seek shelter from sudden gales sweeping over the lake. It added an extra 100 miles to a more direct course. During summer months the chances of *voyageurs* being held up by weather was about one in three. By paddling from headland to headland, with a favourable wind to balloon their square sail, the 400-mile journey was often done in less than a week.

With the wind at their back, they would run up all the sail their craft could handle, and squeeze out every minute of daylight. There was a limiting factor, however. Their bark canoes tended to become increasingly waterlogged with too long an immersion. Since they were loaded down to the gunwhale with either fur packets or trade goods, there was little freeboard. An efficient pair of *bouttes* would continually be checking their vessel's hull.

At the same time, the crossing could stretch into weeks. *Voyageurs* hung the vagaries of weather onto the distaff side by blaming its behavior on the whims of *La Vieille*, the Old Lady.

While driving from Hoveland to Thunder Bay, Edo expressed fears for the crew's safety in crossing Lake Superior. He had heard that the Coast Guard made regular runs across Lake Superior to Michipicoten Island. "Would it be possible", he said, "for the Coast Guard to act as an escort? They could provide you with a mother ship to run to in the event of stormy weather. You might save a few days, and perhaps enough to permit Eastward Ho to make that visit to HMCS Fraser in Halifax."

A call through to Chris Brown of New Westminster, a man of influence with the reigning Liberal Party, stood us in good stead. He in turn contacted Captain Forbes of the Harbours Board at Thunder Bay. Upon learning that Eastward Ho's cruising speed was the same as his ships, Capt. Forbes gave permission for us to tag on behind. The Coast Guard could pick us up in an emergency. We had to be ready to sail at dawn of June 22nd with the lightship tender *Nokomis*.

The City of New Westminster, Host City to HMCS Fraser, had asked Eastward Ho to present a plaque on their behalf to the Fraser's Captain and crew, if the opportunity arose. The frigate class vessel had been converted to a helicopter carrier and the occasion was to acknowledge her re-fit. Since Eastward Ho had picked up so much time in the past two weeks, it was thought four days could be spared to carry out the City's request. The Navy flew all seven to Halifax in a reconnaissance aircraft. The kindness, efficiency, and sense of responsibility by officers and personnel of the Canadian Forces was most impressive. True to their promise, they had Eastward Ho back at Thunder Bay within the four day period.

June 21: The crew was awake early on the longest day of the year. The weatherman seemed unaware that it was officially the first day of summer. Clouds heralded a threat of rain. The wind was snapping the curtains through the open window of the motel. One could imagine what it would be doing to the waves out on the 'Big Pond'.

This was the day we were to canoe north from Hoveland to Thunder Bay, and make ready for tomorrow's early departure behind 'Nokomis'. There were many purchases to make; gasoline, oil, clothing, food, et cetera. Rearranging and packing took all morning. It was noon before Bill could transport us to Hoveland. At the launching site, where we had pulled out of Lake Superior six days previously, waves were breaking heavily onto the beach. We looked to be in for a soaking at the very beginning.

We managed to prevent the waves from sloshing in by attaching the motor on shore and launching the canoe bow first. With no weight up forward the lightened bow rode over the tops of the curlers. When the stern had cleared the beach two of the crew clambered over the sides into the canoe, took it out into deeper water, then turned it around when the stern was beyond the breaking of the waves. The two on shore waded out to pass the supplies aboard. This method was similar to the way the *voyageurs* disembarked. But they didn't have the luxury of rubber boots.

By mid-afternoon we were heading north-east, keeping the coastline well in sight. At first the lake seemed very rough. Large rollers welled up from the south to strike the starboard quarter with a spine-tingling "Smack!" But as the east wind died, the canoe's speed increased in step with the helmsman's confidence. Soon we were bowling merrily along on top of the waves, or roaring down their face into a spray of water at the bottom of the trough. It was exhilarating.

Hat Point was passed to port where the *pork eaters,* six weeks out of Montreal, would put ashore to spruce up and don their bits of finery, a red sash, an unsoiled shirt and perhaps a bit of ribbon to tie in their shoulder-length hair, before rounding into Grand Portage Bay.

Ten miles north of Hat Point the long arm of Pigeon Point served to put a break on the southern swells, providing a quiet trip into Thunder Bay and a berth beside Nokomis.

The skipper told the canoeists: "Be ready to sail at 3:30 a.m., and I suggest you sleep aboard." We bedded down on deck to watch a round orange moon climb above the ship's handrail.

At 3:30 the canoe was lowered from the deck of Nokomis into the waters of Lake Superior and made ready for departure. Precisely at four, Skipper gave the order, "Cast off moorings." Nokomis slid silently away from the dock, a now pale moon waning in the west, dawn's faint light waxing in the east. Clear of the harbour, the First Mate set a course for Marathon. Eastward Ho tucked in behind Nokomis' stern like a duckling in its mother's wake.

The forecast was for winds of 20-25 knots by mid-day; a result of thermal heating, 'they' said. Goodness knows what the sun was warming, but it certainly wasn't the air around the canoe. At high noon it felt as cold as early morning, in spite of long-johns, wool everything else, insulated leather boots and windproof nylon coveralls.

Far from shore and cruising between 12 and 14 mph, we found the wind extremely debilitating, the price paid for speed and protection on the crossing. There was a story floating about, that in the northern depths of Lake Superior the water temperature is barely above freezing throughout the summer. Even here, upon dipping fingers into the water, it felt as cold as ice. Survival time would be measured in minutes if one were to fall in.

Observer Sir Alexander Mackenzie wrote: *Lake Superior is the largest and most magnificent body of fresh water in the world: it is clear and pellucid, of great depth and abounding in a great variety of fish, which are the most excellent of their kind. There are trouts of three kinds, weighing from five to fifty pounds, sturgeon, pickerel, pike, red and white carp, black bass, herrings, &c.&c. ... Last and best of all, the Ticamang, or white fish, which weighs from four to sixteen pounds and is of superior quality in these waters.*

Three of the members could get under the plastic orange tarp to escape some of the icy blast, but there was no protection for the helmsman. The crossing of Lake Superior in an open motorized canoe was the most rigorous part of the trip. Skiing across the Rockies, sleeping out in below zero temperatures, fighting ice flows on the upper Saskatchewan, were pleasurable wintry pursuits in comparison with the hypothermia that resulted from travelling in a canoe at high speed on Lake Superior. It is a pity wetsuits had not been part of our equipment.

We logged a record 140 miles the first day. If the weather cooperates for the remaining Great Lake's portion, our schedule will be eased considerably.

The skipper advised the canoeists that he had a lighthouse call to make early in the morning but would return to Marathon before noon. Marathon is a pulp and paper town as had been evident when approaching it the previous evening; both from the cloying, sickly-sweet odor that assailed our nostrils, and from having to dodge dozens of peeler logs out in the harbour.

There were no known fur trade associations here, but on Lake Superior's northern shore, halfway between Marathon and Thunder Bay, we had passed the large fur trading area of Lake Nipigon. In 1727 La Vérendrye had managed a post at the mouth of Nipigon River, as well as one at the mouth of the Kaministikwia River where Thunder Bay is now situated.

Lake Nipigon may have been visited by Radisson and perhaps it was from here he gained his knowledge of Hudson Bay and the river access routes to James Bay. The north-east shore of Lake Nipigon is just over ten miles from the height of land and headwaters of the Albany River.

To the *voyageurs*, skirting under the beetling cliffs of *le grand Lac Superieur*, the ground between Black Bay and Nipigon Bay was relatively low-lying. Hence they called it *pays plat*, or 'flat country'. The northern coast line of Lake Superior retained many original names, either in French or in an anglicized version of French, which described the shapes and contours of the scenery as the canoemen paddled past. Oiseau Bay, Pic Island, Les Petits Ecrits, Vert I., Sleeping Giant, Thunder Cape and Turtle Head were a few. An excellent account of how the country appeared to the *voyageurs* can be found in 'Conquering Lake Superior In A 17-Foot Canoe', by the late E.W. Morse.

When we woke in the morning, the fog was so thick you could barely see twenty-feet. It dispersed as the sun rose, but the air remained on the cool side.

Nokomis was back in harbour at 10:30, anxious to be off. Our crew had to leave in a hurry, throwing gear and themselves into the canoe, and departing immediately. There wasn't time to arrange the tarp properly, an omission soon regretted.

Outside the harbour the passage was rough, windy and wet, and of course achingly cold. The tarp kept flying up from the gunwales allowing water to spray the interior. Every effort had to be made to stay up with the mother ship who wasn't being very motherly at that point. Don finally managed to gain the attention of Nokomis' First Mate on the walkie-talkie.

"If the sea becomes worse we will have to quit. Our hand pump can't keep up with the amount of water splashing aboard," Don called out.

The Mate came back with, "According to a lighthouse keeper a few miles ahead, winds at his station are light. Try to keep up."

Nokomis' speed didn't slacken. Eastward Ho plowed on through the spray, trying to keep the water level in the canoe down by bailing and pumping.

The lighthouse keeper was right; eventually the sea did improve. The course in the afternoon was practically due south, with a dog-leg to the east at the bottom end of the run. Eighty miles of straight-line travel brought us to Quebec Harbour on the southern shore of Michipicoten Island at 8:00 p.m.

The last two hours of the day were decidedly unpleasant again. *La Vieille* had herself a small fit, similar to the one at departure from Marathon. The crew heaved a sigh of relief as we slid into the mouth of the long narrow harbour.

Quebec Harbour had been the centre of a thriving commercial and sport fishing industry when these waters once teemed with fighting lake trout. Now, the whole place was eerie, reminiscent of a Charles Adams drawing; a few collapsing cabins, a dilapidated hall with a broken-down pool table, a graying grass-tufted wharf. Ghostly reminders of a once flourishing community all seemed to shout, "Memories!"

The lighthouse keeper came by in his boat for a visit. A First Nations person, he was a great raconteur, and kept the crew amused over evening mugs of cocoa. This being the eastern extent of Nokomis' run, the canoeists slept on deck that night, prepared for an early rendezvous with another coast guard vessel.

Their new *shepherd* crept in at dawn, their crew making lines fast under muffled commands. Shaking ice off our sleeping bags, we quickly gathered our things and went to meet the Spray. She was a trim vessel of 65 feet, with lines like the RCMP boats that patrol Vancouver Harbour on the west coast. The skipper and mate, Bob and Jim, were both Scots so Jim Reid felt right at home, his Dad being a Gaelic scholar.

Their cook warmed everyone up with a mug of steaming coffee while we discussed plans for the day.

"We're ready to leave anytime," the canoeists said. "Dave has become proficient at using the coleman under a tarp. We'll eat breakfast in your wake."

Skipper Bob said, "Say, you guys are really eager. We'll shove off right now then."

Goodbyes and thanks to the men on Nokomis were made, and soon Eastward Ho was heading for open water once more, in pursuit of the graceful Spray.

There was little wind that day. Michipicoten Island soon disappeared over the stern. This island had taken its name from a deep bay forty miles eastward and a river that flows into it. The mainland area has a long history in fur-gathering. The headwaters of the Michipicoten River are a stone's throw from the upper reaches of the Moose River which is a sixteen-day canoe journey to James Bay.

We canoed south-east past Cape Gargantua and the island that bestowed the name. Its likeness to a phallic symbol is obvious to earthy *voyageurs*. By noon, the looming hulls of Great Lake freighters could be seen homing into the buoyed channel of St. Mary River.

Spray warned Eastward Ho to stay close by their starboard bow while in the channel, and to tie up alongside when going through the lock at Sault Ste. Marie, with its rise of twenty-one feet.

On reaching the actual narrows of the lock we saw the gesticulating figure of Bill Gifford by the entrance. He was waving frantically and pointing to his right. Looking that way, we could see two canoes with costumed paddlers waiting in front of a palisade log fort. Obviously Bill wanted Eastward Ho to join up with the young men in native garb.

Dave yelled to the skipper for permission to leave.

Skipper Bob shook his head and shouted, "The lock's opening for us right now. We have to go through."

What a dilemma. We realized Edo had probably gone to a lot of trouble in preparing a scene for the film. On the other hand we were loathe to break off from our 'mother hen'. We didn't want to appear ungrateful for Spray's care and hoped they could convoy us to the mouth of French River in Lake Huron. We stuck with Spray, but felt like rats deserting the ship of our own party.

After proceeding through the Sault Ste. Marie locks, Bill arrived and we asked of Edo. "I don't think Edo wants to talk to you guys right now," he replied, "He's so mad. Seeing you canoeing aloofly by after all his effort arranging everything for a colourful 'shoot', really threw the guy. I thought he was going to burst on the spot."

Explanations didn't seem to convince Bill, nor was the manager of the lock much help. "Oh, you could have gone through on your own," he said, "Any time and at no charge."

All we could say was, "We'll know better next time."

It was an emotional moment when we were asked to sign the guest register. *Our canoe was the first transport vessel to come through from the Pacific coast in over a hundred years.*

A replica of the first lock built at Sault Ste. Marie lay beside the one we had just come through. Constructed expressly by the NWC for the thirty-five foot *canots de maître*, it was in operation by 1798. A bronze plaque stated that *coureurs de bois* had passed by here in 1622, a mere seven years after Champlain had found the Lake Nipissing connection from the Ottawa River to Lake Huron.

Replica of canoe lock built for canots de maître

In order to spread the faith of Christ amongst the people here, Jesuits had founded the mission of Sainte Marie du Saut. The natives were Chippewa, or as Henry Jr. called them, Saulteur, because they lived around the *sault* or rapids of St. Mary River. Ranging westward from here to the other side of Lake Superior, they were linguistically related to the Algonquian-speaking Cree nation north of them. Henry had married into a Saulteur family.

That evening we drove to Edo's camper ensconced in a park. He was talking to Bob Andrews who was able to pass on much useful information on the French, Mattawa and Ottawa rivers. Bob was planning a trip from the mouth of French River to Montreal on the first of August, expecting it to take three weeks. He asked Eastward Ho to leave a message for him in a cairn at Recollet Falls.

After Bob had left, and without strangers around, a verbal donnybrook began. All the frustrations built up in Edo broke loose, and not just from the latest fiasco. The canoe group argued. Edo and Bill counter-argued. There was lots of arm waving and shouting back and forth. The only one who kept her cool was unflappable Lorna.

The main objective of the canoe crew was simply *to get there*. Delaying or changing schedule to shoot film, thwarted that desire. With the continuous shortening of travel-time by ice, that impaired our progress from Alberta to Manitoba, filming often seemed like another obstacle. We four felt justified with today's on-the-spot decision, although we did not convince the others.

With the air cleared somewhat, the paddlers agreed to be more cooperative regarding filming in the future. Besides, the pressure of time was easing, and Spray had agreed to conduct us to the mouth of French River in Lake Huron. Baring unforeseen disasters, we could ease up on our travelling intensity.

The next morning we met Edo at the log fort by-passed the day before. Constructed with funds raised by Sault Ste. Marie's Kiwanis Club, it duplicated the setting and routine of a typical trading post of bye-gone days. The staff put on a special performance which Edo captured on film. It was an authentic rendering of what doing business in stores in the hinterland had been like when animal skins took the place of money, and haggling over value was routine. Four of the young lads were Cree from James Bay, working at the fort for summer employment, and seeking a higher education.

Departure next morning was from the government wharf, the course following the U.S.-Canada border which circles Sugar Island then runs south down the west side of St. Joseph Island. The voyageur route had been more northerly, cutting through the island-infested St. Joseph Channel.

South of St. Joseph was another famous and long-established voyageur track. Detour Passage connected the Sault to the oldest trading emporium of the west, the post of Michilimackinac. This mouthful of a name was later shortened to Mackinac.

Mackinac was a missionary and trading station established by the French in 1668, on an island of the same name, in the strait of the same name. It sat athwart the trade route to Lake Michigan and the Illinois River connection of the Mississippi Valley.

It was a sad day for the growth of Canada when, after the American Revolution, by the Treaty of Paris, Montreal merchants lost control of both Mackinac and Fort Detroit. That piece of parchment resulted in the loss of a vast fur-producing area, encompassed by the present-day states of Ohio, Indiana, Illinois, Wisconsin and Minnesota, all which Montreal had controlled for over a hundred years. Canada briefly repossessed Fort Mackinac during the War of 1812 when a combined British-Canadian force seized and held it. The peace treaty, however, restored Mackinac to the Americans.

Mackinac and Detroit were provisioning depots for the southwest and northwest trades. Mackinac provided maple sugar, tallow and gum, while Detroit added flour and corn. 'Mackinac' is said to be a native word for *turtle*, stemming from the shape of the island. The Pontiac Massacre occurred here, part of the uprising organized against the British in 1763 by Pontiac, Chief of the Ottawas, and former ally of the French. Alexander Henry Sr. was a trader at that Fort when the insurrection commenced. He survived after some hair-raising experiences which he described vividly in his journal. It is well worth reading.

That evening we made Little Current on Manitoulin Island. The largest island of Lake Huron's multitude, it contains several good-sized lakes of its own. According to local knowledge, the strong currents that eddy between North Channel and Georgian Bay keep this harbour ice-free most winters.

In Champlain's day, Manitoulin Island was home for a group of natives referred to in history books as the 'Ottawas'. Today, the people themselves pronounce it 'Odawa'. An Algonguin tribe, they were forerunners of La Vérendrye's Saulteurs. Champlain came across several of them picking blueberries when he emerged from French River onto the waters of Lake Huron. He called them: *Cheveux relevés or 'High Hairs', because they had them elevated and arranged very high, and better combed than our courtiers ...*

Upon reaching the many mouths of the French River that flow into Georgian Bay, Eastward Ho will be entering Champlain Country, the most westerly penetration made by our first canoe explorer. In 1615, Champlain came via the Ottawa-French River passage into Lake Huron, in order to support his Huron allies in a siege against the Iroquois of Lake Ontario.

Eastward Ho looked forward to following in the footsteps of their fourth *fifth man*, Samuel de Champlain. His biography follows.

"Courtier, soldier, scholar; eye, tongue, sword".
Hamlet's Ophelia might have described
M. Champlain, 1567 - 1635, thus.

Chapter Seventeen

fifth man **Samuel de Champlain**

E minently qualified to be called the 'Father of our Country', Champlain epitomized the Renaissance Man; intelligent, courageous, direct, a man of action and sensitivity, a man of moral purpose. The son of Antoine de Complain and Marguerite Le Roy, he was born in Brouage, once an important city on the Bay of Biscay, rivalling La Rochelle in size.

During the days of Champlain's youth, Brouage was a busy port of call for the purchase of salt. Foreign ships tied up there; *Boyarts* from Hamburg, Flemish *flutes* and *pinnaces*, Portuguese *caravels*, Spanish *carracks, bargues* from Brittany and the bluff-bowed *hookers* from Bristol, all came a-calling. Their garrulous crews would gibber in unfathomable tongues from all the ports of Europe.

Today, Brouage is a tiny community sleeping behind decaying stone walls set in a sea of marsh grass. The receding ocean has left it high and dry. Now a tourist town, the main resource for Brouage residents is the exportation of *Champlain memorabilia*.

Champlain's first love was for the sea, an inheritance from his father, a ship's Captain. As a lad, Champlain would probably have absorbed some of his father's knowledge while sailing about Brouage's protected harbour in skiffs. He developed an aptitude and a respect for the art of navigation early in life.

Brouage was a town caught up in the religious wars that decimated France in the 16th century. It was under siege when Champlain lived there as a teenager. He learned to cope with hunger, terror, and death at an early age.

Later, as an officer in the Royal Army of France, he fought under the Governor of Brouage, d' Epinay Saint Luc. The Marshal was impressed by his Lieutenant and introduced him to France's new King, Henry IV of Navarre. The latter must have thought Champlain useful as he awarded him a pension and made him welcome at Court.

There is no documentary proof that Champlain became an intelligence officer for King Henry, but his occupation over the next few years would suggest it. He wrote:

I resolved to embark in one of the ships of the fleet which the King of Spain sends every year to the West Indies; to that end I might be able to make enquiries into particulars no Frenchmen have acquired ... in order to make a true report of them to his Majesty ...

He spent two years on the Spanish Main, returning to publish his illustrated *Brief Discours* in Paris.

At age 33, Champlain's mind and body had been tempered by the sea and by war. He could march without food, sleep in rain or on snow, and he was familiar with death. Doubtless, he had bestowed it upon others. He knew the arts of war: sieges, battles, guerrilla fighting, and hand-to-hand combat. Champlain was well prepared for the life of fortitude he would require for his next commission, one that would occupy the rest of his life.

Since the beginning of the 16th century, perhaps even before the voyages of Christopher Columbus, Basque fishermen had been plying their sturdy boats across the storm-wracked Atlantic in pursuit of the mighty whale. Breton, Portuguese, and Bristol fishermen hauled cod from rich fishing grounds of the Grand Banks off Newfoundland. Some salted their catch in brine, others set up summer drying stations along the coasts of Newfoundland and the Gulf of St. Lawrence.

Sailors began to trade with friendly residents of this vast but sparsely occupied country and over the decades a business was built up that proved profitable to both sides. Native people traded all kinds of furs for a wide range of metal products.

The governing body of France was somewhat skeptical of the benefits of colonization in North America. Such efforts in Brazil and Florida had been disastrous, and certainly both Cartier and Roberval had squandered human life and investment capital with nothing to show for it. Yet by the end of the 16th century, changing times were forcing the hand of even the most conservative of Henry's Court advisors.

France was now largely united behind a wise King who had changed his faith from Protestant to nominal Catholic, bringing peace to his strife-torn nation. The business community was expanding and creating wealth. An improved standard of living accompanied the economic changes. People had money to invest and they felt confident enough in their environment to risk it. Coupled with this, the head of state was an optimistic person. He fostered and encouraged the use of private capital to profit the individual and the state.

Henry's strategy was a forerunner of the colonizing schemes that led to the founding of the New England Colonies. He sensed there was money to be made in the fur trade. He knew also that to reap the potential in metals and minerals which Spain had so advantageously harvested, the land would have to have French settlers. His solution followed the simple expediency of granting monopolies to a merchant or a consortium in exchange for the promise to establish a French presence on the land.

On March 15, 1603, Champlain, representing the King of France, left the port of Honfleur at the mouth of the River Seine. He was aboard a 120-ton ship, La Bonne Renommée, bound for the Gulf of St. Lawrence. The ship's master was an experienced mariner by the name of Pontgrave. Champlain took an instant liking to the bluff sea captain. The respect was mutual, and the two men became lifelong friends.

La Bonne Renommée spent two months making her way across the Atlantic, beating against westerlies and threading past the floating mountains of ice moving southward off Greenland. In the latter part of May they slipped through Cabot Strait, between Newfoundland and Cape Breton, to sight fog-bound Anticosti Island. Sailing on flood tides Pontgrave brought his ship into the semi-protected basin of Tadoussac at the mouth of Saguenay River, long a rendezvous for trade between European fishermen and Algonquian speaking natives who inhabited that part of the St. Lawrence Valley.

Champlain stepped ashore onto land that one day he would nurture and prod into the genesis of a nation; but at Tadoussac he was in the centre of the Montagnais people, whom he refers to as *the Canadians*. That day witnessed a treaty struck between the Montagnais and Champlain, one that would significantly affect the development of New France.

Pontgrave on his previous voyage to these waters had persuaded two young men of the Montagnais nation to accompany him back to mainland France so that they might learn the language and act as emissaries to the New World. There they witnessed the marvels of civilization, apparently quite impressed by the gilded carriages drawn by 'moose without antlers'. They spent some time being interviewed by Court officials, and the King himself.

The visitors from the New World described their lifelong bloody feuds against the Iroquois. They received assurances from the French King that if peace with the enemy were impossible, France would send soldiers to assist the Montagnais people.

On the beach beneath the grim hills of the Saguenay, Champlain made the pact that would bind France for a century and a half to the cause of the Algonquin-speaking nations. Those migrant hunters ranged along the northern shores of the St. Lawrence, from the Ottawa River to the Atlantic, and southward into Maine and New Brunswick. As allies of the Algonquin people, the Hurons would also stand with the French. Their hereditary enemies, the Five Nation or Iroquois people would line up with the English. These alliances would shape and colour the history of all participants.

Champlain has been criticized by some who would will the past to be different than it is. They like to maintain that bloody warfare between Huron and Iroquois was economically inspired by the two main competing commercial groups, the French and the English. They believe that Champlain fomented war by forging a contract with the Algonquins and supporting them in battle.

The reality was, by the time Champlain appeared on the scene, the Iroquois had already decimated their own language kinsmen, the Hurons. They had chased them back up the St. Lawrence to their agricultural homeland on Lake Huron, far from Stadacona and Hochelaga (Quebec and Montreal) of Cartier's visitations.

The day Champlain landed on Canadian soil, combined forces of the Etchemins and the Montagnais were celebrating a great victory over the Iroquois with feasting and dancing; a *tabagie* they called it.

Their trophies were one hundred bloody Iroquois scalps dangling around the waists of the dancers. Champlain had landed smack in the middle of a war of extermination between two fierce antagonists. It was an ongoing war which had nothing to do with European influences. For his own cause to survive he had to choose sides. The alternative was annihilation by both forces.

It is here, at the mouth of the Saguenay, where Champlain made his key observation regarding the validity of overland travel by canoe:

Every man in a trice took down his lodge and the said grand Captain was the first to begin to take his canoe and carry it to the water, wherein he embarked his wife and children and a quantity of furs; and in like manner were launched well nigh 200 canoes, ... for though our shallop was well manned, yet they went more swiftly than we. When they wish to go overland to get somewhere they have business, they carry them.

Not only canoes caught the commander's eye. He spotted some light-weight, narrow wooden frames, interlaced with leather thongs, adorning the inner walls of the Montagnais' lodges. They aroused Champlain's curiosity. He questioned the owners as to the purpose of what resembled the tennis racquets used by the leisure class in France. To his surprise, those questioned plucked the rackets off the wall, put them on their feet and proceeded to clump about the clearing. By sign language they managed to convey to Champlain that the footgear was used when the snow lay deep upon the ground.

On his first day in Canada, Champlain found out the two basic methods of transportation for all-season wilderness travel, the canoe and the snowshoe. Later he would urge young Frenchmen to adopt these techniques in order to travel freely throughout North America.

Champlain also took an intense interest in native geography, recording how the Montagnais, following a ten-day journey up the Saguenay River, bartered for beaver and martin skins with tribes from the north who told them:

They are in sight of a sea which is salt. I hold that, if this is so, it is some gulf of our sea which overflows in the north into the midst of the continent.

He anticipated Henry Hudson by seven years, and seemed to grasp a more accurate mental picture of this vast unknown than many explorers who followed in his wake. In spite of a desire to find a route through to the Pacific Ocean he didn't confuse the Western Sea with the Northern Sea as had La Vérendrye and others, when they piled wishful thinking on top of misconstrued local information.

After three weeks in the Saguenay area, Champlain and Pontgrave set off up the River of Canada in a longboat, towing a skiff behind. The further he went, the more impressed he became with what the land had to offer. The expedition was stopped by the barrier of Lachine Rapids, of which Champlain said:

It is beyond the power of man to pass with any boat, however small it be. ... He who would pass must provide himself with canoes of the savage, which a man can easily carry. ... By directing one's course with the help of the savages, a man may see all that is to be seen within the space of a year or two.

Champlain was optimistic to think that he could see all of Canada in a year or two. Neither he nor any one else in his day could comprehend the immensity of the land. Although his E.T.A. was wrong by nearly 200 years, he was the first to point out both the correct method and the proper direction.

Champlain made a full report of his findings in this new world to Henry IV. The King, pleased with his Lieutenant's map, was impressed with the immensity of the primitive country and the potential for mineral exploitation. Surely he must have dreamed of emulating his rich and powerful neighbour to the south into whose lap poured gold and silver from New Spain. No doubt his critical eye caught Champlain's expressed hope for a water route across this new-found continent that stood in the way of sailing ships bound for the Orient.

As a step toward realizing these assets for France, Henry decreed that colonization should take place. Holding a small purse, Henry formed a policy of granting monopolies to licensed consortiums. *For purposes of settlement let individuals take the risk. The losses will be theirs but the gains will be for France.* If Henry had not been cut down by an assassin in May of 1610, a greater future might have been in store for France. He understood the need to encourage both the creation and the distribution of wealth. It is unfortunate that those two traits are so seldom found together in individuals who wield political power.

A name that is missing from most English-Canadian history books is that of Pierre du Gua, Sieur de Monts. He was a gentleman from Champlain's province of Saintonge who had fought under the flag of Henry of Navarre. With improvement in economic conditions as a result of peace and the sensible fiscal policies of the new ruler, he was able to make his fortune in the shipping trade. He operated out of Normandy and Brittany. Of the Protestant faith, he and Champlain nevertheless became firm friends. Without the backing of De Monts, who spent most of his hard won fortune in Canada, Champlain would not have been able to accomplish all that he did. The noted Canadian scholar, Marcel Trudel, said: "Without De Monts there would not be a Champlain."

Lack of space does not permit a fuller account of Champlain's focus for the next thirty-two years but he has been well covered by competent authors such as Professor Trudel, N.E. Dionne, the late S.E. Morison, and Morris Bishop. The most comprehensive work of all is the six volume set of Champlain's papers, published by the Champlain Society in French and English, and available in most libraries.

Over the next three years, Champlain carried out extensive exploration and mapping programs along the indented coastline called Acadia, fighting thirty-foot high tidal races and the dreaded scurvy. This area would one day become Nova Scotia and Maine.

Then, on July 3rd, 1608, a red letter day for Canadians, Champlain landed below the beetling promontory of Quebec to build his 'Habitation' on a point of land covered with a grove of nut trees. He spent the winter there in order to complete three two- story buildings, plus a warehouse and a pigeon loft.

Appreciating the fruits as well as the beauties of nature's bounties, Champlain laid gardens in ordered patterns outside the compound. A walkway from the entrance gate led down to a pier built into the bank of the St. Lawrence. Atop the highest building, a glistening sundial carried a flagstaff from which the lilies of France waved proudly in the breeze.

Winter came early. The first snowstorm whitened the land in November, a bleak month when two men died from dysentery. By February scurvy had spread its insidious sickness, even hardy Champlain contracting it for the first time. Eleven of his men died.

The green shoots of April finally put an end to their misery. Only eight sickly survivors, one third of the original party, made it through that winter of 1608-9. Two of them were young men by the names of Brûlé and Marsolet. Champlain diagnosed the debilitating condition as resulting from too great a dependency on salt meat: *I hold it to be true that with good bread and fresh meat, one would not be subject to it.*

In this supposition he was correct. Once colonists had learned to preserve their animal kills by subjecting them to nature's deep-freeze, little was heard of scurvy in New France.

Warm June weather heralded the arrival of ships from France and Champlain was soon in council with Pontgrave. They decided to ask the Montagnais of the lower St. Lawrence, the Algonquins of the Ottawa River and the Huron people, for guidance in exploration. In return, Champlain promised weaponry support in an attack on the Iroquois of the upper Richelieu River.

At Crown Point in Lake Champlain on July 30th, 1609, the managed confrontation took place. It did not last long. The shot from Champlain's *arquebus* felled three Iroquois Chiefs that summer morning. The sound from the explosion echoed up the green tree-clad hills surrounding the lake. It would continue to reverberate down all the valleys of the St. Lawrence, heralding a century-long conflict of massacre and bloodshed. The colonists of New France now had an implacable enemy, the Five-nation Brotherhood (later Six) of the Iroquois.

Champlain's victory in this first of three battles against the Iroquois had the effect that he sought. His native allies felt obliged to render some assistance, albeit grudgingly, to Champlain's bid for western exploration. Toward that end, Champlain persuaded the Huron and Ottawa tribes to accept a young Frenchman for a winter season. Etienne Brûlé would be exchanged for a Huron youth named Savignon who would journey to Europe with Champlain.

Brûlé was the first known European to penetrate Indian country west of Lachine Rapids. Over the next twenty years Champlain would send out a dozen young Frenchmen to learn the language and ways of the indigenous people. One was Jean Nicolet who arrived in Canada in 1619 to become an interpreter. He rendered a great service to civil authorities here and stayed on to father a large family whose many descendants are with us still.

Once Champlain had established his base at Quebec he formed an alliance with those who controlled the road toward the great unknown. He journeyed up the Ottawa in 1613 as far as present-day Morrison Island, the home of the principal chief of the Ottawa tribe. Surrounded by rapids, the island just below present day Pembroke, housed an armed guard which exacted a toll from all who passed.

Unable to proceed further that year, he stated: *I had to return, my desire unfulfilled to see the 'northern sea', where by this time the*

English had wintered. One might be amazed that Champlain would be apprised so soon after Henry Hudson's discovery of Hudson Bay in 1610. It demonstrates that he moved in high scientific and naval circles.

Two years later Champlain returned to journey up the Ottawa, this time in company with Brûlé and half a dozen soldiers. He came to map the country and to assist the Hurons of Georgian Bay in an attack upon the Iroquois. That historic trip westward via the Ottawa and French Rivers opened up the Great Lakes containment area to adventuresome Frenchmen. Fur traders in pursuit of mammon and zealous priests in search of souls would follow Champlain's road. Thanks to his efforts, the first section of Canada's Canoe Highway was in place and affixed to maps of an expanding North America by the year 1616.

For the rest of his life, Champlain remained dedicated to the settlement he had established that July day in 1608, on the northern shore of The St. Lawrence River. He made twenty-three crossings of the Atlantic, and wintered in Canada thirteen times. His last sailing was from France to Canada in 1633. It was a one way ticket. His once tough wiry body, worn out by thirty years of privation and frustration, had had enough. Suffering a debilitating stroke in November, 1635, the tired fighter laid down his life's burden on Christmas Day in Quebec.

As La Vérendrye had been prevented from finding a route through to the Pacific Ocean by jealous merchants and petty government officials, so too was Champlain held back from building upon his achievements. Champlain suffered a marked withdrawal of support from France after the assassination of Henry IV. Intrigues at Court and the inherent negativism of bureaucracy followed the loss of a strong leader. They were forces that combined to hold back the growth of his colony. The capture and invasion of Quebec by the five Kirke brothers in 1629, was the last straw. It marked the permanent breakdown of peaceful international relationship between France and Great Britain.

Champlain had to spend an inordinate amount of time travelling throughout France seeking political and financial help for his Canadian project. It is useless to speculate on 'what might have been', but there is little doubt that had Champlain received anywhere near the level of support Henry IV had granted, before his senseless murder by a religious zealot, much more would have been accomplished for Canada.

In a speech to the august Royal Chamber of Commerce, Champlain provided a revenue forecast for various industries that could be established in France's new realm. For fisheries, forestry, farming, mining and the fur trade, he set a production figure of 5,000,000 livres annually. In those days a livre was equal to a pound. later development would prove his figures were not just the mouthings of a visionary.

Champlain never witnessed his dream of greater grandeur. When he passed away, Quebec was still a small community of 200 hardy souls, struggling to survive under the rock that guarded the River to Canada. Yet, as founder of this nation, his life would cast a long shadow over us.

Fathers Le Jeune and Lalemant, Jesuit priests who respected and loved him dearly, gave the official blessing to a man mourned by natives and Frenchmen alike. He was buried in his 'City of the Narrows', Quebec.

The River of the Algonquins, from Sault St. Louis
to the vicinity of the Lake of the Bisserinis:
In it are more than 80 rapids great and small to pass.
Samuel de Champlain

Chapter Eighteen
The First Road West

On June 27, the fifth and final day of our Great Lakes crossing, Eastward Ho left Little Current, Manitoulin Island in the wake of Spray. The weather was perfect. Keeping up with our guide, however, meant we had no time for side trips. We should have investigated the multiple use of the name La Cloche, the Bell, applied to several land forms in this area: mountains, islands, and peninsula. Dr. Bigsby surveyed through here with David Thompson in the 1820's. The source, according to the good doctor, is a large, glacier-deposited, basaltic rock, perched on a lonely beach alongside the *voyageurs* track running between Great La Cloche and Manitoulan Islands. *Voyageurs* swore that the stone, when struck sharply, emitted a very audible bell-like ring.

By mid-afternoon, Eastward Ho was west of the Bustards, a cluster of tiny islands marking one of the many exits of the French River. Presumably, the islands were a stopping place for the migrating Canada geese which herald our spring and fall seasons. Skipper Bob stopped opposite a navigational beacon on one of the islets, and gave us a bearing to run north past Cantin Pt. to Main Outlet of the French River. Here we said a fond farewell to Spray's Captain and First Mate.

French River enters Lake Huron via four outlets; Western, Main, Eastern, and one it shares with an arm of the Pickerel River. Main Outlet had navigational markers and was the most direct route for Eastward Ho.

Voyageurs took the Western Outlet when entering or leaving Lake Huron. Returning from Mackinac or Sault Ste. Marie, and hugging the northern shore of Georgian Bay, they would round Lake Huron's welcome landmark of Pointe Grondine, a stony promontory whose poetic sounding name echoed the endless moaning of a restless sea that thrashed its skirting shoals. Once around it and behind a screen of islands, *voyageurs* could forget *La Vieille* for the rest of the homeward journey. They then entered Voyageurs Channel, the first of a three-pronged Western Outlet. This entry saved them eight miles of open water, a decided preference to the Main Outlet used by Eastward Ho.

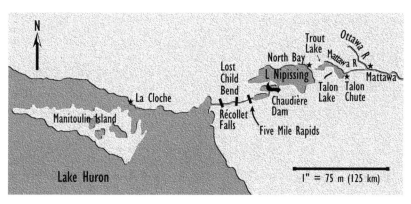

French – Mattawa Rivers

Champlain was impressed by the size of Lake Huron. He himself did not travel west of the mouth of French River, but his guides described it for him. He lumped Lakes Superior and Huron together when writing: *It is very large, being nearly 400 leagues in length from east to west and 50 leagues wide and because of its great size I named it the Freshwater Sea. It abounds in many kinds of excellent fish, ... and principally in trout which are of monstrous size; I have seen some that are as much as four and a half feet long ... Also pike of a like size and a certain kind of sturgeon, a very large fish and marvelously good to eat.*

Our *fifth man* was reporting on a body of water whose size would astound the average European. Almost half of France could be floated on our combined five Great Lakes.

Champlain met the *Cheveux relevés,* known collectively as the *Ottawas,* at the mouth of the French River. They would supplant the Hurons in the Great Lakes trade with Montreal, after the latter had been first Christianized by the church, then all but annihilated by the Iroquois.

French River rapids below Récollet Falls

Not far into the confines of the French River, we had to make a décharge up through a narrow, fast moving chute. Within six miles the track turned eastward at Wanapitei Bay, then came the CNR bridge, the First Rapids, and the approach to Récollet Falls.

Eric Morse described the French River as a rattling good run for downstream paddlers, but for travelling upstream he recommended the more placid Pickerel River which parallels the French.

We carried out our promise made to Bob Andrews in Sault Ste. Marie, depositing a note in a rock cairn near the Récollet Falls. A wooden ramp has replaced the original portage path of forty-five paces.

These falls were named for Récollet priests who came to Quebec with Champlain in 1615. They belonged to an order of

Franciscan monks from a convent in Brouage, Champlain's home town. They were the first missionaries to arrive in the valley of the St. Lawrence River. Two of the friars, Fathers Denis and Joseph, have the distinction of conducting the first mass held on that historic waterway.

The first known European to see this country was Etienne Brûlé. In June of 1610, he accompanied a party of Huron warriors back to Lake Huron to spend the winter learning their ways and language. The second was the overly eager Father Joseph Le Caron who had pushed on in front of Champlain to Lake Huron. Le Caron's precipitate action in leaving for the *pays d'en haut* brought forth a mild rebuke from Champlain. After arriving at Lachine Rapids in July of 1615, he wrote:

They told me that Father Joseph had set out with twelve Frenchmen who had been loaned to the savages to assist them. (In the attack against the Iroquois). This news troubled me, seeing that had I been there, I should have ordered many things for the journey which I was now not able to do, both in respect to the small number of men and also because there were not more than four or five who knew how to handle firearms, seeing that in such an undertaking the best are none too good.

Had Champlain been provided with the kind of military support he had originally planned for, in the combined operations against the Iroquois in the south-east corner of Lake Ontario, history books might have been written differently. He did not consider the campaign against the Iroquois a success.

Champlain was not impressed with the terrain bordering the French River. He had an eye for potential agricultural sites and never failed to put a 'French garden' in his settlements; a garden that nourished a combination of fruits, vegetables and flowering plants. Quite the loveliest kind of gardens, they are still prevalent in France today. But of the French River, he stated:

Having rested two days with the chief of the said Nipissings, we re-embarked in our canoes and entered a river flowing out of this lake and made some thirty-five leagues along it. We passed several little rapids, some by portaging, others by running them, as far as Lake Attigouautan (Huron). This whole region is even more unprepossessing than the former; for I do not see in the whole length of it ten acres of arable land, but only rocks and a country somewhat hilly.

The river and its landscape have remained relatively unchanged since Champlain's day. The only lasting crops are summer tourists who add colour and noise to the river every July and August.

Ross Cox's Columbia River party passed through here on the first of September, 1817, having left Fort George, the NWC post at the mouth of the Columbia River, on the 16th of April. Their journey from the Pacific Ocean to Montreal took five months and three days which was the average elapsed time for a transcontinental canoe brigade. Such constancy speaks well for the transport efficiency of the fur trade.

That evening, Eastward Ho met Hugh McMillan and his family travelling in a twenty-five foot voyageur canoe. Hugh, an archivist with the Province of Ontario, was collecting material for the Northwest Museum at Williamstown. He was also organizing a canoeing venture consisting of paddlers whose ancestors were Nor'Westers. Hugh was a descendant of James McMillan who clerked under David Thompson, and who, in 1827, journeyed from the mouth of the Columbia River to the Fraser River to establish Fort Langley. He went on to became a Chief Trader with the HBC.

Three miles east of Highway 69, the course took a sudden jog northward, then straightened out on its east-west track. This sharp right angle is labeled Lost Child Bend. The reason for this provocative title is contained in the journal of Daniel Harmon, a NWC fur trader making his first journey to the *pays d'en haut*. His explanation was as follows:

Several years since, the natives, being encamped here, lost a child, for whom they made diligent search, but in vain. They imagined however that they heard its lamentations in the bowels of the earth; whereupon they commenced digging. But to no purpose. Their reasoning was that the 'Bad Spirit' was continually carrying him from one place to another in the earth. Many large holes have actually been dug in the earth, as our people have shown me.

Daniel Harmon also commented on the number of white crosses bestrewn upon the banks of the canoe route wherever a particularly notorious rapid was found.

The Canadian Voyageurs, when they leave one stream to go up or down another have a custom of pulling off their hats and making the sign of the cross, upon which one in each canoe, or at least in each brigade, repeats a short prayer. The same ceremonies are observed when they pass a place where one of their own has been interred and a cross erected. Those who are in the habit of voyaging this way are obliged to say their prayers more frequently than at home. For almost every rapid we have passed since leaving Montreal, we have seen a number of crosses erected. At one I counted no less than thirty.

There have been some name changes since the days of the *voyageurs*, but essentially the rapids are the same today as when Champlain was conducted through here by native paddlers. Collectively called Five Mile Rapids, Eastward Ho passed through Crooked, Big Parisiene, Double Rapids, and Big Pine.

With those rapids under our belts, one final effort called for a mile portage around Chaudière dam spillway. After completion we dropped our canoe into Lake Nipissing. As darkness was almost upon us, we stopped at the first likely looking camping site, a small island in the southern portion of Lake Nipissing.

The air was oppressive and still, like a prelude to the frequent thunderstorms which blast in without warning to roil up the lake. This area is notorious for those life-threatening summer squalls, and the *voyageurs* referred to the crossing as la Grande Traverse.

It was a scratchy night. Not only had all the mosquitoes of the island gathered with us on this grassy promontory, but in the dying light of day we had inadvertently pitched the tent on top of a nest of ants. We left earlier than usual the next morning.

Eastward Ho's destination was North Bay, although the *voyageurs* headed toward the mouth of a shallow stream they called *Rivière des Vases,* Muddy River. This insignificant stream had historic connections. For weary paddlers who, for centuries had been heading homeward from the *pays d'en haut,* it marked the final stint of upstream work.

The low-lying height of land provided one final mud-sucking carry which would put the *voyageurs* onto the Mattawa River, a tributary of the Ottawa River system. Soon they would be applying their brakes by back-paddling through several wild downhill runs on their way to families and friends of the St. Lawrence Valley.

La Vase is a landmark on the Champlain Trail. From the mouth of this 'Old Muddy', Samuel Champlain himself caught his first glimpse of Lake Nipissing. Here he rested to write:

We entered the Lake of the Nipissings in latitude 46°15'. This done we reached the lodges of the savages where we stayed two days. They gave a kind reception and were in goodly number.

In North Bay, where we celebrated Canada's birthday, Eastward Ho received the same kind hospitality from their Nipissing hosts as had Champlain in 1615.

For the first time since departing New Westminster three months earlier, we had a few days in reserve. We decided to remove our motor, with its accompanying gas and oil tanks, and paddle the Mattawa River.

A three mile trek was made from Lake Nipissing to Trout Lake. A tail wind gave an assist along the Lake to what used to be a constriction called Décharge de la Tortue. This has since been rock-blasted to provide a boat channel. A down-river dam keeps it navigable throughout the year. The small lake entered from Trout was called Turtle Lake on our maps, but Mackenzie and others applied 'Turtle' to both.

Champlain provides little detail of the short Mattawa River but Mackenzie refers to it as *'La Petite Rivière'*. The first portage was called, *Mauvaise de la Musique*.

Mackenzie referred to it as a dangerous place that had disabled many young men, and Ross Cox from his passage eastward in 1817, recounted a grisly tale that occurred there.

A *voyageur*, carrying his share of a *montreal* canoe, tripped and fell awkwardly when passing a large rock. The canoe sliced across his neck, completely severing the head. Cox saw the *voyageur's* grave in the middle of the pathway, which served as a warning to over-hasty portagers.

The next carry brought us to mile-long Lake Robichaud, out of which another portage, *Portage des Pins de la Musique*, put us into McCool Bay of Talon Lake.

Curiosity was aroused by the repetitive use of the word 'Musique', but no explanation was found for this reference to the English word 'music'. A friend said, "'Musique' is sometimes used in a figurative sense to mean 'repeating', as to say, 'Here's that song again'." Far-fetched perhaps, but it may explain the use of 'musique' for two adjacent portages.

At the bottom end of Lake Talon, we encountered the nefarious Talon Chute about which all west-bound *voyageurs* complained. *Observer* Mackenzie said: *Talon Chute is 275 paces, which for its length is the worst on the communication.*

For Eastward Ho, the Talon Chute was not too arduous. Without the motor we got by with two carries in place of the *voyageurs'* five portages. Although our canoe never seemed light, we eventually became more adept at handling it. The technique was for three to hoist it onto their shoulders, upside down, one man under the stern, two on opposite sides nearer the bow. This took up minimum width on a narrow trail, and left one man free to rest a few paces before stepping in to relieve.

Generally, only four *voyageurs* were required for those huge *canots de maître*. They were almost twice as long, and weighed three times as much as our Big Red.

The waterfalls and steep trails of Talon Chute were picturesque. One trekker of the Mattawa, our familiar Dr. Bigsby, when accompanying a canoe brigade up from Montreal, described an unusual scene:

Picking my steps carefully as I passed over rugged ground, laden with things personal and culinary, I suddenly stumbled upon a pleasing young lady, sitting alone under a bush, in a green riding habit and white beaver bonnet. Transfixed with a sight so out of place in the land of the eagle and the cataract, I seriously thought I had a vision.

Having paid my respects, with some confusion (much amused she seemed), I learned that she was the daughter of an esteemed trader, Mr. Ermatinger, and on her way to the falls of St. Mary with her father, who was then with his people, at the other end of the portage. And so it turned out a fortnight afterwards, I partook of the cordialities of her Indian home, enjoyed the excellence of her tea, and the pleasantness of the evening.

Our map showed three portages which Mackenzie listed in descending order, all within a single mile: *de la Cave, de la Prairie* and *des Paresseux.*

Eastward Ho did not find it necessary to use the well marked portage trails. Wearing running shoes, we jumped out to guide the canoe by hand over a riverbed of rounded boulders. Unlike B.C. and Albertan glacial rivers, these lake-fed streams do not turn your legs blue. The canoe left a few tell-tale red streaks behind on the stones, but suffered no real damage.

In the *décharge de la Prairie* one can see the cascading white sheen of *Petite Paresseux Falls* entering the Mattawa River. Set against a multi-green forested background of ash, spruce, birch and poplar, it made a *picture postcard.*

Big Paresseux Falls followed, before the river bent eastward. The view, looking down the lush, green valley stretching toward the twenty-foot waterfall presented a marvelous sight. Portaging around its base was not so lovely. The trail was steep, narrow, and rocky.

Paresseux can mean '*slow* or *lazy*'. A reference perhaps to the deliberate way water seems to drop over these falls, or it may have been the way in which the *voyageurs* tackled this particular carry. *Observer* Harmon called it *lazy portage.*

Lunch was eaten on Bouillon Lake, where presumably *voyageurs* had a soup break. Then came several minor rapids. Travelling in the same direction as Eastward Ho, Ross Cox had listed them as *décharges*, but Mackenzie, coming uphill, described them as *portages.* The map showed *Les Epingles, des Roches,* and *Campion,* in descending order.

Two early impediments known by Mackenzie as *Décharge des Roses* and *Portage du Plein Champ* are buried under water backed up by a coffer dam at the lower end of Chant Plain Lake. The dam was the last carry on the Mattawa. We passed Mattawa City, camping above the railway bridge across the Ottawa River. Ahead of us flowed Champlain's *la Grande Rivière du Nord.*

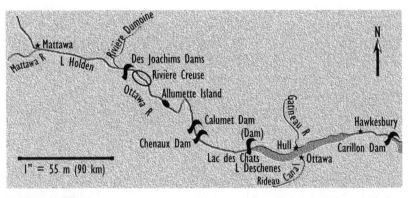

The Ottawa River

That evening called for a double celebration. It was Bill Gifford's sixty-first birthday, and Eastward Ho was now poised on the Ottawa River, the last major communication link between the Pacific Ocean and the St. Lawrence River. The long-sought goal was barely a week away.

The Ottawa River originates in Lake Capimitchigami, 400 canoe miles north-east of Mattawa. From Mattawa to the St. Lawrence River, a distance of 300 miles, it drops 470 vertical feet. It is the St. Lawrence River's largest tributary.

Due to its horseshoe-like shape, the Ottawa forms many connections with other drainage systems. The upper reaches of the Abitibi River are nearby to float canoes north to Hudson Bay. The Gatineau and the St. Maurice Rivers provided an eastern corridor for the far-ranging Algonquian people when they had to by-pass the vigilant Iroquois on the St. Lawrence River. The forebears of those who showed Champlain the way had used these and dozens of other routes for centuries. *La Grande Rivière du Nord* was truly the gateway to the *pays d'en haut.*

The Ottawa of the *voyageurs* was not a gentle winding stream, but a dangerous and unforgiving river, exacting a heavy toll in men and equipment. It remained a challenge until the building of canals and dams in the mid 1800's tamed its raw power. For the *coureur de bois* and the professional *voyageurs* who followed, there were eighteen formidable portages.

The river also had resolute guardians. An Algonquin clan, stationed on Allumette Island, attempted to exercise control over those wanting to use the Ottawa for trading purposes. They turned Champlain back on his first venture up the Ottawa in 1613.

In 1634 Champlain sent Jean Nicolet up the Ottawa to look for the China Sea. Nicolet was so confident of catching a whiff of the Orient he even packed a Chinese kimono in order to 'dress for the occasion'. He did not reach the 'far-east', but he came closer to it than anyone else by coasting along Lake Michigan to Green Bay and Fox River. One wonders if he ever donned his attire to impress the locals.

The Ottawa has long been a military river. Champlain himself used it in his 1615-16 campaign against the Iroquois of Lake Ontario. Adam Dollard's small band of heroes fought their last battle on the banks of that river. In 1686, the Chevalier de Troyes led 100 men up the Ottawa and down the Abitibi River to capture all the Hudson's Bay Co. posts in James Bay.

During New France's troubles with the Iroquois, and later in the Canada-U.S. war of 1812, the Ottawa was an access route to the Great Lakes that could be maintained from Montreal.

Following the surrender of Montreal to General Amherst in 1760, the Ottawa River quickly reverted to its use as a trade corridor. British entrepreneurs from New York, having furnished Amherst's army in the field, remained to work with French merchants who were the long standing experts in the fur trade. The English supplied the capital and markets, the French had the manpower and the know-how.

Men such as Alexander Henry Sr. linked themselves with Canadian interests and followed the Ottawa track. In 1767, more than 120 westward bound canoes cleared the warehouses at Mackinac, carrying trade goods with a book value of £40,000 sterling, a sizable investment in 18th century monetary values. Expenditures like this had a tremendous impact on the total economy of Canada. Risks were great, but so were profits.

Enterprising men of both tongues formed relationships beneficial to each party. True bilingualism and capitalism were working partners in an early, united Canada.

It may interest the reader to have some idea of what men in the field were paid. The financial career of Jean Baptiste Bernard, Gov. Simpson's guide during his 1828 trans-Canada tour, can be traced in Simpson's '1828 Journal to the Colombia', published by the Hudson Bay Record Society. Bernard was hired by the NWC in 1811 at an annual wage of 300 Livres, in North West Currency. That was equal to £25 Halifax Currency or £22.10s. Sterling. By 1820 he was receiving £65.16.3d. Sterling. After amalgamation in 1821, he received £90 Sterling from the HBC.

At that time, £1 was the equivalent of $5.00. A conservative estimate of inflation for the 200 year interim between then and now would be somewhere around 100 times. Thus his salary would be at least $50,000.00 a year. Perhaps double that. Jean Baptiste was a valuable man, and at the top of his category.

Not only itinerant fur merchants, soldiers, and explorers followed this water highway. From the moment it was open, men dedicated to the greater glory of 'God the Spirit', toiled along this trail of suffering. Récollet and Jesuit Orders tried mightily to ease the inevitable strain in the clash between European and native cultures. The stories of their sacrifices are lessons in courage.

Récollet Father Le Caron wrote: *It would be hard to tell you how tired I was, paddling all day with all my strength, among the Indians; wading the rivers a hundred times or more, through the mud and over the sharp rocks that cut my feet; carrying the canoe and luggage through the woods to avoid the rapids and frightful cataracts; and half starved all the while, for we had nothing to eat but a little sagamite, a sort of porridge of water and pounded maize, of which they gave us an allowance every morning and night. But I must needs tell you what abundant consolation I found under all my troubles; for when one sees so many infidels needing nothing but a drop of water to make them children of God, one feels an inexpressible ardour to labour for their conversion and to sacrifice to it one's repose and life.*

Such an attitude can move mountains. In pursuit of a Holy Grail, those 'men of God' beat their way through snagging brush, pulled themselves in and out of canoes a dozen times a day, and slept shivering in flea-ridden camps. They did so while clad in long wool robes that dragged on the ground and became heavier and heavier as they sucked up water like a sponge. Sharp stones bruised sandal-covered feet, and made them bleed like those of their beloved leader, who sacrificed himself in order that they might be inspired.

Eastward Ho departed Mattawa on the 4th of July in a dampening drizzle which soon turned into a downpour. But happily the wind was at our backs. With a favourable wind and current, and the 'voyageur' strapped to our stern once more, progress was rapid. Conditions conspired to ease our way now that there was time to spare.

The next body of water was Lake Holden, a backup from Des Joachims Dam. A carry across its spillway was the only hurdle to slow us down that day. Des Joachims was the first of six dams encountered on the Ottawa River. They have brought benefits of course, but they have removed much beauty and many exciting challenges.

Under man-made Lake Holden, *voyageurs* had faced eight river obstructions. The first three were within twenty-miles of the Mattawa River, and the name of the uppermost one has received at least four different spellings: *Levellier* according to Mackenzie; corrected to *La Veillée* by Dr. Lamb; referred to in the adjectival form by Cox as *L'Eveillée;* and in the infinitive by Morse as *l'Eveiller.* All conveyed the same meaning, *be alert* or, *on guard.*

Next was *Décharge du Trou* (the Hole) and finally *Deux Rivières portage.* In another twenty-mile section Eastward Ho cruised over what was once the portage of mile-long *Roche Capitaine Island* of which *observer* Harmon wrote:

This portage is so named from a large rock that rises to a considerable height above the water in the middle of the rapid. During the day we have come upon several difficult ones where many persons have drowned. At this place I saw no less than fourteen crosses.

Captain's Rock was followed by a *décharge* and a rapid which required at least two trips. *Voyageurs* often stopped to do business at a trading post built by the De Moyne family at the forks of a tributary called *Rivière du Moine.* A fortified post during the French regime, in the early days of the NWC it was the first place of commerce east of Sault Ste. Marie.

Within nine miles of De Moyne's river, *voyageurs* would make two difficult carries known as *Des Joachims*. The upper one was 1400 yards and the lower one about a mile. In between was a small pond covering perhaps fifty yards. Here the 'old-timers' did a little leg-pulling at the expense of the 'new-boys'. The 'juniors' were forewarned that, "Often canoes can't make way against the terrific head-winds that blow on the *expansive* lake you are about to see."

Below the Joachims, the Ottawa River ran straight and deep for thirty-two miles through a section that was referred to by a different name. In fact, it was treated almost as another river. They called it *Rivière Creuse* or Deep River. After miles of heartbreaking toil, where every foot gained required extreme physical effort, to come upon a sudden transition of unhampered progress would probably give the feeling of entering a new river.

There was also a long, sandy point of land referred to as *Pointe au Baptême. Observer* Daniel Harmon remembered it:

The Voyageurs, as the men are called, have many of the customs of sailors; and among them the following. By all those on board who have never passed certain places, they expect to be treated with something to drink; and should a person refuse to comply with their requisitions, he would be very sure of being plunged into the water, which they profanely call, baptizing him. To avoid such a disaster I gave the people of my canoe a few bottles of spirits and porter, by drinking which, they became very merry and exhibited the reverse of their appearance a few days since, when, with heavy hearts and weeping eyes, they parted from their relations.

As the Ottawa River breaks out of the rocky grip of the Laurentian Mountains, it slows into south-east trending Allumette Lake, so named for the reeds that grew there which were used as tapers by the First Nation population. A diversion leaves the main body of water a few miles into the lake and runs due east for fifteen miles. This route begins with the *Culbute Rapids,* then rejoins the Ottawa after both streams have encircled Allumette Island. Eastward Ho went by way of Allumette Lake to camp overnight at Pembroke. Across the lake was Morrison Island which our *fifth man* Champlain reported first visiting in 1613.

Eastward Ho, after leaving Pembroke, had to find a way through the Allumette Rapids which rushed past Morrison Island. They aren't as formidable now as they were in the early days before water levels started backing up from the Calumet dam, but there was enough white water to make it exciting. We chose the far left or Quebec side and hustled down through the wild, white passage, paddling and stemming our way around the largest curlers.

We saw no hint of the Paquette Rapids which were marked on the map. Then came Lac Coulonge. After Fort Coulonge the turn was sharply east, entering a narrow passage that led into the voyageur's track called Grand Calumet Channel. Quebec Hydro gave us a boost by trucking the canoe around.

Calumet Dam was built upon the longest portage the *voyageurs* faced this side of Grand Portage, over a mile and a third. Our *fifth man* said: *The stones in the rapids surrounding Calumet Island were like alabaster.*

Observer Alexander Henry Sr. noted: *... the pierre a calumet was a compact limestone, soft enough to be whittled into pipes or 'calumets' by both Indians and Canadians. The ascent of this carrying-place is not more fatiguing than the descent is dangerous. In performing it, accidents too often occur, producing strains, ruptures and injuries for life. A charitable fund is now established in Montreal for the relief of such disabled and decayed voyageurs.*

It is eight miles across Lac du Rocher-Fendu to Chenaux dam which created the lake. Translated it means 'split rock' or a 'gorge'.

The four rapids drowned by Lac du Rocher-Fendu were *Décharge of the Derigé*, the *Mountain Portage*, the *Décharge du Sable* and *Portage du Fort*.

One can see how generations of fathers and sons would develop intense feelings about a river which had touched their families and friends in such intimate ways. Not unlike the attitude that ocean-going fisher-folk had toward the sea, which brought them both life and death.

Eastward Ho came to shore on the Quebec side of Chenaux dam. Next was twenty-mile *Lac des Chats*. Two miles below the dam on the west side of the lake was the mouth of a stream coming down from Town Lake. This was the turnoff that Champlain took to bypass the Ottawa River. Champlain had a difficult passage, with portages to be made between Olmsted and Muskrat Lakes. An even longer carry put him back on the Ottawa River at the deep bend of Lake Allumette's horseshoe. It was a killer of a trip; sixteen-miles of canoeing, eight-miles of bush-whacking. It had to have been pretty difficult for the stoic Champlain to gripe over travel conditions. He had windfalls to drag canoes over, mosquitoes thick enough to drive a man crazy, and a primitive, coarse diet to put in his belly.

Champlain is purported to have lost an *astrolabe*, (a type of sextant for surveying) in these woods. In August of 1867 near Green Lake, a fourteen year old lad stumbled upon just such an artifact. Champlain himself said he was toting: *three arquebuses, an equal number of paddles, my cloak and some petites bagatelles.*

On his downstream return trip, Champlain's party stayed with the Ottawa, choosing the course that ran them down the western side of Ile Calumet. He must have been glad he was in the company of the son of Chief Tessouat. The rapids which his native guides took him through were impressive enough for him to write: *... a most unpleasant country. I saw clearly that had we come up this way, we should have encountered many more difficulties and should barely have got through; ...*

On his initial venture up the Ottawa, Champlain was attempting to liaise with Nipissing people further northward, as well as hoping to get a glimpse of Hudson Bay which the doomed Henry Hudson had sailed into the summer of 1610. In Lake Allumette Champlain came upon a group of Algonquins jealously guarding this portion of the standard canoe route. From their headquarters on Morrison Island, they controlled Allumette Rapids, and thus traffic on this part of the river. They exacted tolls from all who wished to go this way.

Their chief, Tessouat, did not want to anger Champlain with an outright refusal. They had met at Tadoussac beside the mouth of the Saguenay River ten years before. Tessuoat respected those pale-faced men and their arms that disgorged fire and death. At the same time, his council of elders did not want their position as guardians of the river preempted. Thus they politely dragged their feet. It took two more years before Champlain could return to challenge Tessouat with a stronger hand.

Meanwhile, to register the presence of France in this new-found wilderness, our *fifth man* had a cross built and erected on the bottom end of Allumette Island. He described it thus: *Of white cedar, bearing the arms of France, which I set up on a prominent place on the shore of the lake.*

After planting his flag, Champlain issued an invitation to all those present: *Come to the St. Louis rapids where lie four ships loaded with all sorts of merchandise and where you will receive good treatment.*

A fair deal in other words. His customers must have taken Champlain at his word. By the time the inducement had been passed around from camp to camp, he had a flotilla of eighty canoes sweeping down the Ottawa with him.

By evening, Eastward Ho had reached the bottom of Lac des Chats and the dam where the former Portage des Chats lies buried. The Chats were a mile across and Bigsby called them *Magnificent in time of flood, second only to the incomparable Niagara*.

The 1966 Spring edition of the Beaver said: "*Chat sauvage* had long been the popular name for the raccoons that once teemed here when the cascades were called the Sault des Chats Sauvages." Could it have been because *the rapids spat and roared like angry raccoons?*

Twenty-mile Lake Deschênes, (Lake of Oaks), was next. We pulled out at Britannia Bay Yacht Club around noon to inspect the Deschênes Rapids. They didn't appear particularly awesome. We decided to take them on the right hand, or south side of the river.

The *voyageurs'* track was on the north side of the river, but the backing up of the Ottawa has changed the relative difficulties. Some 'dear soul' mentioned to us that a large canoe party had met disaster here a short time ago, which resulted in several drownings. We re-inspected the projected course, but saw no reason to change.

We pushed off into the bubbling stream. Since the course chosen looked pretty shallow, we had removed the motor. Paddling around a bend we came onto the top of the first chute which displayed plenty of white water. We dropped over a ledge hitting the step below with a resounding crack, then continued on along the south side of the Ottawa River to Remic rapids, passing small islands, and gliding underneath the Hull-Ottawa Bridge. The Remics were less than the Deschênes, and were followed by the final drop of Little Chaudière Rapids, runnable on the Ontario side. We stopped in Nepean Bay.

Ottawa is a lovely city but the natural scenery was even more spectacular in the days of the *voyageurs*, with the Chaudière falls providing the main attraction. 'Chaudière', which to the *voyageurs* meant a boiler or kettle, was a favoured name, and had been applied to three other waterfalls Eastward Ho had passed. Mackenzie used that term for what is now Lake Deschênes, referring to the latter as *Lac des Chaudières*. He said the portage was 740 paces, and for goods only. He listed it as the topmost of three *Chaudière portages*. The rapids had a descent of nine feet. He doesn't mention the Remic rapids, doubtless because they were neither portaged nor décharged but generally poled through with full loads. His second *Portage de Chaudière* was a carry of 700 paces, for lading only. The canoe was lined up as in a *décharge*.

All early travellers were mightily impressed by the view that lay before them as they journeyed upstream to this meeting place of three rivers, the Gatineau, Rideau, and Ottawa.

Champlain described the approaches, although names of the tributaries wouldn't come for several years. First, he mentions entry of the Gatineau river whose headwaters provide access to the St. Maurice River. The name Gatineau came from Nicholas Gatineau of Trois Rivières who, in 1650, to avoid the lower Ottawa river, went up the Gatineau and down the St. Maurice River to the St. Lawrence. At that time, parts of the Ottawa River were controlled by Mohawks, members of the Six Nation Iroquois Confederacy.

Our *fifth man* speaks of what would be the Rideau River, entering from the south: *At its mouth is a wonderful waterfall. From a height of 25 fathoms it falls with such impetuosity that it forms an archway nearly four hundred yards in width. The Indians for the fun of it pass underneath this without getting wet, except for the spray made by the falling water. ... The surrounding region is filled with all sorts of game so that the Indians like to make a halt here. The Iroquois also come here sometimes and surprise them.*

Eastward Ho and Parliament Buildings

Passing on, Champlain's party advanced towards Chaudière Falls: *At one place the water falls with such force upon a rock that with the lapse of time it has hollowed out a wide deep basin. Herein the water whirls around to such an extent that the Indians call it 'Asticou' which means 'boiler'. This water fall makes such a noise in this basin that it can be heard for more than two leagues away.*

Before leaving Ottawa, on July 11th, Eastward Ho had to walk the mail from the termination point in Nepean Bay to the river in front of the parliamentary library building, where the bags were placed in the canoe.

We continued on past Rockland, Thurso and Montebello and under the bridge between Grenville and Hawkesbury. While camped at Hawkesbury that evening, we met an interesting young man named Pierre Maisonneuve. His distinguished surname was shared with the founder of Montreal, and he was well versed in the French period of early Canada.

Eastward Ho was indeed passing over history in this brief stretch of the river. The twelve miles below Hawkesbury comprised what *voyageurs* called the Long Sault. It was made up of three sets of rapids. Looking downstream, the first was the five mile *Long Sault* proper, with a 1,000 yard portage. Next in line was *Chute a Blondeau*, 140 yards. Then *Carillon Rapids* with an 1120-yard portage. Ross Cox said the navigation of these rapids was so dangerous that special pilots were made available to take brigade canoes through.

Our *fifth man* had some difficulty here, as he tells us: *So great is the swiftness of the current that it makes a dreadful noise and falling from level to level produces everywhere such a white foam that no water at all is seen ... In tracking my canoe 1 nearly lost my life. The canoe turned broadside into a whirlpool and had 1 not luckily fallen between two rocks, the canoe would have dragged me in. 1 could not quickly enough loosen the rope which twisted round my hand, which hurt me very much and nearly cut it off. In this danger 1 cried aloud to God. ... and having escaped, 1 gave praise to him.*

Carillon Dam has eradicated all the above mentioned river challenges. Completed in 1960, it dwarfs the five previous dams carried over. Its single lock has a vertical range of sixty feet. Descending while afloat on top of the dropping water level was like plummeting into an open mine shaft. Dark concrete walls loomed above, their sides covered with slithering black eels, and wriggling grey-green lampreys clinging unsuccessfully to the ever increasing height of the enclosure. The lock could accommodate several large motor cruisers but the Eastward Ho canoe was the only vessel on this ride.

Carillon Dam drowned the site of Canada's most venerable shrine, the blood-strewn ground where the New-world Battle of Thermopylae took place in the summer of 1660. It was on the Quebec shore at the foot of these rapids that twenty-three heroes laid down their lives for New France. The brave twenty-three were Adam Dollard, sixteen young Montreal companions, a single brave Huron Chief, and five stalwart members of an Algonquin tribe. They died to a man to save the citizens of Montreal, Three Rivers, and Quebec from a threatened siege by the mighty Iroquois. It is a story every Quebecer knows by heart.

Perhaps today's children of western Canada are better informed than we were from our early schooling. Out west my generation missed many truly exciting episodes of Canadian history. Pages from the French period literally ring with peals of heroism and sacrifice. Is it any wonder that in the development of Canada, they see themselves as a 'distinct society'? The Quebec Act of 1774 confirmed it. As a Canadian of British heritage I'm proud of my inheritance, but I expand my own dimensions by sharing in Quebec's uniqueness.

Emerging from the bowels of the lock, we passed Pointe Fortune, then Pointe au Sable, and Carillon Island. On the more open water of Lake of Two Mountains, higher waves started breaking over the canoe. Many yachts passed on their way up the Ottawa, bound for the Great Lakes via the Rideau Canal. The countryside began to level out.

From the Oka Reserve we hustled across the widest expanse of Lac des Deux Montagnes to the church of Ste. Anne de-Bellevue on the western tip of Montreal Island, entering the canal beside it. For *voyageurs*, the journey to the *pays d'en haut* began here, and not where they started their canoes at Lachine, fifteen miles downstream. At *la petite chapelle de Sainte Anne*, the guardian angel of all travellers over water, they received the blessing of the priest and dropped their mites into the collection box.

With these observances attended to, the men would carry on a little further, camp, and then proceed to get uproariously drunk in one final farewell to civilization.

Eastward Ho ran down the canal where once the *voyageurs* had to make a décharge, then continued into Lac St. Louis and the junction of the Ottawa with the St. Lawrence. We had reached the thirteenth, and at the same time the *first* river of "Canada's Forgotten Highway."

On the north side of the St. Lawrence, we paddled through tall reeds to locate the house of a friend who had agreed to let us camp on her front lawn. We were hoping for an early get-away in the morning. As we parted the last screen of reeds, there was Bill Gifford, ensconced on a lawn chair, taking his ease. He greeted us with, "Well, if ain't the canoodlers. What took you so long?"

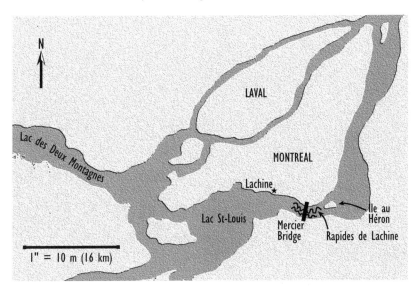

Montreal

*At length we arrived at the entrance of the rapid
and came to an island, almost in the midst
of the said entrance. I named it Isle Ste Hélène.*

Samuel de Champlain

Chapter Nineteen
Journey's End

The Lachine rapids have changed little since Champlain's day. He referred to them as the St. Louis rapids, after a young Frenchman named Louis who drowned there in the summer of 1611. Louis had been bird hunting on Ile au Héron with two native companions, one of whom was Savignon, the Huron lad Champlain had introduced to the Royal Courts of France. Savignon was the lone survivor after their overloaded canoe capsized in the rapids.

Champlain commented on the accident: *The following day I went in another canoe to the rapid to see the place where the two had perished. ... I assure you, when Savignon showed me the spot my hair stood on end. ... I was astonished that the victims had been so lacking in judgment as to go through such a frightful place.*

Sleep did not come easily to Eastward Ho on this last night beside the river. Tomorrow would be the day we had worked toward for the past three and a half months. The last river hazard would not be the place to break down, to be late, or to lose the canoe and canoe-mail.

Montreal Island is the hub of the wheel for many interfaces. Two mighty rivers, the Ottawa and the St. Lawrence join forces to create several rapid infested channels and four verdant islands, the largest of which is Montreal.

Long before Champlain arrived on the scene, this area had witnessed First Nations contending for control of Hochelaga, Cartier's name for the island of Montreal. And as the people before them, European merchants saw Montreal's potential as a great trading entrepôt. The Church of Rome also recognized its value as a place from which to spread the word of God. Christian faith created the story of Ville Marie.

On a lovely May morning, under the inspired leadership of Sieur de Maisonneuve, a small band of dedicated followers came ashore with him to 'cast their grain of mustard seed'. The *Société de Notre-Dame de Montréal* established the site of Montreal in the spring of 1642.

The departing prow of Eastward Ho's canoe separated the green reeds lapped by the St. Lawrence River. The upper rapids were less than a mile away. A press boat lingered off shore for a last minute interview. A helicopter hovered overhead, broadcasting our progress down the rapids.

There was a mile of white water between us and Mercier Bridge, which joins Caughnawaga to La Salle. We kept to the middle of the river and came through unscathed.

Three miles of fast moving but relatively smooth water brought us to Ile au Héron along St. Lawrence's northern shore. Ahead the sight of wild horses tossing their white manes set Eastward Ho back-paddling furiously. To no avail. The canoe slipped closer to the whirling vortexes.

"You'd better get the motor going," Jim called out, "If we're to stay away from that mess!"

With a silent prayer of, "Let it start," I pulled the cord. Our faithful voyageur roared into life. We spun around, headed upstream, and glided across the river above the rapids, looking for a less formidable slot to enter. Seeing none, we heeded Champlain's advice and went over to the south shore of the St. Lawrence River.

Everywhere angry waves stretched across our path. But we had to get through. The helmsman once more turned the canoe downstream toward the rapids. He raised the motor. Each man took up his paddle and mentally crossed his fingers. The river was simply snorting along, dropping over shallow rock ledges in a series of vertical falls. The canoe plummeted through a mixture of air and foam, and came down hard on its keel, throwing us momentarily off balance, and tipping enough to take in a little St. Lawrence water over the side.

A few more spine-tingling rushes, another couple of bumps, and suddenly it was all over. Once past *Ile au Héron,* all the rapids were behind us. The same God's Providence that looked after David Thompson, took care of Eastward Ho. We had met the challenge of the Lachines.

The St. Lawrence flowed under Champlain Bridge, dropping through a series of baffles which guarded against winter's drifting ice flows. Victoria Bridge followed. Straight ahead lay Ile Sainte Hélène and the channel to Bridge of the Isles.

We met a hovercraft in quite the narrowest part of the Chenal Le Moyne. It came right at us, bounding across the top of the water, enshrouded in a mist of its own creation, and roaring like a pride of lions in a cave. For a first-time view it was a terrifying sight, for all the world like a machine straight out of Buck Rogers. We scurried from the path of the snorting monster, then turned bow-on to meet the onslaught of its waves. The din from its motors was ear-splitting.

Left of the centre pylon of the causeway called 'Cosmos Walk', we had to run a steep sluice. Looking down from the top it had a tilt that gave the appearance of a waterfall. With a rush we hurtled down to the bottom where all was calm, then paddled across choppy water under Jacques Cartier Bridge, and the Expressway, to enter Port Sainte Helene. On the far shore, a large crowd waited beside a wharf. Passing a line of tooting motor cruisers, we arrived at the finish line at two p.m., right on schedule.

Families were there, along with friends from home and many sponsors who had connections in Montreal. The bank was lined with photographers. After clambering from the canoe and shaking hands with the Mayor's representative, Mr. Laliberté, I was promptly seized from behind by three pairs of hands, and tossed into the river. Before I could return the compliment the other three dove in.

After interviews, Chestnut Canoe Co. and Outboard Marine were contacted and advised that their sturdy products were still intact. Neither seemed unduly surprised to learn their wares had survived, relatively unscathed, a trip across Canada,.

With mixed emotions, Eastward Ho lifted their canoe out of the water for the last time. It was as if we were saying goodbye to 'home sweet home'. That twenty-foot canoe had been our transport and shelter for three and a half months.

No other type of vessel could have taken its place. It had carried us through rapids and across stormy seas. It had been paddled, motored and pushed through hidden sandbars. We had pulled it as a sled over the snow and dragged it up and down rough ice jams on frozen rivers. We had carried it shoulder high from stream to stream. It had protected us from the rain at night. Truly a remarkable craft. As far as I know, the only water-craft to span a continent, it now lies in an honourable resting place at Westminster Quay. Fittingly, Simon Fraser's bust stands outside, guarding the canoe and the departure point for Eastward Ho's Trans-Canada journey.

Next day there was one final duty to perform; the delivery of four bags of canoe mail to the main post office building in Montreal. By pre-arrangement, our stamped letters were to receive a special cancellation stamp, created for the Eastward Ho Canoe Expedition by Canada Post. Immediately after use the stamp would be destroyed to give the envelopes a unique frank.

Dave was relieved of the responsibility of postman, a position he had taken seriously. Under his watchful eye the forty pound burden had not been taken lightly. He saw to it that the mail was carried by *shoe or canoe only,* every inch of the way between New Westminster and Montreal.

The majority of Canadians, the ones we met in the schools, beside the rivers, or while hiking along the highways, didn't need explanations to provide help and encouragement. In every conceivable situation, they provided wonderful contacts with warm humanity. Their ongoing interest helped sustain Eastward Ho many times.

We've become jaded with the promises of politicians, a cynical press, screaming pressure groups vying for attention, or by the antics of those who create havoc in our society. How refreshing it was to make contact with average Canadians of all colours and creeds.

Letters, telegrams and congratulatory notes greeted us on our return home. One from Bill and Irene MacLean of The Pas encompassed the attitude of many who had befriended the expedition.

"Several groups passed through The Pas, some bent on competition, some a little commercial, but none, we thought, equalled your group in any measure."

How fortunate we are to live in a country that has the wealth to create leisure and the stability to permit freedom of action. There are few places in this world where a small group of people can come together for a few months in order to dedicate their lives in a non-destructive, purposeful pursuit.

Canadians can be grateful to the waterways which determined the *where,* to the beaver which supplied the *why,* and to the *First Nations people* who showed the *how.* These factors, coupled to the energy of *newcomers* put the first Trans-Continental Waterway in place. It was truly a *united* Canadian effort.

Some people needed a little coaching to appreciate the purpose behind Eastward Ho, but such was not the case at the post office where the canoe mail was delivered.

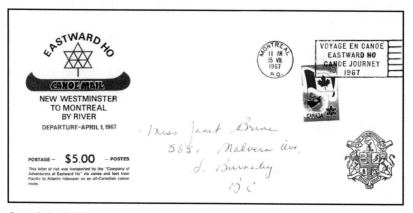

One of the 2,000 canoe-mail envelopes carried

A few moments in a grey, gargantuan government building, evidencing all the warmth of a slab of concrete, provided the most touching moment of the entire journey.

At this facility, the foreman in charge of the sorting floor called all the workers within shouting distance to assemble. They formed a circle of fifty or so around Eastward Ho.

He said to them, in English for the crew's benefit: "These gentlemen have brought this mail from the Pacific Ocean, all the way across Canada, *in the manner of our forefathers; by canoe!*"

You could have heard a pin drop. No one spoke. Then gently they began to clap their hands; then louder, and louder. These mail sorters had names like Regner, Leclerc, Landry, Turcotte, and La Chapelle. As memories of French-Canadian heroes and heroines sped through their minds, their emotions spread out to envelop us. Most had forebears who once challenged the wilderness head-on. It was an environment that showed no mercy to the weak.

Their ancestors had paddled to the *pays d'en haut,* and to far off Athabasca, where the glossiest beaver roamed. They had marveled at the crackle and snap of sub-arctic Northern Lights, and remembered the breaking of ice around a high mountain tarn. They had witnessed the morning mist rising, had heard the loon's call fading, and had hated that pre-dawn shout of *Levée! Levée! Levée!,* when tired bodies had to be reassembled for another twelve hour day at forty strokes a minute.

These Quebecers could hum "La Claire Fontaine", or the bouncing "en roulant ma boule, roulant", the *chansons* of the *voyageurs* who sang as they dipped paddles into Canada's lakes and rivers with thrusting sinew. They could relive those days of long ago, when everything seemed possible to the young and strong. In memory they had climbed and sweated their way up the Talon Chute or the Grande Portage.

Their names were under those white crosses that dotted the border of so many wild rivers. In their mind's eye they had witnessed the wilderness highway Eastward Ho had followed. Quite simply, the people standing together on that cold concrete floor knew why Eastward Ho had come by canoe.

Tears came to everyone's eyes. The air was charged with electricity, and for one brief, unforgettable moment, all were united by a bond of history. These Montrealers sensed how one could be 'swung on the pendulum of an idea' for three and a half months. They understood the enterprise. This outpouring of affection let Eastward Ho know that all their trials and tribulations had not been in vain.

Canada's Forgotten Highway has illustrated how people once travelled across the northern part of this continent before airways, roadways and railways added their communication lines. Invoking memories of a few Canadian canoe explorers should spark an interest in a panoply of others.

The men and women who created the transcontinental waterway laid a framework for the future. Will our generation do the same? We can hope that 'the true north strong and free' of our national hymn will long continue as a meaningful phrase.

Drink a farewell toast to four great Canadians; Samuel de Champlain, Pierre La Vérendrye, David Thompson and Simon Fraser. They were dedicated men who gave whole-heartedly of themselves when living, and in death, enriched Canada's soil with their bones. Their journals re-opened *Canada's Forgotten Highway,* and each in turn became a *fifth man* to Eastward Ho.

We bid them now a fond "Adieu"!

Chapter Twenty
Summing Up

*W*hen the five surviving members of Eastward Ho were asked to make a statement on their involvement in a trans-Canada canoe trip, they wrote the following:

It was *inspiration* and *perspiration*, from the sharing of an idea and a dream, through to the adventure of a lifetime. Momentous and unforgettable.

If memory serves me right, my association with "Canada's Forgotten Highway" started during five-mile runs around Queens Park, New Westminster, B.C. I often accompanied Ralph Brine on those thirty-five minute circuits. Our discussions were many and varied, but one had a lasting influence, which was, Ralph's vision for celebrating and experiencing Canada's Centennial.

An enthusiasm, tempered somewhat by his gasping for air on the uphill stretches, aroused my curiosity. I peppered questions at this would-be adventuring historian, knowing the answers would take longer than the questions. Jogger's one-upmanship at work.

Undaunted, Ralph vividly linked an adventure by canoe, shoe and ski, from New Westminster to Montreal. He wished to experience at first hand the magnificent and challenging landscape of Canada. His idea was to recapture some of the history of canoe exploration by travelling on the highways of the fur trade.

The spiel was tempting and timely. I was hooked. Bonnie, later to be my wife, encouraged this unexpected and unique opportunity. Her support bode well for our future together.

Soon, others made a like commitment. Not only the adventurers were involved. Their families and friends became part of the action. It was sharing and teamwork at its finest.

Now, it's fond and lasting memories; a pride in Canada and Canadians; and how one person's dream does have an impact.

Dave Chisholm

Eastward Ho was one of the highlights of my life.

To be together with six other individuals, to spend months of planning and preparation, and to participate in a canoeing adventure across Canada, was very special. Support from my wife, children, friends, and my employer, the B.C. Telephone Company, made it possible for me to be part of Eastward Ho. I am most grateful to them all.

We enjoyed many great moments, seeing the beauty and feeling the history of our nation at first hand. I think the most vivid time for me, was the last day; shooting the Lachine rapids in the St. Lawrence River; entering the Marina at Expo where family and friends waited; and to be part of a successful adventure.

All those things, plus the fact I was returning to my home province of Quebec, twenty-years after departure, made it a day to remember.

The last day also made me think, like it did the mail sorters in Montreal who relieved us of the 2,000 canoe-mail envelopes, of all those who had gone out from Quebec before. I felt an attachment to the exploring fur traders and coureurs de bois. I can sense now how they must have felt, after a season spent adventuring in Canada's *pays d'en haut*, of being reunited with families and friends

Don MacNaughton

When asked if I would be interested in joining a small group of men to canoe across Canada, I knew it was an opportunity I could not pass up. I unhesitatingly said, "Yes."

From the first organizational meetings I attended, to the present day, I have never regretted that decision.

The planning and effort that went into the expedition, from its conception to its successful conclusion, was a learning experience which continues to benefit me.

All seven members of Eastward Ho, the four canoeists and the land party threesome, threw away self-interest for the duration, and concentrated on working toward a group objective. Sharing dangers and difficulties with others was a rewarding experience. It has also been the source of many wonderful memories.

Some members of our group of seven are no longer living. Those that are, have moved apart. We will always, however, share the close relationships we developed during our canoeing adventure.

I will never forget the encouragement and assistance we received from the thousands of well-wishers who met us, or came out to wave to us, along the way. Throughout this broad land of ours, there is a feeling of pride in being Canadian.

Few people have had the opportunity to experience the *manitou*, or spirit, of Canada, as we did on a canoe trip from New Westminster to Montreal.

Jim Reid

Following Canada's canoe road on a three and a half month journey by camper and trailer was an experience never to be forgotten.

The venture made Edo and I realize what a vastly beautiful country Canada is, and how lucky we were to be living in it.

Playing den-mother to six men was really something, but we got on well together. My only regret is, my beloved Edo and my good friend Bill Gifford, are no longer here to share the wonderful memories we collected.

Lorna Hemmes

What a great team we had. Dave Chisholm: His medical expertize and boundless energy kept us on the move. Don MacNaughton: His strength and endurance helped us realize our goal. Jim Reid: His river skills and courage in the face of danger made him irreplaceable. I could travel anywhere with any of them.

Lorna Hemmes: Her quiet calm and constant good humour were ever at work to augment the success of the expedition. If the camper was parked near the river we often crowded into her six-by-nine-foot mobile house for a hot meal or toddy.

Edo Hemmes: He had never driven an off-road vehicle in his life. At age sixty he learned how. Truck and trailer were always ready with supplies. As well as taking care of our necessities, Edo devoted hundreds of hours before, during, and after the trip, producing a beautiful movie entitled "Canada By Canoe".

Last, but not least, Bill Gifford: He was always there waiting, beside a river or by some distant lake, whether it meant digging out his station wagon on the muddy road to Mica or finding the right logging track to an agreed rendezvous. Bill also acted as Chief Cop around urban campsites. He had that certain look in his eye, marking him ready to tackle anything and anyone.

The three and a half months spent travelling across Canada with Eastward Ho formed a special bond between us. I purposely down-played their exploits in this book in order to emphasize the role of the men who developed Canada's forgotten highway.

Everyone has a reason for doing what they do. Apart from the old ego, which controls all of us to some degree, one persistant goad to my natural lethargy has been the subject of national unity.

None of the seven members of our expedition would have dreamed that a decade after completion of our trans-Canada adventure, politicians and talk-show hosts would be speaking openly about the break-up of Canada.

As you can gather from the remarks of the other members of Eastward Ho, we all became very aware that most ordinary Canadians have a deep and abiding love of country. Whether you speak in Hebrew, Inuit, Cantonese, Italian, Halkomelem, French or English, when the chips are down, that love translates into a desire to remain united under the umbrella of Canada.

A Quebecer may express his or her feelings differently than say, an Albertan, but when emotions relate to the realities of family, job, friends, and health, they both think "Canada".

If we could turn down the frequency and volume emanating from certain politicians and some of the doomsayers in the media, whose very existence is dependent upon hype and moral finger-pointing, we would be able to hear the voices of ordinary people throughout this vast country of ours.

If more Canadians go public with their experiences, and express themselves in stories, poetry and song, the country as a whole will benefit.

Ralph Brine

Appendix

Itinerary   page 238

Biographies of the Observers   page 239

Friends of Eastward Ho   page 242

Bibliography   page 243

Index   page 245

Itinerary

Place	Area	canoe miles	shoe miles	total	mileage	carry	days
New Westminster							
Lytton	Fraser River	148	2	150	150	3	3
Spences Bridge	Thompson R.	5	20	25	175	5	
Ashcroft	Thompson R.	35		35	210	2	6
Kamloops	Thompson R.	70		70	280		7
Sicamous	S. Thompson	105		105	385		9
Revelstoke	Highway #1		45	45	430		11
Mica dam	Columbia R.	95		95	525	2	13
Blaeberry River	Columbia R.	70	40	110	635	5	22
Sask R Xross	Howse Pass		60	60	695		28
Rocky Mtn H.	N. Sask. River	125		125	820	2	
Edmonton	N. Sask. River	205		205	1025	6	
N. Battleford	N. Sask. River	325		325	1350		
Pr. Albert	N. Sask River	125		125	1475		
Cumberland h	N. Sask River	225	35	260	1735		
The Pas	N. Sask. River	85		85	1820		53
Portage La P.	Lake Manitoba	268	77	345	2165		63
Winnipeg	Assiniboine R	85		85	2250		
Ft. Alexander	Winnipeg R	90		90	2340		65
Kenora	Lake of Woods	135		135	2475	8	
Rainy River	Rainy River	70		70	2545		
Ft. Frances	Rainy River	75		75	2620		
South Lake	Pigeon River.	201	4	205	2825	33	74
Hoveland	Lake Superior	20	20	40	2865		
Thunder Bay	Lake Superior	80		80	2945		
Sault St Marie	Lake Superior	380		380	3325		85
French River	Lake Huron	200		200	3525		
North Bay	French River	98	2	100	3625	5	
Mattawa	Mattawa River	39	1	40	3665	3	94
Dorval	Ottawa River	280		280	3945	5	
Ile Ste Helene	St. Lawrence	16		16	3961		105
		3655	306	3961	3961	74	105

Byte-sized Biographies of the *Observers*

Bigsby, Dr. John J. (1792 – 1881) Born Nottingham, England. Died London Eng. Graduate Edinburgh University M.D. To Canada 1818 with British army. An interest in geology led to appointments in boundary-survey work on the Canadian-American border. The chief Canadian surveyor was David Thompson. Dr. Bigsby had several scientific papers published from 1821-25. Returned to England 1827 to practice medicine. In 1850 published a two-volume memoir entitled The Shoe and Canoe, a delightful travelogue of incidents and accidents during his survey work with Thompson. Elected to the Royal Society in 1867.

Cox, Ross (1793 – 1853) Born in Dublin, Ireland. Crossed to North America, joined Astor's Pacific Fur Co. in 1811 as clerk. Spent six years at mouth of Columbia River, first with the PFC, then the NWC, after the 'takeover' of 1813. During that interim he travelled up and down the Columbia River eight times. His final ascent was with the eastbound canoe express of 1817. Returned to Ireland. Published his entertaining journal, 'The Columbia River' in London and New York.

Harmon, Daniel (1778 – 1843) Born in Bennington, Vermont, same area as Simon Fraser. Signed on as clerk with the NWC in 1800. Spent much of his working time in the New Caledonia area. Retired in 1819 as Chief Trader and partner. His "Voyages and Travels", printed in 1820, contributed a rich vein of information to fur trade annals. Believed to be buried in Montreal.

Henry, Alexander the Elder (1739 – 1824) Born in New Jersey. Started a career in the mercantile trade in Albany. Moved down the St. Lawrence River as a supply merchant to General Amherst's army in their attack of 1760 against Montreal. Saw the potential of the north-west fur trade. Remained in Montreal to form partnerships with French merchants. In Michilimackinac he was captured and held prisoner for a year during the uprising of the Pontiac Rebellion. After his release, he continued in the Indian trade forming a partnership with M. Cadotte of Sault Ste. Marie. He and Cadotte journeyed to the Saskatchewan 1775-76 and formed a loose co-operative with Peter Pond and the Frobisher brothers. This liaison was a forerunner of the North West Co. of which Henry became a founding member. Remained in Montreal as a respected man of business and civic affairs. Published his "Travels" in 1809.

Henry, Alexander the Younger (1765? – 1814) Nephew of Henry Sr. Clerk with NWC 1792, partner by 1801 along with Simon Fraser. Spent several years in Lake Winnipeg area. Assisted D. Thompson in his search for the Athabasca Pass. In charge of Rocky Mtn. H. until his move to Ft. George at mouth of Columbia River. Drowned while crossing the sound from Tongue Point to Baker Bay. Left an amazingly detailed and objective journal, begun in 1799 and kept up to date until the day of his death. Two excellent editions of his voluminous diary; the first by Elliott Coues 1897; the second by Barry Morton Gough. The latter published by The Champlain Society in 1988.

Kane, Paul (1810 – 1871) Born in Ireland, arrived in Canada as a youngster. Learned the trade of a cabinet and furniture maker. Pushed by artistic talents he turned to the decorative side of the trade. Travelled to Europe to learn from the 'Old Masters'. Catlin's paintings in London of the American west persuaded Kane to paint a similar environment in the Canadian north-west. Obtained passage on the HBC canoe express bound from Ft. William to the mouth of the Columbia River, and Ft. Victoria on Vancouver Island. He was two years on this project, 1846-48. He returned with over 700 sketches of people and scenes from the untamed wild-west. His paintings are world famous. Published "Wanderings of an Artist", a most readable account of his journey, in 1858.

McDonald, Archibald (1791 – 1853) Born in Glenco Appin, Scotland. Caught the eye of Lord Selkirk who put him in charge of a shipload of Scottish emigrants bound for York Factory on the Bay, thence to the Red River Settlement. The trip began in the summer of 1813, but it was an unmitigated disaster. A typhoid epidemic broke out in the holds of the ship Prince Rupert. It took McDonald two years to get one third of his charges to the questionable safety of the Red River Colony. In 1820 he signed on as clerk with the HBC. Sent to Ft. George on the Columbia. In charge of Thompson River district 1826, made Chief Trader 1828. Left Ft. Okanagan first April that same year with Edward Ermatinger York Factory Express, arrived at York end of June. Turned around to accompany Gov. George Simpson on his trans-Canada dash of 1828. Reached Ft. Langley on the Fraser River Oct. 11th. All told, McDonald travelled over 5,000 canoe-miles in six and a half months. Discovered silver on Kootenay Lake, later to be the site of the Blue Bell Mine at Riondel. Appointed Chief Factor, retired 1848. Drowned when the carriage he was driving across the ice, broke through.

Mackenzie, Sir Alexander (1764 – 1820) Born Stornoway, Isle of Lewis, Scotland. Arrived in New York 1774, family moved to Montreal. Started with fur trading firm of Gregory & MacLeod who merged with the NWC 1787. Worked under Peter Pond in Athabasca country. The two established Ft. Chipewyan. Down north to the Arctic Ocean in 1789. Made his way to the Pacific Ocean in 1793 - first overland crossing of full width of North America.. Became a senior partner NWC. Published his marvelous "Voyages" 1801, knighted the following year. A man of vision, he tried unsuccessfully to amalgamate the NWC and the HBC. Had he been able to do so, the map of Canada would be a great deal larger today. Retired to Scotland.

Simpson, Sir George (1792 – 1860) Born Ross-shire, Scotland. To London as clerk in West India trade. To Canada with HBC 1820. His management capabilities displayed in Lake Athabasca area soon brought him to the forefront. In 1821 he was put in charge of the merger of the NWC and HBC. Five years later he was Governor-in - Canada of the entire North America operation of the HBC. A man of exceptional energy and drive, he made the HBC a productive and efficient organization. Knighted 1841, he died from a stroke at his home in Lachine, Quebec.

Friends of Eastward Ho

"The City of New Westminster would like to officially thank the firms and individuals who assisted the Eastward Ho Canoe Expedition."

Mayor Stuart Gifford

B.C. Tel	Westminster Pharmacy
Bank of Montreal	Inga Nelson Sportwear
Dad's Cookies Ltd	Bolex Camera
Dinty and Harold Moore	YM – YWCA
Royal Outboard	Earl Peterson
Outboard Marine Corp.	The T. Eaton Co.
Les Palmer	Woodwards Ltd.
Bill Hill of Fogg Motors	George Sigismund, Seagrams
Ford Motor Co.	Liptons Ltd.
Eldorado Campers	MacKenzie & Fraser
Road Runner Trailers	The Carnation Co.
Scotty Scott's Service	Bullock's Helicopter
Jones Tent and Awning	B.C. Hydro – Mica City
Radio Station CKNW	B.C. Honey
Greb Shoe Co.	Chamber Commerce, N. W.
Rikk Taylor, The Columbian	Royal Towers Hotel
Aero Club of B.C.	Canada Ropes Ltd.
Canadian Inn, Kamloops	Travelodge, Revelstoke
Chamber Commerce, Revelstoke	Tom Ryall
Stanfield's Ltd.	Copp's Shoe Store

Bibliography

* star indicates frequent references from:

Journals:

Champlain, Samuel de	H.P. Bigger, The Champlain Soc.*
Vérendrye, Pierre La	L.J. Burpee, The Champlain Soc.*
Fraser, Simon	W.K. Lamb*
Thompson, David	J.B. Tyrrell, The Champlain Soc.*
Cox, Ross	E.I. & J.R. Stewart, University Oklahoma Press*
Harmon, Daniel	D. Haskel, Allerton Book Co. USA*
Henry, Alexander Sr.	J. Bain, Burt Franklin U.S.A.*
Henry, Alexander Jr.	E. Coues, Ross & Haines U.S.A.*
Kane, Paul	J.W. Garvin, Radisson Soc. Canada*
Mackenzie, Alexander	W.K. Lamb , Haklyut Soc. Eng.*
McDonald, Archibald	M. McLeod, Hurtig Ltd.
Simpson, George (1828-9)	E.E. Rich, Hudson's Bay Record Soc.*

General Reading:

Douglas, David	Royal Horticultural Soc. Eng.
Macdonell, John	C.M. Gates
Five Fur Traders	C.M. Gates
Ross, Alexander	K.A. Spaulding
Franchere, Gabriel	W.K. Lamb
Bark Canoes of North America	Adney & Chapelle
Behold The Shining Mountains	J.G. MacGregor
Blankets and Beads	J.G. Macgregor
Blood Red The Sun	W.B. Cameron
B.C. Chronicle 1778 – 1846	G.P. & H.B. Akrigg
Canada Under Louis XIV	W.J. Eccles
Canada, An Outline of History	J.A. Lower
Columbia, The	S.W. Holbrook

Fist In The Wilderness	D. Lavender
Fraser, The	B. Hutchison
Fur Trade In Canada	H.A. Innis
Fur Trade Routes of Canada	E.W. Morse *
Historic Forts & Trading Posts	E. Voorhis
History Northern Interior B.C.	A.G. Morice
History Bank of Montreal	M. Denison
Honourable Company	D. MacKay
North West Company	Marjorie Wilkins Campbell
Yale Gazette Vol. 24 #2	D. Bridgewater
Samuel de Champlain	E. Morison
Two Bennington-born Explorers	John Spargo

Index

A

Abitibi River, 215
Albany River, 166, 190
Alder Flats, 110
Allumette Lake, 218
Angle Inlet, 168
Anklevitch Point, 138
Appalachian Mountains, 2, 5
Arrowhead Trail, 182
Ashcroft, 57, 59
Athabasca Pass, 20, 63, 80, 82, 83, 84, 97, 103, 124
Athabasca River, 16, 70, 84, 124
Atnah, 55
Aulneau Peninsula, 167, 168

B

Baptiste River, 109, 110
Basswood Lake, 176, 177
Batoche, 134
Battle River, 132
Bigsby Island, 169
Bigstone River, 140
Black Canyon, 45, 58, 81
Black Sturgeon River, 166
Blaeberry River, 89
Boat Encampment, 15, 62, 64, 73, 76, 80, 81, 82, 83, 84, 90, 124
Boggy Hall, 103, 111
Borden Crossing, 133
Boston Bar, 37, 48
Bottle Portage, 176

Brazeau Range, 103, 106
Brazeau River, 111
Bridge of the Isles, 228
Brosseau, 128
Brouage, 196, 197, 209
Buckingham House, 129, 132
Bustards, 206

C

Cadotte, 137
Camchin, 26, 51, 52, 55
Canada Post, 229
Canoe River, 73, 83
Cape Gargantua, 192
Carrot River, 142
Caughnawaga, 227
Cedar Lake, 154, 155, 156, 157
Champlain Bridge, 228
Champlain, Samuel de, 2, 3, 4, 12, 16, 18, 21, 192, 195, 196, 197, 198, 199, 200, 201, 202, 203, 204, 206, 207, 208, 209, 211, 215, 219, 220, 222, 223, 226, 227, 231
Chant Plain Lake, 214
Chenal Le Moyne, 228
Chenaux dam, 219
Clearwater River, 70, 108
Coast Range, 2
Cole Rapids, 136
Columbia Lake, 71, 76
Columbia River, 9, 10, 11, 13,

14, 15, 20, 34, 38, 43, 49, 51, 52, 53, 60, 62, 63, 64, 65, 71, 72, 73, 76, 77, 79, 81, 83, 84, 90, 92, 124, 210
Conway Creek, 99
Coutamine, 54, 55
Cox, Ross, 84, 210, 212, 214, 223
Crane Narrows, 157
Crooked Lake, 176
Cumberland House, 69, 131, 136, 140, 141, 142
Cumberland Lake, 139, 140, 141
Curtain Falls, 176

D
Death Rapids, 81, 82, 84
Detour Passage, 194
Doubt Hill, 96
Downie Creek, 77, 80
Drayton Valley, 110, 111, 112, 113
Duck Bay, 155
Duck Lake, 129, 134

E
Eagle Hills, 133
Eagle River, 20, 61
Edmonton, 14, 108, 114, 117, 123, 124, 125, 126, 130, 134, 137
Elk Point, 129
Ely, 176, 177
Emory Creek, 39
English River, 166

F
Fort Albany, 166
Fort Alexander, 162

Fort Alexandria, 9, 43, 51
Fort Assiniboine, 84, 124
Fort Astoria, 9, 10, 60, 73
Fort Bourbon, 157
Fort Carlton, 130, 134
Fort des Isles, 129
Fort Detroit, 7, 194
Fort Edmonton, 14, 108, 123, 124, 125
Fort Frances, 170, 171, 174
Fort Garry, 136
Fort George, 13, 26, 43, 50, 82, 129, 210
Fort Hope, 38
Fort La Corne, 136
Fort La Montée, 134
Fort Langley, 34, 36, 52, 210
Fort Maurepas, 161
Fort Okanagan, 43, 60
Fort Pitt, 129, 130
Fort Saskatchewan, 125
Fort St. Pierre, 174
Fort Vancouver, 13, 15, 34, 38, 52, 53, 54, 63
Fort Victoria, 14, 39, 53
Fort William, 13, 14, 21, 73, 131, 176
Fowl Lake, 182, 184
Fraser River, 2, 9, 20, 24, 26, 27, 34, 35, 36, 37, 38, 41, 42, 43, 49, 51, 52, 53, 54, 58, 61, 77, 210
Fraser, Simon, 8, 9, 12, 22, 23, 28, 29, 30, 31, 36, 37, 39, 41, 47, 49, 52, 53, 71, 229, 231
French Portage Narrows, 168
French River, 3, 14, 73, 192, 193, 194, 195, 204, 206, 207, 208, 209
Frog Lake, 129

G

Gap Creek, 103
Garth, 108
Golden, 77, 87, 89, 94, 160
Grand Portage, 14, 70, 149, 174, 176, 182, 184, 185, 188, 219
Great Falls dam, 164
Gunflint Lake, 178, 180, 181

H

Harmon, Daniel, 126, 210, 218
Harrison Lake, 36, 37
Harrison River, 36
Hawkesbury, 223
Henry Jr., Alexander, 103, 107, 108, 130, 136, 137, 140, 162, 174
Henry Sr., Alexander, 137, 142, 195, 216, 219
Honfleur, 198
Hoveland, 182, 187
Howse Pass, 20, 49, 71, 72, 83, 92, 93, 96, 98, 103, 111
Howse River, 99
Hudson Bay, 2, 4, 7, 8, 13, 51, 67, 99, 115, 124, 125, 134, 137, 141, 147, 166, 181, 204, 215, 216, 220
Hull, 221

I

Ile au Héron, 226, 227, 228
Irving Island, 176

J

Jacques Cartier Bridge, 228
James Bay, 166, 190, 194, 215

K

Kaministikwia River, 4
Kamloops, 36, 43, 53, 54, 59, 60
Kamloops Lake, 53, 59
Kane, Paul, 80, 84, 124, 127
Kenora, 166, 168
Kettle Falls, 174
Kinbasket Lake, 64, 81, 83, 85, 86
Kitchen Rapids, 89
Knife Lake, 177
Kootanae Appe, 119
Kootenay Plains, 101, 102, 128

L

La Cloche, 206
La Vérendrye, Pierre, 4, 5, 12, 117, 136, 145, 147, 150, 154, 168, 231
Lac Coulonge, 219
Lac des Chats, 219, 221
Lac du Bonnet, 164, 165
Lac La Croix, 174, 175, 176
Lac Seul, 166
Lac St. Louis, 224
Lachine, 4, 148, 201, 203, 209, 224, 226
Lachine rapids, 226
Lacs des Prairies, 154, 167
Lady Franklin Rock, 40, 41
Lake Deschênes, 221
Lake Holden, 217
Lake Huron, 14, 192, 194, 195, 199, 207, 209
Lake Manitoba, 156, 157, 159, 160
Lake Nipigon, 166, 189, 190
Lake Nipissing, 14, 211, 212

Lake of the Woods, 4, 14, 53, 160, 162, 165, 166, 167, 168, 170

Lake of Two Mountains, 150, 224

Lake Robichaud, 212

Lake Superior, 4, 14, 70, 110, 131, 145, 147, 149, 153, 166, 168, 171, 173, 174, 175, 176, 181, 182, 183, 184, 186, 187, 188, 189, 190, 193

Lake Winnipeg, 2, 5, 6, 13, 14, 15, 101, 128, 133, 145, 152, 153, 154, 156, 157, 159, 161, 171

Lake Winnipegosis, 154, 155, 156, 157

Lamb, Dr. W. Kaye, 30

Little Dalles, 77

Little River, 61

Loon Lake, 175

Lost Child Bend, 210

Lytton, 20, 26, 30, 48, 49, 51, 53, 54

M

Mackenzie, Alexander, 8, 24, 29, 70, 129, 135, 162, 164, 171, 174, 177, 189

Mackinac, 194, 195, 207, 216

MacMillan Island, 34

Magnetic Lake, 178, 180

Main Outlet, 207

Malakwa, 61

Mali', 29

Manchester House, 131

Manitou Rapids, 164

Manitoulin Island, 195, 206

Maraboeuf Lake, 178

Marathon, 188, 189, 191

Martel, 57

Massacre Island, 168

Matsqui, 35

Mattawa, 14, 193, 206, 211, 212, 213, 214, 217

Mattawa River, 14, 206, 211, 212, 213, 217

Mauvaise de la Musique, 212

McArthur Falls dam, 164

McCauley Bay, 169

McDonald, Archibald, 34, 36, 43, 47, 48, 51, 52, 54

McFarland Lake, 182

Mica, 62, 63, 64, 65, 81, 82, 85

Michipicoten Island, 187, 191

Minaki Bridge, 166

Mississippi River, 16, 70

Mistaya River, 100

Montreal, 4, 5, 8, 10, 11, 13, 14, 17, 20, 22, 24, 32, 60, 61, 62, 70, 73, 74, 77, 82, 84, 90, 108, 109, 117, 124, 125, 132, 136, 141, 148, 150, 156, 162, 166, 169, 171, 185, 188, 193, 194, 199, 206, 208, 210, 211, 213, 215, 219, 223, 224, 226, 227, 228, 229

Morrison Island, 203, 218, 220

Mossy Portage, 157

Mount Conway, 93

Mummery Glacier, 93

Muskrat Lake, 219

Musqueam, 28, 29

N

N. Saskatchewan River, 112

Namew Lake, 141

Natalie Lake, 165

Nelson River, 2, 8

Nepean Bay, 221, 223

New Westminster, 17, 19, 20, 27, 39, 135, 153, 170, 187, 212, 229
Nicaumchin, 55
Nicoamen River, 55
Nicola River, 55
Nipawin, 136, 137, 138
North Bay, 211, 212
North Lake, 181
North West Angle, 168

O
Oka, 224
Old Channel, 139, 140
Ottawa, 3, 7, 14, 15, 16, 73, 162, 193, 195, 199, 203, 204, 206, 211, 214, 215, 216, 217, 218, 219, 220, 221, 222, 223, 224, 227
Ottawa River, 3, 14, 15, 16, 73, 199, 203, 211, 214, 215, 217, 218, 219, 221, 222
Overflowing River, 155

P
Paresseux Falls, 213
Pasquia River, 142
pays plat, 190
Peace River, 2, 8, 24, 106, 141
Pickerel River, 207, 208
Pigeon River, 4, 182, 184
Pine Falls, 162, 164
Point Fortune, 224
Pointe de Bois, 165
Port Sainte Helene, 228
Portage de Traite, 141
Prince Albert, 109, 129, 133, 134, 135
Puget Sound, 34

Q
Quebec Harbour, 191
Quetico River, 175
Quluxen, 29

R
Rainy River, 4, 14, 167, 168, 170, 171, 173, 181
Ram River, 107
Recollet Falls, 193, 208
Red Deer River, 118
Redgrave Canyon, 89
Remic rapids, 221
Revelstoke, 20, 61, 62, 63, 65, 73, 77, 89
Rideau River, 222
Rocky Mountain House, 72, 101, 106, 108, 109
Rocky Mountain Trench, 63, 71, 76, 81, 85
Rocky Mountains, 2, 12, 20, 31, 65, 68, 71, 72, 73, 82, 83, 89, 90, 92, 96, 97, 99, 105, 108, 115, 141, 142, 150
Rose Lake, 181
Rubber Island, 168
Ruby Creek, 33, 36, 38, 48

S
Saddle Rock, 27, 42
Saganaga Lake, 175, 178
Saguenay River, 198, 200, 220
Saskatchewan River, 5, 14, 16, 69, 90, 92, 99, 101, 103, 105, 106, 109, 112, 123, 124, 125, 130, 132, 136, 137, 139, 140, 141, 142, 143, 144, 149, 150, 152, 153, 154, 155, 157
Saskatchewan River Crossing, 99, 101

Saukamappee, 117, 118
Sault Ste. Marie, 186, 192, 194, 207, 208
Savona, 53, 59
Selkirk, 63, 64, 65, 71, 72, 76, 77
Shaw Springs, 54, 57
Shunda Creek, 105
Shuswap Lake, 20, 60, 61
Simpson, George, 13, 39, 51, 84, 123, 141, 175
Snipe Hills, 126, 127
Soldiers Point, 174
South Lake, 181, 182
Spences Bridge, 54, 55, 56
Spuzzum, 43
Squaw Rapids, 137, 138, 139
St. Joseph Island, 194
St. Lawrence River, 2, 74, 132, 204, 209, 214, 215, 227
St. Mary River, 192, 193
St. Maurice River, 147, 215, 222
Sturgeon Fort, 134
Sturgeon Lake, 166
Sturgeon River, 125, 134, 166
Sullivan River, 85
Surprise Rapids, 86

T
Tadoussac, 198, 199, 220
Talon Chute, 212, 213, 231
Tearing River, 140
The Pas, 133, 142, 143, 145, 152, 153, 154, 155, 166, 229
Thompson, David, 8, 10, 11, 12, 15, 17, 19, 26, 27, 49, 60, 64, 65, 66, 67, 70, 71, 76, 77, 80, 81, 83, 90, 92, 97, 101, 102, 105, 107, 108, 111, 114, 115, 117, 119, 122, 123, 126, 131, 136, 145, 153, 168, 170, 176, 206, 210, 228, 231
Thompson River, 20, 22, 42, 43, 49, 51, 52, 53, 54, 57, 59, 60, 81, 179
Thunder Bay, 176, 186, 187, 188, 189
Town Lake, 219
Trout Lake, 212

V
Victoria Bridge, 228
Ville Marie, 227
Voyageurs Channel, 207

W
Wallachin, 55, 59
Waterhen River, 156, 157
Western Outlet, 207
Westminster Quay, 229
White Dog dam, 166
White Earth Creek, 126
Whonnock, 27, 35
Wilderness Retreat Lodge, 182
Winnipeg Canoe Club, 160
Winnipeg, City of, 160, 161
Winnipeg River, 152, 161, 162, 164, 166
Wood River, 83

Y
Yale, 31, 34, 39, 40, 43, 51, 52, 53
Yellowhead, 60, 73
York Factory, 13, 68, 124, 131, 140

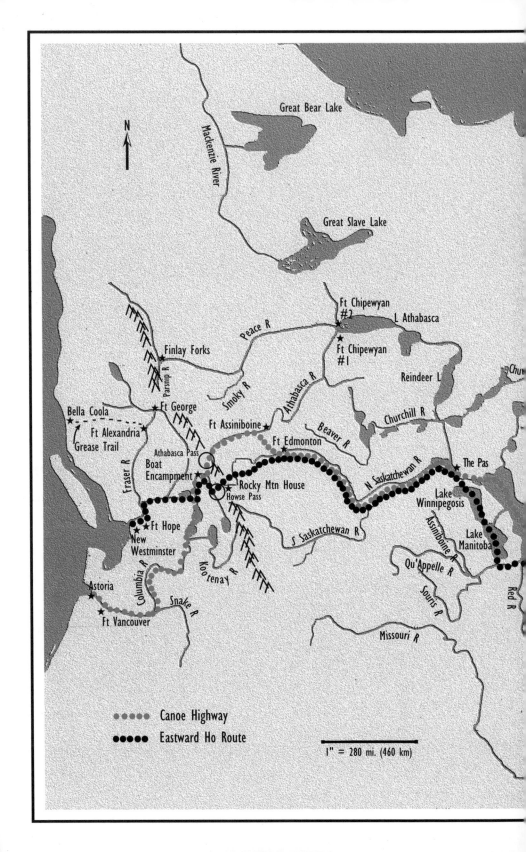

Great Bear Lake

Great Slave Lake

Mackenzie River

N

Peace R

Ft Chipewyan #2
L Athabasca

Finlay Forks

Parsnip R

Smoky R

Athabasca R

Ft Chipewyan #1

Reindeer L

Chu

Churchill R

Bella Coola

Ft George

Ft Assiniboine

Ft Alexandria
Grease Trail

Athabasca Pass
Boat
Encampment

Ft Edmonton

Beaver R

The Pas

Fraser R

Rocky Mtn House
Howse Pass

N Saskatchewan R

Lake
Winnipegosis

Ft Hope

New
Westminster

S Saskatchewan R

Assiniboine R

Lake
Manitoba

Astoria

Columbia R

Kootenay R

Qu'Appelle R

Souris R

Red R

Ft Vancouver

Snake R

Missouri R

●●●●● Canoe Highway
●●●●● Eastward Ho Route

1" = 280 mi. (460 km)